on track ...
Opeth

every album, every song

Jordan Blum

SONICBOND

sonicbondpublishing.com

Sonicbond Publishing Limited
www.sonicbondpublishing.co.uk
Email: info@sonicbondpublishing.co.uk

First Published in the United Kingdom 2022
First Published in the United States 2022

British Library Cataloguing in Publication Data:
A Catalogue record for this book is available from the British Library

Copyright Jordan Blum 2022

ISBN 978-1-78952-166-5

Typeset in ITC Garamond & ITC Avant Garde
Printed and bound in England

Graphic design and typesetting: Full Moon Media

Acknowlededements

More than ever, I'd like to thank Stephen Lambe, not only for offering me another opportunity to write another 'On Track' book, but more importantly, for granting me far more time to get it done than either of us expected. His genial patience and understanding were blessings during the entire process, and I can't thank him enough for allowing me to create the best book possible on my own schedule.

In terms of personal contributions, thanks to all of the artists, writers, and other people in the music industry who chatted with me about Opeth; whether or not your responses are explicitly referenced, know that your feedback was invaluable in helping me shape my research and responses. Equal thanks to everyone who submitted previously published interviews, articles, and/or pieces for the photo section, especially Christophe Largeau, Chris Conaton, and Michael Ainscoe.

Thanks to all of my online acquaintances (whose constant interest in and advice for this project helped me remain focused and confident along the way). That goes double for my closest fellow progressive metal-loving buddies – you know who you are – for the countless conversations, debates, and laughs. Most importantly, thank you to my immediate family and dearest friends, without whom I almost surely would have succumbed to an excessive combination of laziness and self-doubt. (I kid, I kid.)

Lastly, thank *you* for taking the time to read this book and maybe even tell a few friends about it. No matter how often or infrequently our opinions align, I appreciate your interest and support. In the end, we can both agree that Opeth's inspiring story and singular sound are the stuff of legend, and we'll always have them in our time of need.

on track ...

Opeth

Contents

Introduction 7

Orchid (1995) 11

Morningrise (1996) 17

My Arms, Your Hearse (1998) 22

Still Life (1999) 29

Blackwater Park (2001) 38

Deliverance (2002) 50

Damnation (2003) 59

Ghost Reveries (2005) 66

Watershed (2008) 77

Heritage (2011) 89

Pale Communion (2014) 102

Sorceress (2016) 114

In Cauda Venenum (2019) 124

Roundup – Live/Video, Compilation, and Extra Tracks 132

Bibliography 137

Jordan Blum's ultimate Opeth Playlist 140

Opeth albums ranked from best to worst 141

Introduction

There has never been – and never will be – another band like Opeth. Sure, that may sound like a cliché and/or hyperbolic way to begin, but it becomes increasingly deserved and indisputable the deeper you dig into their unique catalogue and appreciate their boldly resolute journey. Formed in Stockholm, Sweden, circa late 1989, their roughly thirty-year career showcases a melding of diverse influences; prevailing commitment to songwriting and instrumental excellence; and unwaveringly chameleonic vision – no matter the cost – that's unmatched by *any* contemporary act aiming for a similar style. Be it their earliest and most unashamedly brutal LPs, their multifaceted and near-faultless mid-period opuses, or their somewhat polarising recent glimpses into macabre 1970s-esque prog/jazz rock eccentricity, mastermind Mikael Åkerfeldt and company continuously create records that push themselves, their audience, and progressive music as a whole forward. The result is already one of the most extraordinary, dependable, and laudable legacies in modern metal.

Although the group technically began at the tail-end of the 1980s (or during the first half of 1990, depending on who you ask), Åkerfeldt wasn't always its leader. In fact, he wasn't even an original member! You see, Opeth – whose name was inspired by the word 'Opet' from Wilbur Smith's 1972 novel *The Sunbird* – was founded by David Isberg. He was a teenager who went to the same school as Åkerfeldt and had a stronger love for, and awareness of, under-the-radar death and doom metal acts. In contrast, Åkerfeldt was gravitating toward bigger and – in some instances – more accessible options (Deep Purple, Iron Maiden, Metallica, Celtic Frost, Slayer, Scorpions, Judas Priest, Black Sabbath, etc.) while jamming with other people in his first ensemble, Eruption. As he explains in *Book of Opeth*: 'We'd seen each other around but never really talked until we met each other skateboarding, and I saw he was wearing a Wehrmacht T-shirt'. Åkerfeldt was just beginning to play guitar – his parents insisted that he take recorder lessons first – and was intrigued by Isberg's drive, knowledge, and confidence. Seeing him equally as a friend and mentor of sorts, Åkerfeldt decided to make a go of it with Opeth, bringing along Eruption drummer Anders Nordin – who stayed through 1996's *Morningrise* and preferred 'boogie-woogie piano' over most metal – for good measure.

Humorously and serendipitously, Åkerfeldt was recruited to play bass since Isberg was having second thoughts about their current player, Martin Persson. However, no one else in the band knew that – including Persson – so Åkerfeldt's introduction was awkward, to say the least. 'At my first rehearsal, it became obvious that the other guys ... didn't know that I was replacing the bass player – and neither did the bass player, who also showed up – so everyone was asking who the hell I was', he recalls. An argument ensued while Åkerfeldt waited outside; before long, Isberg came out and told him that he'd fired everyone else, leaving Opeth as a duo in which Isberg wrote the lyrics while Åkerfeldt wrote the music.

Over the next couple of years, various other musicians – such as guitarist Andreas Dimeo; bassists Nick Dörin, Johan De Farfalla, and Stefan Guteklint; and guitarist Kim Pettersson – would come and go while Opeth played local gigs (including at least one with another important up-and-comer, At The Gates) and worked on original music. In 1991, the first two major Opeth line-up changes occurred. First, Åkerfeldt was introduced to guitarist Peter Lindgren (whose girlfriend was best friends with Åkerfeldt's girlfriend); just like Åkerfeldt, though, Lindgren was initially hired to play bass. Then, Åkerfeldt and Isberg went on a skiing trip to Switzerland, during which Isberg divulged that he was going to quit Opeth to work on other projects. He'd already been displaying a swelling disinterest in the group, so the decision wasn't too surprising. Thus, Åkerfeldt became the formal frontman and architect of Opeth, with Lindgren moving over to guitar, Nordin remaining on percussion (and piano), and De Farfalla eventually coming back as a session-turned-official bassist.

For the sake of brevity – and to leave room for the finer details in the introductions to each studio collection – suffice it to say that Opeth spent the rest of the 1990s infusing their black/death metal foundation with gradually more varied and ambitious styles and scopes – prog rock, folk, jazz rock, etc. – that demonstrated Åkerfeldt's growing affection for pioneering prog rock darlings like Yes, Genesis, King Crimson, Camel, and Jethro Tull. (His love for wholly unrelated artists like ABBA and Joni Mitchell likely played a part, too.) Despite some poor promotion and support on the part of labels Candlelight (UK) and Century Media (US), their first trio of LPs – 1995's *Orchid*, 1996's *Morningrise*, and 1998's *My Arms, Your Hearse* – illustrated an ever-evolving knack for interweaving vicious and mellow aesthetics within lengthily complex song structures. The latter 'observation' – as Åkerfeldt famously calls them – even showed them attempting the genre's requisite narrative framing; the following year, and after going to Peaceville Records, they'd perfect it with the downright Shakespearean *Still Life*, which many devotees – myself included – consider one of the greatest progressive metal concept albums of all time.

By now, the classic quartet of Åkerfeldt, Lindgren, bassist Martin Méndez, and drummer Martin López was in place, and they were really starting to see some major critical and commercial achievements, as well as major touring opportunities. Plus, they'd switched labels once again, to Music for Nations / Koch, and recruited Steven Wilson – himself gaining much-deserved acclaim as the head of Porcupine Tree – to produce and contribute parts here and there. Hence, 2001's *Blackwater Park* was significantly more polished, focused, assorted, and balanced than its predecessors, paving the way for the ingeniously dissimilar one-two punch of 2002's hellish *Deliverance* and 2003's heavenly *Damnation*. Recorded simultaneously, they essentially reveal the two polar opposite sides of Opeth's palette, cementing their unsurpassed skill at juxtaposing tranquil ballads and terrifying aural assaults. Of course, that compromise was also splendidly documented on their first live album/video, *Lamentations: Live at Shepherd's Bush Empire 2003*.

The second half of the 2000s saw them swap labels and producers once more – to Roadrunner Records and Jens Bogren, respectively – for 2005's magnificent *Ghost Reveries*. In addition, Spiritual Beggars keyboardist Per Wiberg turned Opeth into an official quintet, too, and helped give that eighth LP much of its orchestrally gothic splendour. Sadly, López announced his departure the next year because of health concerns; he was replaced by Martin Axenrot, who'd previously joined death metal supergroup Bloodbath right after Åkerfeldt first left it. Subsequently, Opeth's 2007 sophomore concert release, *The Roundhouse Tapes*, proved noteworthy not only for how its venue – the Roundhouse in London – signified how successful and celebrated Opeth had become, but also because it marked the departure of Lindgren due to his declining passion for the project. Ex-Arch Enemy guitarist Fredrik Åkesson took over for him afterwards, and the group focused on creating what would become their final record with any semblance of death metal vocals and music, 2008's *Watershed*. Naturally, and understandably, it was their most divisive effort at the time fanbase-wise, and while it was at least a tad inconsistent and unfocused, it was still majorly satisfying. More importantly, it served as a partial stylistic segue into Opeth's current sonic landscape.

They didn't welcome in the new decade with a new studio effort, however. Instead, 2010's *In Live Concert at the Royal Albert Hall* presented a commemoration of their twentieth anniversary via an expansive setlist and elaborate performance. Unsurprisingly, 2011's *Heritage* was arguably even more contentious than *Watershed* since it silenced any speculation admirers might've had about what direction they'd go from there. Rather than maintain their heaviest roots, the collection was commendably – if unevenly – adventurous, retro, and vibrant, bringing an almost avant-garde sense of challenge and brazenness to their arsenal. It was also the mutually agreed upon swan song of Wiberg, who was succeeded by Joakim Svalberg to round out the present-day line-up. The consequent three full-lengths – 2014's full-bodied *Pale Communion*, 2016's stark *Sorceress*, and 2019's ghoulish *In Cauda Venenum* – expanded upon the *Heritage* blueprint in various ways, and to varying degrees of success.

Along the way, Opeth continued to try out new producers amidst moving to Nuclear Blast Records, starting their own label (Moderbolaget Records), and issuing another live set, 2018's *Garden of the Titans: Live at Red Rocks Amphitheater*. In 2015, they even came up with their own beer, XXV Anniversary Imperial Stout, to honour their twenty-fifth anniversary. Åkerfeldt promoted the venture by stating: 'Even if we're musicians firstly, we're beer drinkers secondly... So when we were approached by the fantastic Northern Monk brewery to do an Opeth signature beer, we simply could not turn it down'.

Obviously, deeper dives into the accolades earned, festivals played, and other crucial events should be saved for when they come up chronologically. For now, it bears repeating that Opeth have amassed one of the most idiosyncratic, admirable, and reliable discographies in modern progressive metal. Never content to simply repeat themselves or sell out for more mainstream victories, their daring eclecticism has resulted in not only countless protégés citing them as influences, but also innumerable other members of prog rock royalty showering them with praise. In the October 2017 issue of *PROG* magazine alone, Mike Portnoy, Steve Hackett, Steven Wilson, and Ayreon architect Arjen Anthony Lucassen shared their esteem for what Opeth have accomplished.

Throughout their periodic shifts in players, sounds, and representation, the band have sustained a singular vision, with Åkerfeldt's unapologetic sense of purpose, development, and humour guiding them every step of the way. That unparalleled artistry is precisely what this book will discuss. With a combination of historical insights and original assessments, we'll go album-by-album and track-by-track to provide fair judgments on what makes Opeth's one-of-a-kind journey as monumental as it is masterful. Let's get to it.

Orchid (1995)

Personnel:
Mikael Åkerfeldt: lead vocals, acoustic and electric guitars
Peter Lindgren: acoustic and electric guitars
Johan De Farfalla: backing vocals, acoustic and electric bass
Anders Nordin: drums, percussion, piano on 'Silhouette'
Additional Personnel:
Stefan Guteklint: bass on 'Into the Frost of Winter' (bonus track)
Torbjörn Ekebacke: artwork, photography
Pontus Norgren: co-production on 'Requiem'
Dan Swanö: engineer, mixing
Produced at Unisound Studio in Finspång, Sweden, March – April 1994 by Opeth and Dan Swanö.
Release date: 15 May 1995
Highest chart places: UK: none, USA: none
Running time: 65:26 (reissue 71:49)
Current edition: 2020 Candlelight Records / Spinefarm Records Record Store Day pink marble swirl 2 x vinyl with bonus track

While the departure of Isberg was unexpected and quick, it wasn't entirely upsetting for the rest of the band. As Åkerfeldt reflects: 'David had stopped showing up for rehearsals [before he quit] and I was starting to take it all more seriously; I was really becoming the leader of the band ... If I'm being honest, there was a sense of relief when he left'. Lindgren concurs, adding, 'At that time, David was a bit troublesome; he didn't make friends with people and didn't even try. On stage, he would insult people and we'd tell him we thought it was unnecessary'. They were even thinking of reforming under a new name and leaving Isberg to fend for himself. Fortunately, that never had to happen, and with Isberg out of the picture, they had free rein to give Opeth a fresh start.

For the next year or so, Åkerfeldt, Lindgren, and Nordin wrote and rehearsed about half a dozen times per week (and sometimes in complete darkness to help establish a sense of control and atmosphere). Along the way, they brought in bassist Stefan Guteklint – who didn't stay for long – and took promo photos to 'feel like a real band', as Lindgren puts it. Although they still looked to extreme metal for inspiration (not only musically but also in terms of work ethic and promotional tactics), Åkerfeldt knew that they wanted to 'be a heavy metal band that could really play', too. So, he started collecting second-hand vinyl records of progressive rock acts such as King Crimson, Camel, Van der Graaf Generator, Yes, Wishbone Ash, and even Dream Theater because their photos reminded him of classic rock and metal giants like Led Zeppelin, Deep Purple, and Black Sabbath. He 'loved the length of the songs, the moods, and movements' so much that he decided to incorporate those attributes into a revised Opeth formula that wittingly strayed from the typical and ubiquitous Swedish death metal sound.

Boldly, they decided against recording a demo, choosing instead to try and get a record deal from the rehearsal tape that they'd be handing out wherever they could. Luckily, a few notable people – Jonas Renkse of Katatonia, Samoth of Emperor, and Candlelight Records founder Lee Barrett – heard it and agreed. (Of course, this also led to Åkerfeldt and Renkse becoming great friends.) Specifically, Barrett heard a snippet of 'The Apostle in Triumph' on a tape of miscellaneous unsigned black metal bands and decided to pursue signing them. Shortly thereafter, Åkerfeldt received a letter from Barrett saying that he wanted to put out an EP. Just as he finished reading it – feeling excited but also disappointed at not getting offered an LP – Barrett called and said to ignore the letter because he wanted to do a full album.

At first, Åkerfeldt thought that this would lead to him living the ideal rock star life; but, after taking the contract to a lawyer, he realised that 'the trips to Malibu' may not come very often. Nevertheless, they were happy to finally see their hard work pay off and get the chance to show the world what they could do. As is often the case, though, that meant reassessing the line-up once more and deciding the Guteklint needed to be replaced. Happily, former bassist Johan De Farfalla – who'd played one show with Opeth before leaving to spend more time with his girlfriend – accepted the role of session musician. With the quartet of Åkerfeldt, Lindgren, Nordin, and De Farfalla now in place, it was time to create what would become *Orchid*.

Because they'd had roughly three years to perfect the songs – and already wrote all the material except for 'In Mist She Was Standing' – they entered Unisound Studio (located 'in the cellar of a small house, right in the middle of a field') well prepared to nail the official versions. In fact, they booked two weeks of sessions but needed only twelve days to get it all done. Åkerfeldt admits: 'I was a bit underwhelmed when we arrived ... as I'd imagined it would have had recording booths and all of the other elements I thought a professional studio would have – but it was a cellar with a 16-track and cheap console with a quarter-inch tape machine'. Even so, they found working with Swanö easy and exciting, if also a bit anxiety-inducing, and they were even able to record much of it live and simultaneously. Having just turned twenty years old, Åkerfeldt encouraged substantial partying as well, and since they were staying at 'a little flat' near the studio, it didn't really impact their productivity.

Lyrically, the LP establishes Åkerfeldt's then-interest in the occult – albeit 'in no serious manner', he clarifies – but he concedes that the focus was more on the music than the words. As for the cover, he'd been following photographer Torbjörn Ekebacke for a while and thought that a simple but evocative image would work. The first pressing didn't feature their quintessential logo, though, and 'the lyric pages were totally the opposite' of what they wanted. The photographs on the back were taken at Åkerfeldt's 'childhood place' in Sörskogen during an especially lovely sunset; while there were 'several cool shots', the silhouette ones were picked as the best.

Unfortunately, *Orchid* wasn't the ground-breaking success that they'd hoped for. For one thing, and as Åkerfeldt explains, Isberg's 'influence' and 'some bad shows' resulted in Opeth having a 'bad reputation' in Stockholm. In addition, it took more than a year for Candlelight Records to put it out, and once they did, they didn't do enough (in the band's eyes) to promote it or get them many touring opportunities. Yet, there was at least some positive feedback in a handful of fanzines, and according Åkerfeldt, some of the other artists who worked with Swanö and heard the LP were 'blown away' to the point of 'hav[ing] band meetings to rethink what they were going to do'.

Since its release, *Orchid* has been praised as a seminal collection not only for Opeth, but for the larger scope of progressive death metal overall. John Serba of *AllMusic* called it 'a far-beyond-epic prog/death monstrosity exuding equal parts beauty and brutality', whereas *Decibel* magazine's Chris Dick said that the album 'changed death metal forever'. Looking back, Åkerfeldt confesses that although some of it makes him 'cringe' now, he finds to be a 'genuine', direct, 'pretentious', and 'energetic' image of who they were at the time. 'Essentially, it sounds like one of our rehearsals but with much better sound ... I don't have a solitary regret about it and am really proud of [it]', he notes.

To say that *Orchid* is the worst Opeth album is both true and misleading, as it implies that it's also a bad album. Far from it, the record is immensely go-getting and wide-ranging, continually infusing its black/death metal core with healthy doses of folk, jazz, classical, and prog rock accentuations. Those features, coupled with Åkerfeldt's rudimentary yet striking ability to play dual roles as devilish and angelic denouncers, means that *Orchid* contains everything that'd come to define Opeth as an outstanding creative force. It's just that they'd already advanced so much by the time it arrived, which is why they were able to follow it with the significantly superior *Morningrise* a mere thirteen months later.

'In Mist She Was Standing' (Åkerfeldt, Lindgren)

Reportedly, it's about a nightmare and was inspired by Erich Engels' 1951 crime film, *The Lady in Black*. It's both the last song completed for *Orchid* and the lengthiest of them all, with elements stemming from a demo called 'Eternal Soul Torture'. Not a moment is wasted, however, making it a thrilling and illustrative way to begin. A rush of continually changing blast beats and guitar riffs set the stage for the extreme metal ire that Opeth deliver so well (especially this early on). Åkerfeldt and Lindgren's exceptional ability to complement and contrast each other's playing is immediately apparent, with Nordin and De Farfalla proving to be a strong rhythm section. Plus, Åkerfeldt's ghostly whispers and chants add an effectively haunting layer that foreshadows the eerie nature of 1998's *My Arms, Your Hearse*.

His screams and graceful words – 'Contorted trees are spreading forth / The message of the wind / With frozen hands I rode with the stars' – reveal how adept he was with those trademarks. Correspondingly, the wild electric guitar solo is emblematically feisty yet melodic, making room for a seamless transition into a brief and serene bridge. The acoustic guitar arpeggios are basic but successful in bringing a gentle coldness to the environment, and they wisely transform it into a harsher rendition of the same melody. A second, more fragmented electric guitar solo segues into an embellished reprise of the bridge before moving onto an entirely new movement.

That surreal passage captures the feeling of being stranded in a dark forest on a moonlit night, and it gives way to more clever guitar counterpoints as De Farfalla's malevolent bass rests in the centre. After some more enticing hecticness and demonic verses, more fierce and speedy changeups take over, displaying great dexterity. Then, a folky interlude appears to appease with handsomely harmonised acoustic guitar lamentations, leading to an outro bursting with aggressive anguish. Elementary as it may be compared to later compositions, 'In Mist She Was Standing' confirms that Opeth were aiming higher than their peers from the get-go.

'Under the Weeping Moon' (Åkerfeldt, Lindgren)
Based around 'some kind of satanic worship of the moon', Åkerfeldt has described the lyrics as 'absolute black metal nonsense'. Actually, they're as poetically macabre as pretty much anything else on the LP. Musically, it's understandably similar to its predecessor but with a bit more finesse and tightness in terms of juxtaposing heavy and light segments. There's also a sturdier use of echoed tones and space to yield a creepier vibe. To be honest, the mid-section lull goes on too long, but it nonetheless builds tension well via dissonant textures and periodic instrumental eruptions. When the vehemence returns, it's tremendous, with a lead guitar note ringing out like an impassioned buzzsaw. Likewise, the jazz fusion break around the seven-minute mark is remarkably intricate, just as the coda – 'Burn the winter landmarks / That said I was there' – is tender and ghoulish. All in all, it's another stupendous sign of Opeth's dynamic prowess.

'Silhouette' (Nordin)
The annals of popular music are filled with cases of excellent drummers who could also write and perform excellent piano pieces; here, we get one of the best examples in recent memory. It was recorded hours before they left the studio one day, and Nordin's arrangement is a gothic gem that oozes romanticism, panic, and classical heft. It begins mournfully and patiently prior to embarking on a whirlwind of wicked and uncontrollable alterations. Near the end, it settles back into a leisurely and luscious motif that can't help but get stuck in your head. It's a very rewarding diversion from *Orchid*'s prevailing characteristics, which makes it all the more tragic that Opeth never truly did something like it again.

'Forest of October' (Åkerfeldt, Lindgren)

Parts of it came from the first song Åkerfeldt ever wrote for Opeth, 'Requiem for Lost Souls', and at one point in time, Lindgren called it 'the best song on the album'. While that's quite debatable, it's inarguably another superb addition. Nordin's laidback syncopation does a good job of supporting the alluringly multilayered electric guitar croons at the start; from there, Åkerfeldt's snarls guide more piercing turmoil that's interspersed with bits of tranquillity (including a couple of pleasant lines – 'Gazing unto the stars / Please, take me there' – that hint at his ability to sing cleanly). Gorgeous rustic intervals and hasty frenzies of metal wrath bleed into each other over the next few minutes, with Åkerfeldt's evil explanations taking over from time to time. De Farfalla's bounciness really comes through three-quarters of the way in, just before Åkerfeldt's monotone yet epic chants kick off another stirring solo. It winds down with an acoustic outro – complete with marching drums – that cements 'Forest of October' as a poignant and flexible victory.

'The Twilight is My Robe' (Åkerfeldt, Lindgren)

Formerly known as 'Oath', it's another Satanist dedication, and Åkerfeldt jokes that it's 'a complete rip-off' of 'Fly to the Rainbow' by Scorpions. There are certainly connections to be made if you look hard enough, but the track is far from an overt emulation. Clearly, it harkens back to the empowering directness of definitive Judas Priest, Queensrÿche, and Iron Maiden, with an opening attack of emotional riffs and agitated percussion acting as a declaration of purpose. For a moment, things calm down with a central bass pattern alongside warm guitar strums and clean vocals, but Opeth instantly launch back into their hellish foundation. Likely the nicest acoustic breather yet happens next, and Åkerfeldt's matching narration is sweet – if expectedly timid – as well. Afterwards, De Farfalla and Nordin align to jumpstart more irregular and penetrating instrumentation. The rest of the tune sustains that requisite back-and-forth motion, culminating in a likeable inclusion that undeniably highlights *Orchid*'s forgivable but explicit formulaicness. (The effects during the closing guitar solo are awesome, too.)

'Requiem' (Åkerfeldt, Lindgren)

It's an attractive little folk/jazz instrumental full of elegant interactions between acoustic and bass guitars. True to Åkerfeldt's mission, it sees them reaching new heights as players and composers, integrating more non-metal influences into their artistry. The finished product is even more noteworthy considering the issues they had recording it. As the group explain:

> The only real problem that occurred was that we didn´t have enough time to record [it] properly. We did actually record it first at Unisound, but the result was not at all pleasing. So that particular piece was actually recorded in a studio in Stockholm with a guy called Pontus Norgren as co-producer. He had

earlier been with a rather famous HM [heavy metal] band, called Great King Rat, and I must say that I was kinda impressed with his knowledge too!

In addition, there was a mix-up in the album's mastering process, which is why the end of it is tacked onto the start of closer 'The Apostle in Triumph'. That can be seen as a happy accident, though, since 'Requiem' not only comes across as complete anyway but also feels linked to its successor due to the mishap. In contrast to 'Silhouette', they *would* revisit and improve upon this approach many times over the next 25 years.

'The Apostle in Triumph' (Åkerfeldt, Lindgren)

It's unclear how much of the finished version was a part of the aforementioned demo that made Barrett sign Opeth. (There is also a four-minute *Apostle in Triumph* promo from 1994 that's comprised of poorly recorded segments from 'Forest of October' and 'In Mist She Was Standing'. It was just meant for label executives to hear, but it was eventually leaked to the public.) In any case, its lyrics fuse demonic and nature worship, and the ending of 'Requiem', though there by accident, assuredly works as a sort of Indian raga appetiser to the main course.

The song itself begins with an easygoing and compelling jam that features a few sharper timbres and flare-ups. De Farfalla subtly mimics what Åkerfeldt and Lindgren do while Nordin keeps order. About four minutes in, it dives into black metal bleakness, and Åkerfeldt's guttural decrees (such as 'Rain is pouring down my (now) shivering shoulders / In the rain, my tears are forever lost') are slightly more discernible than usual. Truthfully, it's the most run-of-the-mill portion of *Orchid*, but it's still engagingly grisly and peppy. Halfway through, a wavering and somewhat symphonic tone – joined by delicate drumming and pastoral elements – presents an appreciated change of scenery prior to the return of the disorder. The backing chants are a fine touch and further verify Opeth's aptitude for throwing in new fragments to shake things up. The concluding section is restful but faintly harrowing, too. All things considered, it's not the best track in the sequence, but it is a good way to end it.

Bonuses

The 2000 Candlelight Records reissue – and every edition since then – also houses 'Into the Frost of Winter', an early and raw rehearsal recording that goes back to 1992. Parts of it were recycled for 'Advent' from *Morningrise*, and that alone makes it interesting. There's also some fan debate regarding if Åkerfeldt or Isberg sings on it; Isberg is never credited on any version of *Orchid*, however, so it's safe to assume that it's indeed Åkerfeldt. If the quality weren't so dull, it would fit perfectly well with the rest of the disc because it encompasses the same kind of fluctuations in pacing and temperament. It's a tad less sophisticated and striving, sure, but it's not that far off, either.

Morningrise (1996)

Personnel:
Mikael Åkerfeldt: lead vocals, acoustic and electric guitars
Peter Lindgren: acoustic and electric guitars
Johan De Farfalla: backing vocals, bass
Anders Nordin: drums, percussion
Additional Personnel:
Stefan Guteklint: bass guitar on 'Eternal Soul Torture' (bonus track)
Tom Martinsen: artwork
Lennart Kaltea: booklet, photography
Timo Ketola: layout, logo
Tuija Lindström: album cover
Dan Swanö: engineer, mixing
Produced at Unisound Studio in Finspång, Sweden, March – April 1996 by Opeth and Dan Swanö.
Release date: 24 June 1996
Highest chart places: UK: none, USA: none
Running time: 66:02 (reissue 74:37)
Current edition: 2016 Candlelight Records / Spinefarm Records European CD reissue with bonus track

Undoubtedly, *Orchid* was a creatively successful introduction that fuelled Opeth's desire to outdo themselves with a sophomore sequence; however, it failed to garner sufficient attention from anyone outside of their inner circle and scattered newcomers in 'the US, Poland, Australia, and Japan', so Opeth were far from the household name they desired to be. As previously mentioned, a major reason for why was that the label did little to get the band in front of prospective fans. Åkerfeldt muses that it was the beginning of 'a three or four-year struggle with Candlelight Records where we were questioning why [we] weren't touring, why no one knew who we were, and why we weren't being mentioned next to bands like Emperor who were also on the label – and this lasted for the duration of the contract'.

With little else to do, Opeth hunkered down and completed writing new material that, as Åkerfeldt rightly assesses, 'delved more into the prog side of things' and aimed to 'show all of those who had ignored the first album what they'd been missing'. (Because their debut was delayed for so long, they wrote a significant amount of *Morningrise* before *Orchid* was released, with some of it dating back to 1991.) For sure, the five-song set progresses their sound in every way, especially when it comes to an enhancement in clean singing and fluid multipart structures. It even houses their first and only side-long piece, the twenty-minute penultimate classic 'Black Rose Immortal', which still stands as one of their most beloved tunes. Åkerfeldt and Lindgren also wrote an instrumental piece that they didn't include because they weren't able to finish it.

Regarding the now-iconic cover, it features a photo of a Palladian bridge in Prior Park in Bath, England. Åkerfeldt received a colour postcard from someone at Candlelight Records – likely Barrett – and wanted to modify it to be what it became. As with *Orchid*, Opeth's logo wasn't included in the initial batch of records.

To support *Morningrise*, they managed to book a summer tour with Morbid Angel and a month-long fall tour with Cradle of Filth that stretched from Scandinavia to Spain and Italy (during which they partied only after performances). Lindgren ponders: 'We were opening the shows, so we were able to get off the stage quite early and have time to get wasted every night!' He also gives Cradle of Filth credit for being 'really nice and treat[ing] us well', which eased the sense of defeat they felt playing to crowds that didn't value them very much. Add to that the fact that Barrett wasn't always the most helpful or understanding leader, as he frequently expected Opeth to borrow amps from Cradle of Filth and then blamed them for their inexperience and unpreparedness.

This led to the label and the group agreeing that they should seek a suitable manager. Åkerfeldt reached out to Dave Thorne at Sanctuary Music (who was looking after acts such as Arch Enemy and Spiritual Beggars right before keyboardist Per Wiberg joined the latter in 1998). After several months of silence, he finally phoned Åkerfeldt to compliment the music, criticise the vocals, and make 'no mention of management at all!' as Åkerfeldt states. At the same time, tensions were rising between Åkerfeldt, Lindgren, and De Farfalla due to De Farfalla adopting a 'rock start attitude', resulting in both De Farfalla and Nordin leaving the band. (More on that when we get to *My Arms, Your Hearse*).

Over the years, *Morningrise* has become one of Opeth's most popular records (at least for fans of their darkest persona), with many outlets championing its evolution and impact on the genre. In 2005, *Sea of Tranquility*'s Murat Batmaz professed that it's 'a very, very big achievement and one of the best Opeth albums', due in part to how De Farfalla and Nordin add 'subtle jazz harmonies' to augment 'the psychedelic passages'. To be fair, several major magazines – like *Loudwire*, *Decibel*, *Metal Injection*, and *Stereogum* – rank it below *Orchid* and consider it far from Opeth's finest project, but they also show gratitude for what it does. Specifically, *Stereogum*'s Jonathan Dick avowed: '[It's] like a listening exercise in just how many times a band can change dynamics during the course of one song. . . . *Morningrise* offered a perspective on the virtually limitless musicianship of Opeth'.

Although the LP could be viewed as the second half of *Orchid*, there's enough refinement, exploration, and captivation to deem it a substantial step forward. It's an all-around more fetching and confident effort whose songwriting, musicianship, and even vocals outclass its forebear. The first four tracks expertly mature their merging of hard and soft components within sizeable frameworks, while the finale 'To Bid You Farewell' endures as a top-tier Opeth acoustic ballad. Therefore, *Morningrise* surpasses *Orchid* while remaining an ancestor to the start of their true artistic breakthrough.

'Advent' (Åkerfeldt, Lindgren)

Using bits and pieces from a few demos – 'Into the Frost of Winter', 'Poise into Celeano', and 'Eternal Soul Torture' – 'Advent' is a thunderously prophetic opener. Its twenty-second echoey set-up alludes to the grave cinematic nature of *My Arms, Your Hearse*, and the ensuing influx of jackhammer percussion, sinister riffs, gruff announcements, and smooth segues are like a coarse preview of the sleek violence that dominates *Deliverance*. The rhythm section is expressly exciting and inventive, with De Farfalla's springy movements accompanying the acoustic and electric guitars as they reveal a polished ability to reinterpret the same themes.

Åkerfeldt's singing has developed as well, with his first friendly sung section – 'But you were beyond all help / The folded message that wept my name' – indicating vast composure. The subsequent arrangement maintains *Morningrise*'s already evident upgrade in terms of interweaving vicious and meek timbres with nuance, resonance, and professionalism. In total, 'Advent' filters nearly all of *Orchid*'s specialities into a snugger and more arresting concoction, with De Farfalla's perpetually flexible patterns, mesmeric acoustic guitar fingerpicking, and brief but lovely harmonies near the end increasing that finely tuned expansiveness.

'The Night and the Silent Water' (Åkerfeldt, Lindgren)

Knowing that it was written about the death of Åkerfeldt's grandfather gives extra substance and clarity to stanzas such as 'And so you left us / Jaded and gaunt, some September / Wilted with the seasons / But hidden inside the delusion'. That melancholia also shines through in the simultaneously cathartic and crunchy lead-off, wherein Åkerfeldt's throaty agony is coordinated with sombre rhythms and shrilly downtrodden guitar work. His secluded whisper – 'All your words are misgiven' – plays into the ethereal nature of Opeth's initial trio of records, and the consequential combination of jazzy acoustic outlines and remorseful thoughts produce the most touchingly lush movement in Opeth's catalogue thus far.

Naturally, that sensitivity bookends more anger midway through; it's an unassuming but useful demonstration of their talent for affectively mirrored guitar lines. Resourcefully, a wall of twangy chords coincides with thumping rhythms to spark suspense a few minutes before the track is done. Then, more dreary commotion covers Åkerfeldt's purposefully elongated final sentiment, fortifying the weight of Opeth's first autobiographical venture.

'Nectar' (Åkerfeldt, Lindgren)

The common interpretation of 'Nectar' is that it explores nightmares and the longing for a deceased lover; in doing so, it's practically a precursor to the

plots of *My Arms, Your Hearse* and *Still Life*. Nordin opens it with drumming
that sounds like a click track – which is more of an observation than a criticism
– and the unified blend of electric and acoustic qualities is infectious. De
Farfalla's isolated moment is neat, too, and showcases how much *Morningrise*
emphasises imaginative prog rock flourishes. Sadly, the song gets a bit drab
from there – that is until it paves the way for De Farfalla's lone interruption
(one of the coolest moments on the LP, for sure). Further on, a marginally
derivative guitar solo appeals prior to another burst of enticing time signature
tomfoolery.

Once again, a pleasing vocal harmony – 'Mine is yours' – comes in to
designate how well Opeth can balance heavenly and hellish roles. Their regal
acoustic duet is a cherished addition as well, especially since it instigates such
a sympathetically morose but soothing section that exemplifies how much
they've grown as both individual players and collaborative musicians. Equally,
the belligerent – yet almost funky – climax is an explicit prototype for 'Demon
of the Fall' from the following album.

'Black Rose Immortal' (Åkerfeldt, Lindgren)

Ah, so we've come to the twenty-minute monster that still lives as Opeth's
longest statement. They'd been working on it since 1992, and despite being
a little amateurish, it fully encapsulates *Morningrise*'s advancements. At first,
it's relentlessly malicious, with a downpour of growls and an abrasive score
situating you in the depths of the underworld. Nevertheless, the sporadic
changeups keep you intrigued, particularly when the Jethro Tull-esque
woodland shift shuffles the mood near the start. Also – and not to keep
repeating the same bit of praise – the punchy bass lines really stand out behind
the pungent guitar riffs during this preliminary segment.

Later, sounds of water help make 'Black Rose Immortal' seem like a larger-
than-life fable, as does the splendidly sorrowful acoustic bridge roughly one-
fifth of the way through. As with everything Opeth were doing around this
time, none of it is notably complex, but it never stops keeping you on your
toes, and that's precisely the charm of it. That said, the hyperactive outbursts
and key changes around the eight-minute mark – plus the searing solo within
the midst of that chaos – are staggering in the best way possible. Nordin's skills
are truly put to the test here, too.

Suddenly, Åkerfeldt peacefully sings a reverberated ode – 'Eyes attach to
your mute portrait / We spoke only through thoughts' – that cues a sublimely
stately prelude to a beautiful folk detour ('Sun birds leave their dark recesses
/ Shadows gild the archways'). Hyperbolic as it may be to suggest, it's at this
exact moment that Opeth's songwriting and Åkerfeldt's clean vocals are taken
to the next level, giving listeners a glimpse into how matchless they'd become.
Their adoption of that blueprint into a harsher context works well, too, with
an engrossing new guitar melody layered on top to punctuate the emotional
immensity.

A new acoustic section sets up the concluding quarter of the track with ravishing tension. In typical fashion, it's countered by immense hostility before being enhanced by even more dramatic musicianship. As it finishes, the quartet issue one last flood of fury whose disturbing closing screeches drill directly into the listener's soul. It's frightening and fragile at once, ingeniously capping off the epic trip. If they were able to pull this off at the very start of their career, just imagine how much better they could make another side-long suite today. Either way, 'Black Rose Immortal' is a masterful titan.

'To Bid You Farewell' (Åkerfeldt, Lindgren)

Åkerfeldt and company were certain that 'all metal people would hate it' because of how 'mellow' it is; they didn't care, however, because they 'liked it so much'. That commitment to a singular vision has always been one of the band's biggest assets, and it still pays off since 'To Bid You Farewell' has lost none of its tearful brilliance in the 25 years since it concluded *Morningrise*. Even today, it's among Opeth's greatest compositions.

Admittedly, the wordless introduction takes its time getting to its destination, but it's lovingly majestic along the way (and it plainly foretells of future pieces like 'Benighted', 'For Absent Friends', and 'Patterns in the Ivy'). Åkerfeldt and Lindgren excel at crafting interlocked acoustic structures that exude purification and yearning, and behind them, De Farfalla and Nordin provide refreshing bounciness. As a result, the transition that comes afterwards (and right before the first verse) feels especially troubling.

Åkerfeldt's vocals are pleasantly sincere and kind as he recites plaintive reflections around a nourishing arrangement; in-between, a silky acoustic guitar solo reminiscent of classic Camel (an influence that Åkerfeldt's always worn on his sleeve) boosts the comforting yet woeful vibe. Decades later, it's still one of Opeth's best. Once we reach the middle of the tune, psychedelic wah-wah effects, agitated percussion, and heated chords are added as the heartache swells; it ultimately breaks with a drum fill that prompts a spiteful turnaround. Even so, the vocals are still richly inviting, and Åkerfeldt returns to his most distraught form to utter his last recognition – 'We walked into the night / Am I / To bid you farewell' – escorted by a lingering bundle of gentle strums. It's an exquisite ending.

Bonuses

Like 'Into the Frost of Winter', 'Eternal Soul Torture' is a part of all *Morningrise* reissues. It's a 1992 demo whose lyrics are credited to Isberg (though there's no indication that he played on it). As already pointed out, some excerpts were reused on 'Advent' and 'In Mist She Was Standing'. It consists mostly of wicked guitar work, 'cookie-monster' vocals (as they're often called), and frantic syncopation; honestly, there's nothing special about it aside from those connections. Rather, it's generic and poorly captured, working better as a behind-the-scenes novelty than as a listenable batch of spare parts.

My Arms, Your Hearse (1998)

Personnel:
Mikael Åkerfeldt: vocals, acoustic and electric guitars, bass, grand piano
Peter Lindgren: acoustic and electric guitars, photography
Martin López: drums
Additional Personnel:
Fredrik Nordström: engineer, mixing, Hammond organ on 'Epilogue'
Anders Fridén: engineer
Tom Martinsen: graphic design
Timo Ketola: logo
Produced at Studio Fredman and Maestro Musik/Nacksving Studios in Gothenburg,
Sweden, August – September 1997 by Opeth, Fredrik Nordström, and Anders
Fridén.
Release date: 18 August 1998
Highest chart places: UK: none, USA: none
Running time: 53:13 (reissue 62:45)
Current edition: 2019 Candlelight Records European blue/yellow 2x vinyl reissue
with bonus tracks

Having achieved moderate success with their first two albums – and feeling
creatively satisfied – Opeth were all set to go further than ever with their
third LP. (They'd even signed to Century Media Records while on tour in
Scandinavia, which meant that *Orchid* and *Morningrise* were rereleased
in America under the Century Black offshoot.) Sure, they were without a
manager, but that didn't really deter them. However, there was *another* major
problem that needed sorting out: De Farfalla, whose arrogance had become
incompatible with Åkerfeldt and Lindgren's more grounded personalities.
Lindgren recalls: 'It had been a big deal ... when Johan had joined ... because
he was already a name in the suburb where we lived. He played a six-string
bass and he could really play, but he didn't fit our music and our style'.
    Likewise, Åkerfeldt told Dave Everley of *PROG* in October 2017: 'In the
early days, we didn't make any money, we couldn't live off the music, so
a lot of people simply quit. Other people have been fired, but I haven't
fired anyone based on nothing – there's always been a reason'. So, he
and Lindgren 'rehearsed' firing De Farfalla in Lindgren's kitchen (with his
girlfriend 'playing the role of Johan'). When the actual moment of truth
came, De Farfalla was surprisingly amicable about it, as if he'd also been
thinking about a separation. Oddly enough, it was Nordin who became so
incensed by the decision – partially because he was vacationing in Brazil and
wasn't consulted for his opinion on the matter – that he quit on the spot and
announced his plan to move back to Brazil. That effectively left Opeth as a
duo, at least for a little while.
    Reasonably, Åkerfeldt and Lindgren felt uncertain of the band's future,
but they decided to press on and try to find replacements. They placed

advertisements in music shops and eventually attracted the attention of
Swedish-Uruguayan drummer Martin López (formerly of Amon Amarth),
whom Åkerfeldt describes as a 'super cocky, funny, witty, [and] full of attitude'
musician who 'kind of kicked [him] and Lindgren in the ass ... and essentially
rejuvenated the band'. As it turns out, López had removed all the adverts
he could to ensure that he was the only viable option, which showed 'great
determination', according to Lindgren. Feeling confident about López and the
'bits and pieces' they'd already written, the trio got to work on what would
become *My Arms, Your Hearse*.

Part of that process involved testing López's abilities regarding both intricate
and simple techniques, as well as educating him on acts he wasn't familiar with
(such as Camel) and recording a cover of Iron Maiden's 'Remember Tomorrow'
for a 1998 tribute album called *A Call to Irons: A Tribute to Iron Maiden*.
Although they felt fine proceeding as a trio – at least for this next record –
Åkerfeldt and Lindgren were intrigued when López suggested that his close
friend and roommate, Martín Méndez, audition to be their new bassist. They'd
met in Uruguay but moved to Sweden – where Méndez first encountered snow
– as teenagers primarily to join the death metal scene. Méndez was already
a fan of Opeth, too, and he felt especially lucky being asked to join since he
'couldn't even speak English and spoke very little Swedish'. Lindgren explains:
'It was like dealing with one person: you called one and you got two, which
was very convenient'. Since he became an official member only a week or so
before they started recording, he had no time to learn the material; therefore,
My Arms, Your Hearse remains the only Opeth LP on which Åkerfeldt plays all
of the bass.

With the 'classic line-up' – as Lindgren sees it – in place, Åkerfeldt and
Lindgren became more committed than ever to Opeth. 'We never had any
money; we had to take part-time jobs just to get through the day ... That's
what we were living for – the music – that was all', Lindgren ruminates. They
still wrote together, of course, but Åkerfeldt was already sensing that he was
'advanc[ing] further' and occasionally feeling 'distracted by Peter's suggestions
for whatever [he] was working on', leading Lindgren to scale back his
contributions and enthusiasm. 'It wasn't a very happy record to do', Åkerfeldt
concludes, and at first, even he wasn't pleased with the finished sequence. It
wasn't until he saw how much co-producer Anders Fridén (singer of In Flames)
and Mike Amott (founding guitarist of Arch Enemy) liked it that he began
appreciating it.

Speaking of how the album took Opeth into a new direction, Åkerfeldt
deduces: 'We wanted something heavier, and a lot of that was down to López
joining the band, as he was more of a powerhouse drummer than Anders – so,
as a consequence, [it] became a bit ... [more] extreme and evil-sounding than
what we had done before. It was the beginning of the sound that we would
become known for'. Undeniably, *My Arms, Your Hearse* outshines *Orchid* and
Morningrise in every way, with better production, tighter songwriting, fresher

arrangements, more eccentric timbres, and an overarchingly improved sense of experimentation, focus, and capability. Obviously, a major component of all that is the fact that it's their first concept album, with Åkerfeldt – for the first time – writing the lyrics before any of the music.

In a 1998 interview with *Lamentations of the Flame Princess*, Åkerfeldt broke down the storyline of *My Arms, Your Hearse*:

> [It's] basically about dying and becoming a ghost or spirit trapped in the form of mist on earth, and being confronted with the reactions of those being close. It reaches throughout one earthly year, and during this time, the character tries to affect people and subjects, but without much success. It results only in the character scaring his loved ones to death; thus, he plunges into a wicked state of mind, and wants to bring his beloved with him to the other side.

That plot is one of a few reasons for why the LP also comes across as an overt precursor to 1999's extraordinary *Still Life*. If that weren't enough, *My Arms, Your Hearse* features an additional trick: each song flows into the next, with an abundance of lyrical allusions connecting the parts. It's a very effective and crafty gimmick that makes the LP a treasurable anomaly within Opeth's discography.

As for the change in producers and studio, Swanö had closed Unisound Studio by the time Opeth were ready to go; that led them to look for other options, ultimately settling on Fredrik Nordström and Studio Fredman due to his fine work on At The Gates' *Slaughter of the Soul* about two years prior. They lived there as they recorded as well. In the official session diaries, Åkerfeldt writes that he 'slept on the fucking floor in the recording room for two weeks', adding, 'I needed a fan blowing in my face, as the heat was too fucking intense for me to handle. Peter slept on the couch, and López … that strange man slept on the toilet floor, using a pile of porn mags as a pillow!' Due to issues with mixing, they had to redo some acoustic guitar work at Maestro Musik/Nacksving Studios before returning to Studio Fredman; meanwhile, Åkerfeldt got a cold that, thankfully, didn't mess up his vocal performances.

As with *Orchid*, the release of *My Arms, Your Hearse* was delayed about a year. On the bright side, though, it was their first album to be issued in Europe and America simultaneously (on Candlelight and Century Black, respectively). Critically, it fared even better than its predecessors, with *Chronicles of Chaos* writer Pedro Azevedo declaring, 'Top quality sections just flow throughout the album, making it truly excellent'. (Magazines such as *Terrorizer*, *Sea of Tranquillity*, *Metal Storm*, and *Metal Crypt* have expressed similar assessments.) In 2015, *Metal Injection* named it the third best Opeth album, while 2017 saw *Prog Sphere* rank it at their fifth.

It wouldn't be unjust to view *My Arms, Your Hearse* as *Still Life Jr.* considering that it established a template that Opeth would perfect with that fourth studio collection. Nevertheless, the record does plenty on its own to escape the shadow of its superior successor. It's at once glossier, weirder, and angrier than *Orchid* and *Morningrise* – both of which now seem like mere stepping-stones – and its atypical construction (such as featuring three instrumental passages, including a 'Prologue' and an 'Epilogue') allows it to stay relatively distinctive. Although Opeth would go on to do even stronger projects, *My Arms, Your Hearse* – named after a lyric from Comus' 'Drip Drip' and dedicated to Lee Barrett – was indubitably their first truly great full-length effort.

'Prologue' (Åkerfeldt, Lindgren, López)

Right away, *My Arms, Your Hearse* goes farther than its predecessors in terms of scope and ambition, with this minute-long run-up setting the gorgeously gothic stage. Sounds of rain and wind introduce dejected piano chords that ascend slowly, conveying the great tragedy at hand (the ghost watching his lover mourn for him at his funeral). Although it's an instrumental track, there are unsung lyrics that go along with it and validate that implication, such as: 'Still clinging to vast, old memories / And I would marvel at her beauty / Playing through the rain / The coffin is beautifully engraved'. Overall, there's almost nothing to 'Prologue', but it's quite alluring as a set-up for what's to come, with Åkerfeldt's intensifying bellow acting as a bridge into the true start of the tale.

'April Ethereal' (Åkerfeldt)

His crooning swells to its breaking point, giving way to a torrent of outraged observations and instrumentation regarding the protagonist watching his beloved suffer as he becomes a spirit. He questions how deeply she's affected by his death, leading to a transitional passage that foreshadows 'The Funeral Portrait' from 2001's *Blackwater Park*. True to Åkerfeldt's intention, it's probably the most uncompromisingly destructive song Opeth has done thus far, yet the acoustic guitar fingerpicking a couple of minutes in adds a moment of earnest sadness. Shortly thereafter, López's quick breakdown reveals his unique style.

Following a few more fast and complicated movements, López delivers a modest fill that instigates Åkerfeldt's soulful proclamation: 'I will endure / Hide away / I would outrun the scythe / Glaring with failure'. It provides a wonderful breather prior to a fiery guitar solo, and after more grief-stricken riffs, Opeth jump back into their penchant for jazzy balminess before the hectic misery returns. In fact, the arrangement borders on thrash metal here, albeit with more gracefulness. As it fades out, a calming new electric guitar part enters and leads us into 'When'.

'When' (Åkerfeldt)

Easily the top track on *My Arms, Your Hearse*, 'When' is ahead of its time since its immaculate fluidity and absorbing melodies wouldn't be out of place on something several years in the future (such as 2002's *Deliverance*). As *MetalSucks* contributor and YouTuber Tristan Pratt (aka TheMetalTris) states, the song finds the main character suspecting that his partner has been unfaithful, yet he still wants to 'bring her into this ghostly world'. Åkerfeldt elaborates: 'Her grieving is complete, but not to his satisfaction. He hears voices from somebody else than her. Unable to figure out if it's imagination or not, he expects the worst, and the story unfolds'.

With that in mind, it's no wonder that his earth-shattering scream – likely the greatest jump scare in metal – cuts off the 'April Ethereal' segue. Then, it erupts into a fascinating display of wrath that solidifies how reinvigorated and gifted the new trio are, resolving with a categorically hypnotic combo of succulent harmony – 'to find my way back home' – and evocative electric guitar solo. It glides into tenderly stacked acoustic guitar work and spectral murmurs before bringing back the tempting aggression. The instrumental revving up halfway in is a swift but awesome example of Opeth's enlarged knack for creating spellbinding musical jigsaw puzzles.

Similarly, there's enhanced melodic dignity in the six-string set-ups (electric and acoustic) for Åkerfeldt's chief epiphany – 'Once inside, I heard whispers in the parlour' – which he sings affectionately. Naturally, the character assumes that his lover has already moved on, so he becomes infuriated, caringly pondering his plans ('When can I take you from this place?') as the group compellingly drives us toward the LP's fleeting and imperial intermission, 'Madrigal'.

'Madrigal' (Åkerfeldt, Lindgren, López)
Initially, a cloud of meshed, nonchalant guitar notes bears the ghost's anguish; along the way, extra coatings hint at eventual danger and retaliation. As with 'Prologue', there's not much to it, yet it too prospers at heightening the theatricality of the sequence. Without it, the record wouldn't come off as much like a cultured multi-act play.

'The Amen Corner' (Åkerfeldt)
That vulnerability is transformed into vulgarity as 'The Amen Corner' – whose name may be a nod to the 1960s Welsh psychedelic/pop rock ensemble in addition to its obvious religious connections – commences. The man continues to wallow in the wish that their bond remained, as well as wonder if the other man is there to support or seduce her. It's a grimy and antagonistic outbreak of tones that gives way to Åkerfeldt's diabolical yelling. (It's worth noting the advancement of seasons, too, as we've moved from springtime to 'white summer', illustrating how he's been stalking and judging her for a while.)

Troubled acoustic arpeggios – accompanied by a velvety and uplifting riff – soon take over, signifying Lindgren and Åkerfeldt's evolving synergy. The previous indignation reappears instantly, though, only to be upended again by another liberating section ('The celestial touch / From grey to black') that's backed by hasty heavy metal solos. He indicates communicating with his lover via 'eerie circles upon the waters' as spurts of ferociousness cascade around him. Finally, he decides that the only way to fully confront her is to become the 'demon of the fall', initiating a decorative and restful outro that starkly juxtaposes the bizarreness to come.

'Demon of the Fall' (Åkerfeldt, Lindgren)

This one begins with fittingly otherworldly dissonance bleeding into brash and steadfast resentment. It's a logical means of representing how the woman is (as Åkerfeldt clarifies) 'being confronted with his spirit, [but] this time [he is feeling] rage due to frustration'. Of course, the story is now situated in autumn – hence the title – and both musically and vocally, Opeth channel the entirety of the hell. Åkerfeldt has never sounded scarier (and wouldn't again until *Deliverance*), unfolding how 'false love turned into pure hate' as he provokes and threatens his former spouse. Rather than alleviate the impending doom, periodic acoustic guitar twangs escalate the nightmarishness inbetween the savage onslaughts. Really, the only relief is at the end, when Åkerfeldt kindly beckons her to 'Run away / Run away'. Haunting fragments – acoustic plucking and patient percussion – then sail into 'Credence'.

Curiously – and not unjustifiably – Åkerfeldt evaluates the composition as 'cool' but 'a bit too linear and streamlined because it only really has one breakdown'. He also calls it 'one of those instant songs' because it 'just came together very quickly' and wasn't 'anything special'. Compared to most of the other tracks on *My Arms, Your Hearse*, it is fairly straightforward, but that's far from a knock against it. Instead, that plainness flawlessly embodies the blinding ire of Åkerfeldt's anti-hero.

'Credence' (Åkerfeldt)

Realising that his darling is afraid of him and wants to move on – as well as the fact that he can't take her with him into the afterlife – the man's depression deepens, and thus we have this lovely ballad. Unsurprisingly, it's a tad suggestive of 'To Bid Your Farewell', with interwoven acoustic guitar patterns and light drumming yielding elegant devastation. Åkerfeldt's pessimistic narration (regarding the ghost watching his widow as she moves throughout her house, seemingly unphased by his absence) is genuine and heartbreaking. Once he finishes singing, the tastefully disconsolate – if also too drawn-out – addendum takes us to 'the once unknown karma'.

'Karma' (Åkerfeldt)

We're now into winter and, in Åkerfeldt's words, the protagonist can 'cross the line to the other side'. It starts heatedly, with all the black metal depravity you'd anticipate for such a bittersweet climax. He agrees to leave his 'rotting body clad in ancient clothes ... behind with a wave of the hand', and a single-note chant (that, however unintentional, conjures the opening of Yes' 'Close to the

Edge') steers Opeth into an tantalisingly new but still vindictive path. Midway in, a softly sung acknowledgment – 'You have nothing more to find / You have nothing more to lose' – and a few fancy acoustic guitar hooks bring solace to the experience. It's rapidly substituted for more ruthless suspense as 'Karma' barrels forward, permitting various musical fluctuations to adorn the spectre's livid descent into his ultimate resting place: the forest.

'Epilogue' (Åkerfeldt, Lindgren, López)

Like a forerunner to *Damnation*'s 'Ending Credits', 'Epilogue' exudes poignant conclusiveness. Nordström's forlorn Hammond organ chords and López's compliant beats travel alongside the weeping guitar phrases like heavenly pallbearers, covering the landscape with equal portions of torment and closure. At the end, a final double-tracked guitar riff acts as the unforgettable bow that ties up the tale for good, leaving the listener thoroughly enthralled. Even though Opeth would make better albums at the turn of the century, they never quite recaptured the theatrical magic of *My Arms, Your Hearse*.

Bonuses

The 2000 reissue (and all future releases) comes with two cover songs: Celtic Frost's 'Circle of the Tyrants' and Iron Maiden's 'Remember Tomorrow'. The former (originally written by frontman/guitarist Thomas Gabriel Fischer and taken from 1985's *To Mega Therion* debut LP) was used for 1996's *In Memory of Celtic Frost* compilation. Interestingly, Opeth reimagine the grungy opening guitar riff via medieval piano echoes before launching into a considerably authentic rendition. Predictably, there's a stronger progressive death metal edge, too, such as with some trickier transitions and a closing acoustic passage that evokes parts of 'Black Rose Immortal'. I dare say it's the superior version.

As for 'Remember Tomorrow' – which Lindgren says López 'struggled' with – it was penned by bassist Steve Harris and vocalist Paul Di'Anno for Iron Maiden's self-titled 1980 full-length introduction. Opeth's attempt is even more faithful than their cut of 'Circle of the Tyrants', as it closely follows Iron Maiden's blueprint but with more angelic bulk. In other words, it's a marginally fuller and faster production whose ability to mirror the original take – musically *and* vocally – is extremely impressive. Cliché as it is to suggest, both inclusions highlight Opeth's cleverness at making other people's material feel like their own, with just enough idiosyncrasies to seem organic without sacrificing anything essential. Seeing as how many cover songs are either too indistinguishable or too different from their inspirations, it's a commendable balance to strike.

Still Life (1999)

Personnel:
Mikael Åkerfeldt: vocals, acoustic and electric guitars
Peter Lindgren: electric guitars
Martin López: drums
Martin Méndez: bass
Additional Personnel:
Fredrik Nordström: engineer, mixing
Isak Edh: engineer, mixing
Travis Smith: album art, photography
Harry Välimäki: photography
Timo Ketola: logo
Produced at Studio Fredman and Maestro Musik/Nacksving in Gothenburg, Sweden, April – May 1999 by Opeth and Fredrik Nordström.
UK release date: October 1999. US release date: February 2001.
Highest chart places: UK: none, USA: none
Running time: 62:31
Current edition: 2018 Peaceville Records European digipak CD reissue

Just as *My Arms, Your Hearse* signified a major change for the group (regarding its line-up), so too does *Still Life*, as the quintet moved from Candlelight Records to another British label, Peaceville Records. (Unbeknownst to them, it would be their *only* album on Peaceville, but we'll get to that with *Blackwater Park*.) As already discussed, they'd been quite dissatisfied with Candlelight and were eager to find a new company. In a 2019 interview with *Invisible Orange*'s Jon Rosenthal, Åkerfeldt explains: 'We felt at home with [them] and were really good friends with Lee Barrett ... but it wasn't what I thought of when I thought of a record label'.

At first, he was torn between Peaceville and Earache Records for different reasons (such as that both were putting out material by artists he liked). He notes that eventually, Peaceville 'matched the advance that Earache were offering'; that, plus him getting along with founder Paul 'Hammy' Halmshaw and being encouraged by Renkse, made the choice clear. 'Jonas and I were best friends – we thought it would be cool to be labelmates. We decided that we'd both sign for Peaceville and our two bands could take over the world together!' he gloats. Peaceville's distribution deal with another company, Music For Nations, was also a benefit because it seemingly ensured that Opeth's music would be carried in more shops.

Obviously, this made the quartet see themselves as more of a 'professional band', which added to Åkerfeldt's growing satisfaction with life in general. He reflects: 'I felt settled with myself about who I was and what I did'. After all, *My Arms, Your Hearse* didn't exactly make them superstars or financially secure – and neither would *Still Life* – but he was comfortable living 'in poverty' if it meant that he could chase his artistic dreams. To that end, he'd been 'sleeping on Jonas's couch for about six months or a year' before finally getting his own very modest flat, which he barely managed to pay for while living off of 'canned meat ... with aspic and dill'. (He still eats it occasionally because it 'left such an imprint on [his] soul').

By this point, Åkerfeldt had fundamentally turned into the leader and mastermind of Opeth, so it's no real shock to learn that he wrote virtually all of *Still Life*. He started working on it while living with Renkse, knowing that it was going to be Opeth's 'last try' before giving up. 'I didn't have much hope then, to be honest, so I figured that we'd go all in. There was some positivity surrounding [it] because we had done three records prior ... and we had signed to a label which we knew about before we were a band', he discloses. Because he had no recording equipment of his own, he'd have to remember and/or write down the arrangements as best he could. Luckily, he was also able to 'record a few demos' at the home of Katatonia multi-instrumentalist and co-founder, Anders Nyström. Nyström enlightens:

[Mikael] came over to my place [on] a couple of evenings and we started recording bits and pieces [of] what was to become Still Life. He told me what kind of beats he was after and I programmed the drum machine and tracked two rhythms, leads, [and] cleans, but no vocals, leaving it all instrumental. So, I got to hear a lot of the riffs before they were actually constructed into proper songs, and [I] made a personal connection with the material. I loved it! It was quite technical and both aggressive and beautiful.

Åkerfeldt was trying harder than ever to 'become more and more progressive' amidst 'distancing [himself] from the metal scene of that time'. As usual, his ever-growing assortment of records helped, with increased interests in jazz artists like Wes Montgomery and Bo Kaspers Orkester alongside Morbid Angel and Nick Drake. The result is, in many ways, Opeth's most complex collection (especially regarding its acoustic guitar work), and its stylistic and compositional growths from *My Arms, Your Hearse* are astounding.

Fortunately, its concept packs a similarly evolved punch. Yes, it also deals with ill-fated love, but from an external standpoint rather than internal; in addition, there's a healthy dose of criticism regarding antiquated theology. In the liner notes to the 2008 reissue of *Still Life*, Åkerfeldt divulges that it began as a short story 'about religious beliefs contra atheism and how it would have affected someone in the old or even ancient days'. He continues: 'The main character was a religious man who ... started questioning his faith and eventually would lose it. He was to be banished by his village ... and would only return years later, [when] his past love, Melinda, was scheduled to be unwillingly married through family pressure. Yes, quite romantic at times, but overall, it was a pretty dark affair that I'm still quite happy about'.

Once again, they'd planned to begin recording at Studio Fredman, but it was being renovated, so Nordström brought them to Maestro Musik/Nacksving, the 'cosy old prog studio' where they'd recorded acoustic guitars for *My Arms, Your Hearse*. Åkerfeldt admits that because they rarely had enough space to rehearse beforehand, they showed up 'very, very unprepared', with the songs 'written, pretty much, on pieces of paper'. Nervous but optimistic, all four members smoked frequently, played PlayStation, and watched ping-pong competitions in-between working, with López feeling 'more at ease' and Méndez doing 'really well too' as they worked with Åkerfeldt. He was particularly thrilled that Méndez played with his fingers rather than with a pick, and he kept turning them on to more progressive rock, as well as Stevie Wonder's *Innervisions*. Méndez comments: 'It was a great experience to be in a real studio. I always knew I wanted to be a musician; I never wanted to be a rock star, so I never expected anything and just wanted to have fun, and it was a great time making *Still Life*'. Meanwhile, Lindgren contributed musically when needed but focused mostly on the recording process itself.

They'd rented engineer Isak Edh's old apartment and cooked for each other daily, leading to a humorous incident in which Méndez and López were tasked with grocery shopping for the first *and* last time. You see, Lindgren and Åkerfeldt expected them to get the basics – 'bread, milk, butter', etc. – but instead they bought 'ice cream, waffles, and chocolate sprinkles'. Another funny occurrence came when Åkerfeldt and Lindgren were putting down vocals one night. They'd been at it for roughly twenty-four hours straight, and they were so tired that they started having visual and auditory hallucinations. The most 'famous' occurrence – as Åkerfeldt puts it – was when he thought that he'd heard a cough by his left ear. 'I got terrified ... literally thought it was some kind of apparition in the works'. It turned out to be Edh in the control room, and supposedly it can still be heard on *Still Life*.

Remarkably, Åkerfeldt didn't have 'a single vocal idea' in mind when they moved to Studio Fredman, so he basically improvised everything he sang. Furthermore, they did it all in one night, starting 'at like 9:00 p.m. in the evening and finishing at six in the morning, and that included ... coming up with all the vocal lines and stuff like that', he recounts. He also chose to use a new guitar tool, the EBow, to take him 'into the keyboard world' and provide 'crazy, scary vibes'. That new element – coupled with López's innovations – made the pair 'the real creative forces' behind the LP and took their sound to broader places.

Even the cover imagery illustrates advancement since it's a commissioned painting rather than just a photograph of something real. It was designed by genre legend Travis Smith, who got the job after Renkse told Åkerfeldt how happy he was with the cover of Katatonia's *Tonight's Decision*. Åkerfeldt recalls: 'I think he delivered a bunch of pictures and I liked the kind of gothic looking style with the Madonna-like statue ... I guess I kind of sent him the concept so he could kind of make up his own ideas from reading those lyrics'. For sure, it's a gorgeous and symbolic piece of art that represents the story and sound of the album exceptionally. For instance, the crying woman represents Melinda weeping at the grave of her partner, and its two main colours (red and black) express the anger, passion, and love inherent to the cautionary fable.

The surrounding touring cycle was about as prosperous as ever (which is to say not very much at all), with them doing only 'two or three shows in Poland'. However, they also played their first America set at the Milwaukee Metal Fest in late July or early August 2000, which was quite eye-opening and inspiring (especially since *Still Life* wouldn't be released in the States until February 2001 due to distribution issues). Granted, they had to travel as tourists and didn't have their instruments ('Katatonia were literally walking off the stage, handing their guitars to us, and we walk[ed] on stage with the exact same sound', Åkerfeldt confesses); yet, it was still a dream come true overall. Åkerfeldt illuminates: 'We didn't play the main stage – we played in a room that held 2,000 people – and it was so packed that they were turning people away, and it was a complete revelation to us'. Previously, Opeth hadn't received 'any mass feedback' like that, with people 'roaring' before they even came out. Understandably, he was uplifted by the reception, particularly because they were still incredibly underknown in Europe: '[We] felt like it was the same old thing again, as it had been for almost ten years by that point. As far as our popularity and profile was concerned, it felt like *Still Life* may as well never have been released'.

Sales-wise, things weren't any more encouraging, and they barely received royalties because the label deal turned out to be 'a bad decision', Åkerfeldt says. 'We had high hopes for the album, with it coming out on Peaceville, but again nothing happened, and it actually felt like we'd taken steps further back'. Méndez shares an alike opinion: 'I was too naïve to think that the album might be the one to make it happen for the band'. Happily, though, most press reviews – albeit from relatively small publications – celebrated Opeth's development, and *Still Life* has only grown in stature since then. In 2014, *PROG* placed it at #83 in their feature on 'The 100 Greatest Prog Albums of All Time', while *Loudwire* placed it at #54 in their 2020 'Top 90 Hard Rock and Heavy Metal Albums of the 1990s' piece. Many other magazines – such as *Metal Wani* – bestow even stronger praise, and countless Opeth devotees (such as I) see it as one of their best works.

Without a doubt, Åkerfeldt is right in surmising that the band 'moved up a level' with *Still Life* and cemented the notion that they were 'doing something beyond' the bands around them. He argues: 'Our contemporaries stuck rigidly to their death metal roots, whereas we, despite having death metal at the centre, went into a lot of other areas. This album was the first one where we took that leap to not limit ourselves in any way and do exactly what we wanted and not worry about the consequences'. In contrast to how its predecessors 'always [had] something ... I wasn't too happy about', Åkerfeldt considers, *Still Life* was 'perfect'. Lindgren concurs, adding, '*My Arms, Your Hearse* was a really big step for us, second-wise and band-wise, and *Still Life* was another big step because it's more musical than *My Arms, Your Hearse*, which is basically a metal album. *Still Life* was much more fine-tuned and polished'.

Simply put, the headway made with *Still Life* remains staggering. Every aspect of Opeth's artistry – songwriting, production, musicianship, lyricism, storytelling, cohesion, vocals, you name it – is just about immaculate here, which is why it remains a crowning achievement. Its myriad segments connect seamlessly and ingeniously as the quintet dish out some of the most mesmerising melodies and instrumentation of their whole career. As such, Åkerfeldt's Shakespearean drama – with all its linked brutality and beauty – is among the finest progressive metal records ever made. *My Arms, Your Hearse* was indeed Opeth's first truly great full-length effort, but *Still Life* was their first masterpiece.

'The Moor' (Åkerfeldt)

By and large, *Still Life* is less impervious with its storytelling compared to *My Arms, Your Hearse*, and this one is a strong example of that. Lyrically, the protagonist poetically yet clearly details his return to his homeland and quest to rescue his love ('The sigh of summer upon my return / Fifteen alike since I was here'; 'I was foul and tainted, devoid of faith / Wearing my death-mask at birth'; and 'There is no forgiveness in these eyes / For any of you but one / Dispel the mist for now / Melinda is the reason why I've come'). It's a gripping account that promptly lets you empathise with his plight.

As with its predecessor's 'Prologue', the instrumental prelude successfully puts you in the mood for the saga. It takes a bit too long to get where it's going – almost two minutes – but its mirrored blend of warm acoustic notes and chilling electric complements is an enticing way to juxtapose the fondness and fury that lies ahead. That exquisite union is taken up several notches when the song really starts, as the intermingling of eloquent acoustic scales, menacing riffs, and firm rhythms are enormously appealing. There's a smoothness and purity to it all that outclasses anything on the prior LPs, and the percussive break just before Åkerfeldt's scream is a small instance of how the playing and writing on *Still Life* is raised. Méndez and López immediately demonstrate that vitality and creativity they bring to Opeth's chemistry.

Moreover, Åkerfeldt's growls are infectiously rich and captivating, backed by an addictive score that silkily moves into the track's first magnificent slice of relief: 'Pale touch / Writhing in the embers'. Even the instantaneous six-string transition between these two parts is subtly cunning, and Åkerfeldt's multilayered singing demands that listeners sing along with all their might. Another resourceful segue leads to more desirable mercilessness and then to an even more divine acoustic passage (the aforementioned 'There is no forgiveness in these eyes' part, plus the back-and-forth chanting afterwards). It's the most breathtaking section of the tune, and it still stands as one of Opeth's utmost amalgamations of clean vocals and acoustic guitar work.

The rest of the piece upholds the satanic and saintly duality, with its final call-back – 'If you'll bear with me / You'll fear of me / You'll never leave me to /

A fate with you' – exemplifying Åkerfeldt's fruition as a songwriter. It's the most agile and keen reprise within an Opeth composition thus far, capping off 'The Moor' as an absolute victory that single-handedly proves how much greatness the 'classic line-up' had right out of the gate.

'Godhead's Lament' (Åkerfeldt)

All of the praise given to the last track applies here, too, as it's just as masterfully envisioned and executed when it comes to spellbinding tonal swings and riveting melodies. The main character has arrived at his village and observes Melinda – now a nun – as he hides and contemplates when and where he should approach her. Contrary to how 'The Moor' eases us into its belligerence, 'Godhead's Lament' hastily explodes with concentrated turmoil. López's syncopation is consistently superb as he guides a distillation of sharp, cyclical guitar lines that shrewdly foreshadow later occurrences.

Next, a penetrating and heartfelt guitar solo ends with glimpse at the song's ensuing pre-chorus – 'Searching my way to perplexion / The gleam of her eyes / In that moment, she knew' – which Åkerfeldt sings lovingly. Another round of stylishly entangled acoustic and electric guitar ornamentation pours into the equally stunning main hook ('Thought I could not leave this place on this imminent day'). It's a striking detour that effortlessly summons more fiercely nail-biting descriptions, as well as a slight trace of jazzy relaxation. The last two minutes further unite brutishness and blissfulness with meticulous self-assurance and sensible reiterations, sealing the fate of 'Godhead's Lament' as a tour de force of Opeth's specialities.

'Benighted' (Åkerfeldt)

Let's address the figurative elephant in the room: the principal guitar pattern of 'Benighted' bears an uncanny resemblance to Camel's 'Never Let Go'. Åkerfeldt has admitted as much in the years since *Still Life* arrived, and while it's perhaps not *quite* as explicit as, say, the link between Spirit's 'Taurus' and Led Zeppelin's 'Stairway to Heaven' (another deeply debated comparison amongst music aficionados), it's an undeniable, if unintentional, connection.

That said, the track is certainly no copycat, as it charts its own course with a surprisingly traditional structure. In a way, it's like a more sophisticated descendant of 'Credence' from *My Arms, Your Hearse* and ancestor to 'Harvest' from *Blackwater Park*. Åkerfeldt's ghostly falsetto depicts the hero's plea for Melinda to run away with him, dismiss her superstitions, and 'atone with [her] lonely soul'. While his singing is moving but comparatively uncomplicated, his fingerpicking is miles above anything he'd done beforehand. Smartly, he lets that elegance stand on its own for a while before adding brisk drumming alongside an admirably bluesy guitar solo and some concluding grandeur. All in all, 'Benighted' is a peaceful and regal gem whose intimacy and intricacy can't help but win you over. It's also a much-appreciated breather before Opeth carry on with their sonic cataclysm.

'Moonlapse Vertigo' (Åkerfeldt)

This fourth entry chronicles the outcast's realisation that 'The council of the cross / Must have sensed [his] coming', so he rushes to flee with Melinda. His panic and zealousness are evident from the get-go via a tuneful assemblage of crashing cymbals, screeching guitar notes, and crunchy chords. It completely arouses an air of now-or-never resolve, making you feel like you're on the run, too. Then, recurrent acoustic guitar arpeggios and fatalistic percussion carry Åkerfeldt's solemn verdicts – 'Kept warm by the light of the lantern / Lost sight of everything tonight' – fabulously, instigating a repeating battle between fiendish and sentimental musical personas.

Halfway through, an easy-going yet quirky and maze-like jam (that alludes to the charming nature of 'Face of Melinda') dissipates into ominous acoustic chords and echoey electric tones. From there, a sweltering guitar solo paves the way for Åkerfeldt's snarls about being discovered; the arrangement persists with destructive delight until his closing cathartic proclamation – 'I turned away my eyes / In pallor escape from the end' – offers another one of the quartet's most attractive melodies to date. It fades out chaotically, preparing you for the terrifically dynamic display of love up ahead.

'Face of Melinda' (Åkerfeldt)

Featuring fretless bass and – as Åkerfeldt declares – 'brush drums, which [were] unheard of in death metal at that point', 'Face of Melinda' is the fan favourite track from *Still Life*. In fact, it still appears in live setlists from time to time, and for good reason. It's an exceedingly accessible, catchy, and vivid song (about the main characters' star-crossed romance) that begins with a sunny but grave disposition akin to that of 'Benighted'. The protagonist wistfully describes Melinda's looks and languished demeanour, mentioning that she'd 'sworn her vows to another' (God) after he was forced to leave her. Åkerfeldt's gentle singing resides impeccably beside the delicate guitar work and rhythms, with Méndez's bouncy timbre adding spooky pep to the proceedings.

Inventively, a fresh pair of tempting acoustic motifs sway around each other to build anxious anticipation, finally crumbling beneath intimidating stabs of syncopation and forceful strumming. What follows is a peak fusion of dazzling riffs and earnest verses ('I returned for you in great dismay / Come with me, far away to stay') whose conversion into acoustic scales – with piercing electric accentuations – is overwhelmingly classy and entrancing. As with much of *Still Life*, it reaches new heights of refined ambition and technique, stretching the band's boundaries to make them best at what they do. At the same time, its glimmer of affectionate reconciliation for the couple is twisted into unadulterated catastrophe when the next chapter reveals that they'll get no such happy ending.

'Serenity Painted Death' (Åkerfeldt)

This penultimate assault was directly influenced by Morbid Angel, and its relentlessly tragic turbulence is apt due to its central topic: the death of

Melinda. Specifically, she was hanged by her community for abandoning the Church in favour of a life with her lover; in response, he kills everyone involved with her murder, ensuring that they die 'choking in warm ponds of blood' prior to passing out from exhaustion, awakening, and being captured by the 'starlit shadows on the wall'. Thus, it's very appropriate for 'Serenity Pained Death' to start off abundantly hostile, with its brief pauses and subsequent textural throttles signalling the resentment that will induce the massacre.

His demonic decrees ('White faced, haggard grin / This serenity pained death'), coupled with the six-string shrieks, are totally awesome; likewise, the emotional pivot into Åkerfeldt's woeful harmony – 'Saw her fading / Blank stare into me' – is enchanting, as is the malevolently psychedelic instrumental movement that's born from it and that goes toward his awe-inspiring irritability. A profound dual-layered guitar solo transports us to a second clean stanza ('Came with the moon / The wayward in conscious state') that's just as stirring as the first. It spirals downward to recap the 'White faced, haggard grin' portion before the piece melts into more tranquil acoustic fingerpicking, rounding out its thrilling mixture of bitterness and yearning.

'White Cluster' (Åkerfeldt)
History shows that a story like this could only end one way: with the outcast also being executed for his perceived crimes. On the bright side, though, he senses Melinda's 'primal touch' as the 'hangman clutch[es] at his tools', so the pair are ostensibly reunited in the hereafter. It's a systematically devilish composition, which makes Åkerfeldt's initial urge to remove it from the record (because 'it felt too poppy' and, like 'To Bid You Farewell', might force fans to 'hate' him) downright silly. Frankly, 'White Cluster' is as transfixingly representative of Opeth's progress as anything else on *Still Life*.

It commences in a similarly absorbing and wicked fashion to 'Serenity Painted Death', with stampeding howls and musicianship indicating how irate the hero is at the situation. López's secluded syncopation burrows into a double whammy of angelic pre-chorus ('This is forgiveness, so I know / Once I repent, I seal the lid') and dominant hooks ('They wear white for me / Seemingly jaded and lost'). Holy outcries steer incensed instrumentation until gloomy acoustic thrums give way to a searing progressive metal freak-out that's underscored by erratic drumming and antagonistic guitarwork. It's probably the most musically challenging moment in the group's arsenal up to this point, and it never stops being amazing. (The flash of acoustic arpeggiation at the end is brilliant, too.)

Consequently, the former two sung sections are retooled, with new lyrics telling that his 'noose is tied' and that there's 'cloak-captured sighs of relief'. It's as handsomely dramatic as possible, putting you in the role of a powerless spectator. The intense outro – which, like the opening of 'The Moor', does a fine job of contrasting airy and aggressive components – drifts away, but 'White Cluster' isn't over just yet, as a neatly played guitar coda sneaks in to wrap up the tale with saddening inevitability. It's the final touch of what makes *Still Life* a work of art

Bonuses

The 2008 digipak edition – remastered by Jens Bogren – comes with a second disc that contains a 5.1 surround sound version of *Still Life* and a 2006 live video for 'Face of Melinda' from *The Roundhouse Tapes*. The concert clip is shot well, with multiple camera angles and a clear picture. The band plays to a large audience adorned with red and purple lights and a projected image of the LP cover. Honestly, the guitar tones are significantly mellow and/or meshed together – even washed out – but Åkerfeldt's voice is sturdy and untarnished. It's also nice to see the crowd clap along and cheer from beginning to end. Obviously, it's a useless inclusion for anyone who owns *The Roundhouse Tapes*, but for devotees who don't, it's a nice bonus.

Blackwater Park (2001)

Personnel:
Mikael Åkerfeldt: vocals, acoustic and electric guitars
Peter Lindgren: electric guitars
Martin López: drums
Martin Méndez: bass
Additional Personnel:
Steven Wilson: engineer, mixing, piano, additional guitar, clean and backing
vocals on 'Bleak', 'Harvest', 'The Funeral Portrait', and 'The Drapery Falls'
Markus Lindberg: egg shakers
Fredrik Nordström: engineer, mixing
Travis Smith: album art
Harry Välimäki: photography
Produced at Studio Fredman in Gothenburg, Sweden, August – October 2000 by
Opeth and Steven Wilson
Release date: 12 March 2001.
Highest chart places: UK: none, USA: none
Running time: 66:59 (reissue: 81:46)
Current edition: 2021 Music for Nations 20th Anniversary Deluxe 2x vinyl/CD
reissue

Although *Still Life* was a monumental creative feat, it only earned its fair
share of acclaim and popularity years later; as such, Åkerfeldt and company
remained a tad disheartened and fraught as the new millennium began.
(In *Book of Opeth*, Lindgren even acknowledges that his father had to help
him pay rent.) However, that shared desperation bonded the boys more,
as Lindgren explains: 'During those years, 1997 – 2001, that defined us so
much as a band – we were very tight ... we were stronger than apart; we
turned into something more than we were as individuals'. As the Peaceville
deal and Milwaukee Metal Fest appearance showed, people both inside
and outside of the industry were truly starting to take notice of Opeth's
craftsmanship and distinctiveness, which – Åkerfeldt reminisces – meant
that they were 'set for something quite amazing'. As it turns out, their
commercial breakthrough was right around the corner, in the form of their
fifth LP, *Blackwater Park*.

Around this time, Åkerfeldt was still living a mostly happy life in his 'one-
room apartment in Aspudden', where he ate cheap meals, smoked cigarettes,
spent time with his girlfriend, and wrote/demoed as Lindgren studied in
cafés and the two Martins lounged around. One day, Åkerfeldt received a call
completely out of the blue from Paul 'Hammy' Halmshaw, who was 'almost
in tears' with some upsetting news: Music for Nations was demanding that
Peaceville let Opeth go so that they could represent them entirely; otherwise,
Music for Nations would end their entire distribution arrangement with
Peaceville. Åkerfeldt expounds:

Feeling a strong sense of loyalty to Hammy, I went berserk ... it seemed like it was almost corruption. I felt like I'd been duped and so I refused to go with Music for Nations, but Hammy ... said that I had to let it go because my stance was obviously going to have an adverse impact on his business – so , reluctantly, we signed with Music for Nations. When we arrived at their office in Latimer Road, we were introduced to about 15 or 20 staff – PR people, designers, distribution, promotion, everyone you could think of – who we were told were all working together for the same goal: to make Opeth happen.

In the previously mentioned *Invisible Oranges* interview with Jon Rosenthal, Åkerfeldt hints at cognitive dissonance in finding kinship with Halmshaw and Peaceville despite realising that they 'blew some nice dreams into [his] head' regarding how big Opeth would become after *Still Life*. When push came to shove, he knew that Peaceville had let him down, and in his heart, he knew that he wanted to go elsewhere. Hence, it wasn't the move itself that bothered him – 'At the time, even if it was a bit frustrating and I was sad to leave, I was excited', he divulges – as much as it was the lack of authority he had in the decision. Ultimately, he saw Music for Nations as a 'better' and 'safe[r]' new home, and his hopefulness for the future of Opeth was reinvigorated.

The group saw themselves continuing to get better as players, too, especially López and Méndez. In the 'Making of *Blackwater Park*' documentary – directed by Åkerfeldt's childhood friend, Fredrik Odefjärd, and included in the 'Legacy Edition' – López states that on *My Arms, Your Hearse* and *Still Life*, he was 'so young and trying to fit in'. After working with Åkerfeldt for a few years, he'd learned to play 'with finesse' and 'slow down and feel the music'. Méndez concurs, adding that Åkerfeldt's direction and input as 'the 'brain' of the band' allowed him to develop dexterity and confidence. Clearly, both men appreciated and respected Åkerfeldt's leadership, which he's quick to distinguish from being something akin to a dictatorship: '[I'm] more like a driving force, [and] all bands have that. Nothing odd, really, and I welcome ideas from the other members', he clarifies in the documentary. With the quartet's techniques, dreams, and relationships elevated higher than ever, they were fully ready to take advantage of whatever Music for Nations could do for them. Part of that involved bringing on a new – and somewhat intimidating – producer: Porcupine Tree founder Steven Wilson.

Today, Wilson and Åkerfeldt are extremely close, but back then, Åkerfeldt was categorically starstruck at the notion of Wilson being involved. After all, Wilson was one of his idols, and Porcupine Tree was 'basically the only [modern] band' that Åkerfeldt cared about. But, Åkerfeldt wanted to expand Opeth's stylistic scope and adventurousness with *Blackwater Park*, and he felt that Wilson ('a musical oracle, an inventor, and ultimately a musical genius', Åkerfeldt asserts) was the proper person to help fulfil that need. As for how they started communicating, it's a simple story: Åkerfeldt received an email from Wilson, who said that he really loved *Still Life*. This shocked Åkerfeldt since, as he avows, Wilson 'seemed very elusive; I'd seen photos of his silhouette and didn't know if he really existed'. In response, Åkerfeldt asked if he'd like to meet up and discuss producing their next album, which is precisely what happened.

They met at a taco bar in Camden, and despite Åkerfeldt feeling a bit daunted by it all (partially because he was 'working class' and 'destined to work in a factory had [he] not [fallen] in love with music', whereas Wilson was 'very educated' and more refined), they instantly hit it off. Wilson remembers establishing 'an immediate artistic connection with Mikael', whom he calls his 'exact double' because of their shared positions as leaders of their respective bands. In other words, they allied not only in terms of musical interests and desires, but also in terms of shouldering the highs and lows of being in charge (such as managing fan expectations, facing resistance behind-the-scenes, and the like). Wilson also admired Åkerfeldt's curiosity regarding the expansiveness of music. 'I think a lot of his fans would be surprised by what he listens to and what inspires him: classical music, outsider music, avant-garde jazz, and all sorts of other areas', he suggests.

Just because they struck up a great friendship and liked the *idea* of cooperating, that doesn't mean that Wilson knew if he was the right person for the job. He discloses in *Book of Opeth*: 'Initially, I was concerned by the prospect of producing a metal band, not knowing what I could do and not knowing much about metal'. Luckily, Wilson continues, 'that was exactly why they wanted me, because they wanted something that didn't just sound like a regular metal record'. Of course, hindsight shows that Wilson not only did a wonderful job on *Blackwater Park*, but ended up being significantly influenced by it as he steered Porcupine Tree toward a heavier direction with 2002's *In Absentia*, 2005's *Deadwing*, etc.

Prior to this alliance, however, Wilson had lost his childhood love for the genre – particularly, bands like 'Saxon, Diamond Head, [and] Iron Maiden' – as he aged and discovered progressive and electronic music. It was only when he was speaking to a journalist (identity unknown) about growing interest in Porcupine Tree from the metal community that Wilson (at the reporter's insistence) decided to check out Meshuggah and Opeth. In fact, the journalist interviewed Åkerfeldt a few weeks earlier, and once Porcupine Tree came up in their conversation, Åkerfeldt gave him a copy of *Still Life* to give to Wilson. Wilson reflects: 'About a week later, we were doing a sound check in Rome and I dug out the CD, which was *Still Life*, and I put it on over the PA and I was just totally blown away by the musicality of it. It wasn't generic, it wasn't basic, or any of the things I'd accused metal of being ... it had made me revise my opinion on extreme metal music'.

A few emails and a taco shop meet-up later, Åkerfeldt and Wilson were ready to get started. But, Åkerfeldt had to clear it with Music for Nations' Managing Director, Andy Black (whom Åkerfeldt humorously likens to 'Gollum from *The Lord of The Rings*, but with black hair, black eyes, and wearing a black suit').

Having not heard of Wilson, Black agreed on the condition that Åkerfeldt pay for it, which he 'reluctantly agreed' to. As a result, and contrary to common misbelief, Wilson wasn't there for the whole recording process; rather, Åkerfeldt illuminates, he just worked on the vocals and lead guitars after Opeth already had 'the basic song structures down – the rhythm guitars, the drums, the bass and most of the acoustic guitars'. Dressed 'like a geeky ninja' and sticking to a diet of 'Cheez Doodles washed down with [Swedish] milk', he stayed on for about two weeks.

For Åkerfeldt, Wilson, and Lindgren – who was also a Porcupine Tree fan, unlike López and Méndez, who weren't familiar with Wilson and weren't really consulted about bringing him on board – working together was joyful and enlightening. Åkerfeldt affirms: 'I let some of my need for control go, since I knew in his hands, we'd be safe. His ideas were worth listening to', while Lindgren muses: 'It was an absurd feeling that [Wilson] was in the studio. It turned out great. It took a day or so before everybody felt comfortable. It was a very pleasant experience'. In an August 2016 chat with *Metal Hammer*'s Malcolm Dome, Åkerfeldt also addresses possible pushback from followers regarding the pairing: 'I know that a lot of fans were worried when they found out we weren't working with a metal producer. But [Wilson] didn't alter our sound, he enhanced it. There would have been no point in us using the same sort of name as everyone else in the metal world. We wanted to take the risk, because that's the only way you get the best out of the songs'.

Wilson echoes the same perspective, concluding that the project exceeded expectations and yielded an extensively well-matched and fruitful partnership:

> I think it's partly because of the musical interests and the musical influences that Mike and Peter have got that there's a much wider spectrum of influences in their sound. Although it's metal, it's actually got a lot of influences from other styles of music, which give it sophistication that other metal music doesn't have. Obviously, just from talking to them and picking up on some of the things they've been listening to, it's been much more compatible than it might otherwise seem to be on the surface. We do have a lot of musical inspirations in common; we just choose to express them in different ways.

Through a mixture of flattery and necessity, Wilson was persuaded to lend his performance skills to the record, too, via backing vocals, piano, and additional guitar work. 'I didn't mean to, but then they kept asking me to sing. I've done quite a lot of singing, actually. I never imagined myself being able to sing over metal music because my voice is not that well suited. I just naturally got involved in the [that] side as well', he gloats. That decision proved to be one of the most important since Wilson's vocal and instrumental accentuations (particularly on 'The Leper Affinity' and 'Bleak') are a key reason for why the LP stands out so much.

One person who *wasn't* keen to have Wilson involved was Nordström, and understandably so given that he interpreted his presence as, well, a slap in the face. Happily, Åkerfeldt says, Nordström was 'a little hurt', but not outright angry, and that he and Wilson ended up on good terms: 'They understood each other, and it was a great partnership. In the end, we allowed Fredrik to mix the album on his own – we all trusted him – and he did a fantastic job'. For sure, one of the most noticeable parts of the record's evolution is its unblemished polish. Whereas the prior four albums – including *Still Life* – were muddled at times (and to varying degrees), *Blackwater Park* sounds immaculately clean, vibrant, and balanced, so Nordström still played a vital role.

Outside of all that, making *Blackwater Park* was mostly business as usual. They had four songs 'virtually ready to go' – according to Åkerfeldt – when they moved into Studio Fredman: 'The Leper Affinity', 'Harvest', 'Bleak', and the closing title track. Those changed along the way, of course, and the rest, he notes, were developed during Opeth's two-week stint in Gothenburg. Afterwards, they briefly stayed on a boat before moving into a flat owned by Dark Tranquillity vocalist (and former rhythm guitarist) Mikael Stanne. Although those environments were quite confined, they also aided them in focusing solely on the music and prevented any distractions from getting in the way.

Even with Wilson's myriad touches and the quartet's own improvements, Åkerfeldt doesn't see the collection as a drastic change from the Opeth norm, as he told Dome: 'I don't think we altered at all with this album. It may seem that way, because we got so much more attention, but if you listen to [*Still Life*], it's in the same style'. In contrast, his *lyrics* this time around definitely shake things up, as they focus far more on autobiographical recognitions. In the official documentary, he confesses: 'I've never written personal lyrics like this before. It was basically afterwards that I understood what they are about. Personally, I avoid other people. I think [there are] so many crazy people out there, and I get harassed by idiots. All this made me write lyrics about how I despise other people. Then I spiced it up to make it more sick!'

Once *Blackwater Park* was finished, the benefits of having Music for Nations behind them became fully apparent. Åkerfeldt cheers: 'It was so fucking great to finally be involved with a label who were getting the music into the shops and to a wider cross-section of people. We were getting attention from parts of the media who didn't know we even existed before, and at last, we got to go on proper tours, playing everywhere. It was a crucial time for us'. Lindgren recalls playing in America (and a bit in Canada) for about seven weeks, most of which were spent warming up Nevermore's audience: 'We were opening for [them], but the crowd was basically there for us. Nevermore were great guys. I remember Warrel [Dane, vocalist] coming up to us and asking if we could please make the fans stay for Nevermore's set!'

They also shared the stage with Amorphis, and afterwards, they played Europe with Katatonia toward the end of 2001. Other stints included

Germany's Wacken Open Air festival, where they played in front of roughly 60,000 people. It was during that time that, at Andy Black's suggestion, Opeth hired Paradise Lost's manager, Andy Farrow, to be their first official manager. In *Book of Opeth*, Farrow states that one of the first things he did was focus on *Blackwater Park*'s secondary marketing campaign (including a reissue with two new tracks: 'Still Day Beneath the Sun' and 'Patterns in the Ivy II'). '[H] e put us where we should have been this whole time. So, we were touring all the time and we had feedback coming in constantly, and Andy made sure that we did interviews and everything you're supposed to do as a proper band', Åkerfeldt smirks.

The record was also Opeth's first to release in North America (via Koch) and Europe simultaneously – well, to be fair, it took another day in the States – as well as their first to have promotional singles, with a shortened version of 'The Drapery Falls' going out to radio stations and 'Still Day Beneath the Sun' later coming out as a vinyl-only single. (Also, Robotic Empire Records put out a vinyl-only 7' EP of 'Patterns in the Ivy II' and 'Still Day Beneath the Sun' in February 2003; reportedly, it sold out in less than 24 hours and remains one of the group's rarest and most sought-after releases.) While it didn't chart in the UK or US, *Blackwater Park* sold well enough to imply that – as with the increased breadth of touring locations and press write-ups – Opeth were quickly getting to the next level as a professional band.

Speaking of *Blackwater Park*'s reception, critics were predictably and uniformly positive. Famously, *The Village Voice* wrote, 'Opeth paint on an epic canvas, sounding at times like... metal's answer to '70s King Crimson', while Sean Palmerston of *Exclaim!* made the same comparison before concluding that it 'might be the best metal record of this year, and it is worth every bit of energy the band has put into the creation of it'. Other outlets, like *Metal Crypt* and *AllMusic*, awarded it five out of five stars upon release, whereas *Pitchfork*, *Metal Sucks*, *Decibel*, and *Spectrum Culture* have championed it in more recent years. Unsurprisingly, *Loudwire* listed it as the best progressive metal album of all time in June 2020, and *Rolling Stone* gave it the #28 and #55 spots, respectively, in their rundowns of the 'Greatest Prog Rock Albums of All Time' and 'The 100 Greatest Metal Albums of All Time'.

Looking back, everyone involved recognises that the sequence was a game-changer for Opeth, if not for the entire spectrum of modern progressive metal. Wilson presumes that they 'created a new language for progressive metal' due to the album's 'real levels of production' and wealth of imaginative layers and textures. Correspondingly, Méndez boasts: 'Life changed after *Blackwater Park* ... We were young and touring around the world, and that's the dream of every young band; to make that happen was an amazing feeling'. In his chat with Dome, Åkerfeldt says that people still come up to him and talk about all of the 'little things' that are buried within the music like subtle secrets, providing 'constant excitement of discovery' unlike any of its predecessors.

Blackwater Park may not be the definitive Opeth album – such a thing isn't possible with a band that's gone through this many phases – but it's inarguably among their most momentous. Beyond being their breakthrough LP in relation to them finally attaining some degree of mainstream success – thanks in large part to Music for Nations and Farrow – it kick-started Åkerfeldt's creative union with another one of progressive music's utmost figures, Steven Wilson. Together, they delivered Opeth's most spotless and exploratory collection so far, as well as sparked an artistic synergy and friendly rivalry that would continue for several years (or, at least until their only official collaboration, 2012's *Storm Corrosion*). More approachable, pure, and multifaceted than anything before it, *Blackwater Park* was the dawn of Opeth as kings of the genre, and although they've changed quite a bit since, they've never relinquished the crown.

'The Leper Affinity' (Åkerfeldt)

Fan interpretations range from thinking that it's about vampires, necrophilia, murder, and/or metaphorical observations of nature. Only Åkerfeldt really knows, and of course, there's also the possibility of its title indicating to a kinship with outsiders (such as those faced with disease). If that's the case, both its subject matter and opening – a foreboding swell of tones giving way to an onslaught of growls, percussion, and guitar riffs – pick up where *Still Life* left off.

True to Åkerfeldt's aforementioned analysis, it's not much different than what the quartet did last time around; it's just a more pristine version of it, with the arrangement, roars, and discussion of 'winter', 'ghosts', 'love', and 'death' being familiar yet as hypnotic as ever. Even so, there's a larger amount of fluidity, conciseness, and purpose here that makes it – like all of *Blackwater Park* – more economical and accessible without sacrificing anything that made Opeth's first four LPs adoringly characteristic. A great example of that comes at the end of the superbly echoey first guitar solo, when an irresistibly twisted mesh of syncopation and chords transitions into a new influx of enticing anger: 'Insanity at its peak / Love me to my death'.

A tenderer solo leads into a lovely acoustic section – 'Lost are days of Spring / You sighed and let me in' – that, too, perfects the milder trademarks of the quartet's aesthetic. Åkerfeldt has never sung more prettily, and his words are equally graceful. After a return to the earlier frenzy (complemented by a pungent six-string overtone and López's resourceful syncopation), downtrodden strums and a sharp closing guitar line punctuate the track's exuberance. Then, Wilson adds a mournful piano epilogue that wraps up 'The Leper Affinity' beautifully. Admittedly, it goes on longer than it needs to, but it nonetheless showcases his invaluable role in widening Opeth's palette.

'Bleak' (Åkerfeldt)

The atmospheric beginning foreshadows 'The Drapery Falls', and it would've been a stronger selection for radio airplay given its fairly standard verse/chorus formula. Effectively a duet between Åkerfeldt and Wilson, its invitingness made it one of three songs (alongside 'Blackwater Park' and 'Ghost of Perdition' from *Ghost Reveries*) contained in the Opeth Song Pack DLC for Ubisoft's *Rocksmith 2014* video game.

López patiently chaperons ethereal guitar coatings until a speedy acoustic arpeggio announces hooky snarls and captivating instrumentation. It's paced exceedingly well with respect to its soft and heavy attributes, as Åkerfeldt's livid couplets are soon cut-off by a seductive segue into Wilson's alternating purification: 'Devious movement in your eyes / Moved me from relief / Breath comes out white clouds with your lies / And filters through me'. Wilson's voice is thin and high, radiating stirring sincerity while Åkerfeldt's fuller timbre supports him.

A nicely rustic and intricate instrumental passage (assisted by a recurrent squealing guitar line that ties *Blackwater Park* together) takes over; following a clever moment of silence, the jazziness becomes wholly serene as Åkerfeldt issues his most soothing request: 'Help me / Cure you / Atone for all you've done'. It's rapidly countered by a crushing yet melodious and sensitive wordless response before Wilson and Åkerfeldt recap their duet. Eerie effects surround Åkerfeldt's fleeting epiphany – 'Night falls again / Taking what's left of me' – and more thunderous agitation sparks a few extra seconds of sonic manipulation. That ending is another instance of Wilson's indispensable fingerprints on the record, and it's alluded to (if not overtly reworked) at the start of *Deliverance*'s 'By the Pain I See in Others'.

'Harvest' (Åkerfeldt)

As a deceptively cheerful folk ballad, 'Harvest' is a noteworthy departure from the first two tunes, as well as a major contributor to the album's marvellous diversity. It's incredibly warm and dense, with an array of luscious acoustic guitar work, feisty waltz rhythms, and gorgeous vocal harmonies (by Åkerfeldt and Wilson) evoking artists like The Strawbs, Renaissance, and Simon & Garfunkel more than any metal peer or precursor. The reverberating spectral notes around all of that encourage a darker subtext, though, and it is another narrative about mortal demise and bereavement, if not unambiguous self-sacrifice. Their voices and melodies exude innocence, longing, and vulnerability, especially in how Wilson's falsetto syllables endure around Åkerfeldt's richer commandments. Just over halfway through, a hip, Camel-esque guitar solo pacifies further, and in general, this one is a thoroughly majestic and poignant treasure.

'Harvest' spawned Opeth's first music video, too. Filmed by Odefjärd, it's just sepia tone footage of them recording and hanging around the studio, but its use of slow-mo and its glimpses into their professional and personal sides (such as playing ping pong and video games) humanises them. In hindsight, it displays how down to earth yet striving they were, so you feel proud – and maybe choked up – about how far they'd come and how much *Blackwater Park* did for them.

'The Drapery Falls' (Åkerfeldt)

The first single from *Blackwater Park*, its central motif sends chills down your spine (which is why it's debatably Opeth's most eminent composition). Its numerous temperament shifts also illustrate one of Åkerfeldt's chief wishes for the LP, as revealed in the documentary: 'I can have a theme from the start and the listener feels safe in that theme. But I don't want the listener to feel safe, [so] we'll choose the opposite direction [in the] next moment'. In that sense, 'The Drapery Falls' is nearly unrivalled in the band's catalogue, as it routinely and seamlessly oscillates between being dreamy and nightmarish.

Case in point: how its initially comforting acoustic chord progression is promptly transformed into a storm of fetching hecticness – complete with diabolical ascensions and frisky bass lines – that metamorphosises into a *different* kind of creepy calm underneath Åkerfeldt's pleading verses. Although typically cryptic, lyrics like 'The silence of your seclusion / Brings night into all your say' propose that Åkerfeldt's referencing the end of a relationship. His merciful singing is slightly spooky, too, and the change in intensity from these sections to his impassioned chorus – 'Pull me down again / And guide me into' – is unnervingly alluring.

Even his melodic 'ah-ah-ah' bellows are considerably powerful, doing a terrific job of setting up the resultant guitar solo (which harnesses *Still Life*'s cutting air of tragedy) and switch to infernal introspection. On the whole, it's an unfussy but compelling dive into vehemence – that is, until the zigzagging instrumental bridge finds López and Méndez dominating a swift start/stop trajectory around dizzyingly cyclical guitar parts. It's astoundingly immersive and rigorous, signifying a truly virtuosic unity amongst the foursome. From there, Åkerfeldt returns to his scratchy judgments, with the final one – 'My gleaming eye in your necklace reflects / Stare of primal regrets / Your turn your back and you walk away / Never again' – also insinuating romantic rejection before an ingeniously applied acoustic riff moves us into perhaps the most peaceful segment of *Blackwater Park*.

As simple and sedative as it is, however, it's nevertheless broken up by disorderly outbursts. Just like every other stark juxtaposition, it's expertly accomplished, with Wilson's verbal accompaniment achieving the same objective as on 'Harvest' when he sings, 'Waking up to your sound again / And lapse into the ways of misery'. The track finishes with a call-back to where it began (albeit with more pulsating heft from López and Méndez), leaving you in amazement as it disperses.

'Dirge for November' (Åkerfeldt, Lindgren)

There's a haunting emptiness to it that's never been felt in an Opeth song. Åkerfeldt's sorrowful claims, acoustic fingerpicking, and use of silence in-between are sparser and kinder than ever, coming across like a forerunner to the unswerving godly heartache of *Damnation*. His playing alone is like an instrumental sonnet – speaking volumes about anguish and futility – and he decorates it with fittingly low-spirited sentiments.

In keeping with *Blackwater Park*'s penchant for combustible ebbs and flows, Opeth personify total obliteration in the aftermath, with weeping guitar tones supplementing jackhammer rhythms and utterly barbaric barks from Åkerfeldt. His delivery is so guttural that his words are virtually indecipherable; however, that's not an issue because of how effectively the band convey their relatively rudimentary but grand hellscape. Subsequently, the track comes full circle by culminating in an acoustic epitaph whose supernatural and spacious melancholy is enveloping. All things considered, 'Dirge for November' isn't as substantial or go-getting as the other selections on *Blackwater Park*, but that doesn't mean it's not a potent step in the journey.

'The Funeral Portrait' (Åkerfeldt)

It's cool how the jittery arpeggiation slithers in prior to the hot-blooded downpour of abrasive riffs, drumming, and vocals. The perpetual key change around the verses makes it expressly gripping, too, as do the continually coarse modifications that the arrangement goes through. In every way, then, the quartet is operating at the height of their nefarious liveliness, with new guitar lines and sly percussive adjustments embellishing the vicious sleekness at every turn. The injection of another acoustic break about four minutes is wise as well, and shortly thereafter, idiosyncratically hard-hitting electric guitar solos offer a climax to the outrage that's been steadily mounting all along.

Opeth reprise the beginning of the tune for some more engrossing savagery before a titillating descent launches the irrefutably magnetic finale: 'And you are just like them all / Stained by the names of fathers / I'm greeting my downward fall / Leaving the throes to others'. Once again, Åkerfeldt and Wilson harmonise exquisitely, with the Swedish mastermind even burying an almost secret set of murmurs – 'I'm slave to this calling inside me / It won't let go / Spirit bewildered and gone / Waves hello' – beneath their clamours. A fresh, doubled-up guitar solo wraps up 'The Funeral Portrait' delightfully, permitting the dimming anarchy to leave a lasting impression just in time for the penultimate slice of short-lived restfulness.

'Patterns in the Ivy' (Åkerfeldt)

Åkerfeldt more or less reimagines *Orchid*'s 'Requiem' while replacing the bass with piano and fully tapping into his love for the transcendental density of Nick Drake (particularly on *Five Leaves Left* and *Pink Moon*). It's an icier and more sophisticated elegy, though, with Åkerfeldt's distraught plucking serving as the stage upon which Wilson's anguished keyboard accentuations dance. Like 'Bleak', it's a faultless duet wherein each player complements rather than outshines the other.

'Blackwater Park' (Åkerfeldt, Lindgren)

Cunningly, it gives the whole collection an extra dose of continuity by setting off almost exactly like 'The Leper Affinity': with a similarly threatening – yet much briefer – tone blooming into a dissonant ambush. It's sort of an all-encompassing reflection on what precedes it, too, as Åkerfeldt told *Metal Update* around the time of release: 'The song 'Blackwater Park' is about how disgusted I am with people sometimes. I just wanted to create some kind of very, very disgusting and very dark kind of mood with that track'. Undoubtedly, he succeeds.

It doesn't take long for that apocalyptic set-up to be interrupted by a sinister acoustic riff; then, an archetypal Åkerfeldt 'ugh!' resumes the bedlam. Following the first monstrous verse, another acoustic detour comes in and (abetted by ghostly overtones and hums) oozes cautionary distress. Such brisk turnarounds mean that this title track is the most hastily bipolar piece on *Blackwater Park*.

The pandemonium arises again via otherworldly sound manipulation, and it's extremely riveting. Åkerfeldt harkens back to the start of the LP once more by singing, 'Lepers coiled neath the trees / Dying men in bewildered soliloquies'. The sheer ferocity of his grumbles, combined with the flexibly in-your-face maliciousness of the musicianship, sees 'Blackwater Park' also acting as a clear walkway into the evils of *Deliverance*. Acoustic chords are added beneath the nifty re-emergence of past themes, yielding a vitriolic whirlwind that's as unrelentingly dreary and adversarial as can be.

His closing comment – 'Sick liaisons raised this monumental mark / The sun sets forever over Blackwater Park' – adds a dash of conceptual weight as the commotion is conquered by one last succinct acoustic arpeggio. Honestly, it's a little undeveloped, obligatory, and clumsily inserted (at least compared to previous changeups), but it does its job well enough and doesn't diminish the lingering magnitude of what's just transpired.

Bonuses

Different editions of *Blackwater Park* have different bonuses, so let's tackle them all here. First, there's the live version of 'The Leper Affinity' from one of their European tours (exact location and date unknown). Åkerfeldt introduces himself as 'a genius when it comes to music' – half kidding, half-serious, I'm sure – and the crowd goes wild when he announces it. Quality-wise, it's more muddled than the studio version, and Åkerfeldt's death vocals are croakier but still satisfying. There are a few adjustments instrumentally (such as some new guitar hammering after the third verse), but it's mostly a one-to-one recreation.

Obviously, Odefjärd's video for 'Harvest' has already been explained in detail, and his *Blackwater Park* documentary goes for much of the same look and vibe. It's only about half an hour long and doesn't offer much insight into individual songs; yet, it's fascinating to see each member (and Wilson) discuss their backgrounds, hopes, assessments, and the like, all the while allowing viewers to see bits and pieces of the recording and production processes. The amateurish quality and approach are quite charming.

Unsurprisingly, both 'Patterns in the Ivy II' and 'Still Day Beneath the Sun' are ravishing acoustic carols deeply influenced by Nick Drake classics like 'Cello Song' and 'Day is Done'. In fact, the latter one is directly referenced in 'Patterns in the Ivy II', whose labyrinthine fingerpicking is as breathtakingly morose as its harmonies and lyricism ('Without you, I cannot confide in anything / The hope is pale designed in light of dreams you bring'). Åkerfeldt's concluding chants are especially pure and affecting. As for 'Still Day Beneath the Sun', it walks the same path musically and emotionally – employing the same techniques for virtually identical outcomes – but with the smallest touch of optimism differentiating it. It's unclear why they were left off *Blackwater Park* (probably something related to pacing and a need to uphold parity between folk and metal attributes), as they're two of the most divinely sombre songs Åkerfeldt ever wrote.

In July 2021, the band re-teamed with Music for Nations for a 20th-anniversary reissue that was pressed onto heavyweight, 'audiophile approved' vinyl – available in several colours, such as dark smoky transparent, green, white, dark grey, clear transparent, silver, and light smoky transparent – and housed in a gatefold artwork sleeve. Deluxe versions also feature an updated artwork booklet that contains updated liner notes, other reflections from the band, rare photos, and more. As for the CD option, it comes in a hardcover book and includes all of those extras, too. Predictably, all editions offer the live version of 'The Leper Affinity' as well. Because this book was completed before this reissue came out, an actual appraisal wasn't possible; that said, it certainly looks like an excellent new way to honour the record.

Deliverance (2002)

Personnel:
Mikael Åkerfeldt: vocals, acoustic and electric guitars
Peter Lindgren: electric guitars
Martin López: drums, percussion
Martin Méndez: bass
Additional Personnel:
Steven Wilson: engineer, piano, keyboards, Mellotron, additional guitar, backing vocals
Isak Edh: engineer
Fredrik Nordström: engineer
Fredrik Reymerdahl: engineer
Andy Sneap: mixing
Travis Smith: design, photography
Ken Seaney: photography
Rex Zachary: photography
Harry Välimäki: photography
Produced at Studio Fredman and Maestro Musik/Nacksving Studios in Gothenburg, Sweden, July – September 2002 by Mikael Åkerfeldt and Steven Wilson.
Release date: 12 November 2002.
Highest chart places: UK: none, USA: none
Running time: 61:45
Current edition: 2015 Sony Music / Music for Nations CD/DVD digibook remix (with Damnation)

The sudden commercial and critical success of *Blackwater Park* was the payoff for roughly a dozen years of struggles and self-doubt. Logically, that prosperity made everyone involved – the band, management, the labels, etc. – confident in and curious about where Opeth would go next. For Åkerfeldt, it meant that their follow-up would have to aim higher and do something unexpected. In *Book of Opeth*, he elaborates: 'I was getting a bit restless. I didn't want to do just another record, but something different… I wanted to do something special. I wanted to do a really heavy record, but I was also writing a lot of acoustic stuff'.

The end result – *Deliverance* and *Damnation* – were the ideal solutions, as they embodied the group's most radical tonal extremes (overpoweringly harsh and unconditionally heavenly, respectively). Specifically, *Deliverance* – whose title was influenced by and dedicated to Ned Beatty and the 1972 film *Deliverance* – is like an entire record of *Blackwater Park*'s most maniacal alleyways. Though still ripe with friendly fragments, it's a wrathful venture that – even without its relentlessly mellow counterpart – comes close to being Opeth's finest assemblage thus far.

At first, and at the recommendation of Jonas Renkse, Åkerfeldt planned to put all the new material into a double album; however, Music for Nations weren't on board because they thought that it'd be too expensive. Justifiably, this upset Åkerfeldt since it meant that that his creative vision was being stifled; smartly, both parties compromised by agreeing to do two albums for the price of one, with the recording sessions happening simultaneously, the recording contract stipulating that the quartet would only be paid for a single album, and the release dates being about half a year apart (allowing Music for Nations to generate more promotional hype and cumulative sales).

As usual, Opeth didn't have a lot of completed material written ahead of time (between two and three songs), but Åkerfeldt's new toy – a Boss BR-8 Digital Record Studio that he bought from Dan Swanö – at least allowed him to record demos at his own pace rather than rely on the equipment and open schedules of friends. Likewise, the group didn't rehearse what they *did* have because, as Åkerfeldt regrettably acknowledges, that was 'a good way to get everybody in the band a bit more involved in the creative process'. Add to all that the fact that they were now also pressured into making two LPs in the same amount of time they usually had to make one (about seven weeks) and Opeth were entering the most gratifying yet stressful recording period of their career.

Lindgren claims that in order to get it all done in time, he and Åkerfeldt spent almost every waking moment in the studio (whereas López and Méndez would go home once they were done with their parts each day). Furthermore, they fell into a cycle in which Åkerfeldt would write at night and then they'd record whatever he came up with during the next day. Hence, the whole *Deliverance* record was done 'extremely spontaneously', Åkerfeldt notes, adding:

> I was not as interested in that record as I was in making *Damnation*.
> *Damnation* was something that we hadn't done before: a whole record of
> progressive songs. That was the stuff I was listening to, calm progressive
> music, so I was much more interested in working on that. I couldn't wait for us
> to finish *Deliverance* so that we could start with *Damnation*.

His shifting musical interests weren't the only reason why he was keen to move on from *Deliverance* ASAP, as he was mentally and emotionally exhausted due to overlapping hardships in the studio. For one thing, Opeth and Fredrik Nordström quickly parted ways due to his fee demands, and Maestro Musik/Nacksving – as well as owner/engineer Isak Edh – were no longer reliable or adequate. In Åkerfeldt's online diary for *Deliverance*, he divulges that they'd 'sacrificed whatever normal lives [they] had at home for this recording', which meant sleeping on the floor and enduring sweltering summer heat. If that weren't bad enough, the studio used an outdated PC instead of an up-to-date MacIntosh, leading to constant problems with Edh's software and recording devices.

While all of this was happening, Åkerfeldt says, Edh 'spent most of his time down at the local bar drinking beer. Literally every time we called him on his cell phone, he was down in the bar'. Lindgren, Méndez, and López have equally negative memories of those days, with López also bringing up (in the 'Making of *Deliverance & Damnation*' documentary) that he argued with Edh because Edh swapped out a good drum mic for an inferior one. Things got so bad that they had several band meetings to talk about what they should do, and Åkerfeldt took on a sort of father figure responsibility as the chief creative force and band leader. Both he and Lindgren admit that virtually all the joy of being in the group was gone, and they worried that it would be the end of Opeth.

Internal tensions between the quartet only intensified those thoughts. Despite all four members suggesting that, as Méndez puts it, they had 'a good relationship as a band', Åkerfeldt was getting the sense that he was the only member who truly shouldered the burden, expressly regarding Lindgren. In *Book of Opeth*, Åkerfeldt states that he was apprehensive about giving Lindgren feedback because Lindgren's confidence was increasingly fragile and his 'nerves were on the outside of his body at this point'. That may clarify why – according to Åkerfeldt in a 2018 interview with *Billboard*'s Christa Titus – Lindgren 'kind of disappeared during that time'. He continues:

> That was kind of the beginning of the end. He went away to a different town to drink beer and to party when we were going to start recording the guitars. Also, you can add to the equation that I'm not good with confrontation. I just kind of clenched my fist in my pocket. But I figured that's showing enormous disrespect to me, to the band, [and] to himself, as a guitar player, to just piss off when we're going to record.

Thankfully, he and Lindgren 'reconnected' and 'cleared the air' years later; meanwhile, Méndez and López were agreeably ancillary as they worked on *Deliverance*. Actually, Åkerfeldt reflects, they brought in 'influences [he] wouldn't have gotten otherwise because they had 'a lot of friends from different cultures who played music for them' (which they then played for Åkerfeldt). He and López had a particularly fun time coming up with drum parts together, too, with Åkerfeldt surmising, 'Once you have the drums down, you more or less know if it's good or not. That was always very exciting, and even if we weren't in a great state collectively, I think there were moments that we really enjoyed, too'. Be that as it may, something major had to be done to rectify those other complications, and fortunately, the answer became abundantly clear: head back to Studio Fredman and bring in Steven Wilson for some much-needed course correction.

Those two choices were more entwined than they may seem, as Åkerfeldt explains – in the documentary – that Fredman had what Wilson needed to work, such as a software program called Logic, and that they 'knew everything would work there'. Once those changes were made and everyone was settled in, Åkerfeldt felt 'the first ray of light during the whole recording'. As for why Wilson came back (aside from his friendship with Åkerfeldt), he jokes that Opeth kept 'bugging' him and that he knew they'd done something remarkable with *Blackwater Park*. (So much so, in fact, that a lot of Porcupine Tree fans who'd previously disliked metal music were 'surprised' at how much the LP appealed to them.) The idea of doing the entirely mellow *Damnation* intrigued Wilson, too, and he foresaw that the duality of both LPs would yield 'a kind of watershed in the Opeth trajectory'.

Opeth had a lot of *Deliverance* finished by the time Wilson arrived, so he was only there for the final two weeks or so; however, because of Wilson's stature and how far behind they were in completing it, the group was very nervous about what Wilson would think of the progress they'd made. Åkerfeldt writes in *Book of Opeth* that he half-heartedly hoped that 'somehow the tapes had been wiped and the studio time ran out, so that it would be all over'. Luckily, Wilson recalls, what he had to work with was far from the 'disaster' Åkerfeldt thought it was, so they got to work on 'the higher end' of it and Åkerfeldt 'started to get more into it'.

As with *Blackwater Park*, Wilson concentrated on putting together the pieces Opeth already constructed in addition to putting their vocals and instrumentation into their 'own sound world that's distinct from all of the other vocals or leads'. Naturally, he also added his own musicianship and voice when beneficial, as well as having lyrical input from time to time. Lindgren remembers that Wilson's direction was quite reassuring and freeing, allowing the quartet to maintain *Blackwater Park*'s experimentation in terms of spawning absorbing sound effects and refreshing innovations. 'Steve saved *Deliverance*', Åkerfeldt concludes, and he also calls Andy Sneap (Sabbat, Judas Priest) of Backstage Recording a 'saviour' for doing the best he could when mixing and mastering the album.

Predictably, Åkerfeldt wasn't very enthused about writing lyrics, as he told Titus:

A lot of those songs aren't about anything ... I didn't enjoy writing lyrics. I hated writing lyrics, actually. I didn't have anything to say. I felt like I said everything I wanted to say with the music itself, but then, of course, you need something to sing, so it's going to be either some random shit that doesn't mean anything or something with a bit more substance.

That doesn't mean that there's nothing to dig into about *Deliverance*'s subject matter – especially regarding the title track – and we'll get there soon. In the documentary, Lindgren addresses another often asked question about the band's artistry: how he and Åkerfeldt decide who gets to do certain guitar solos. Lindgren claims: 'We split [them] in half, more or less, unless one of us has a favourite part that we really want to do a solo over. One of us starts and, since we usually only have 24 hours to do everything, we each get 12 hours'. Within that time frame, they continuously listened to the same segments until they were happy with the 'melodies' they laid down. Seeing as how *Deliverance* has some of the best guitar solos in Opeth's whole discography, their efforts were very well spent.

Because Music for Nations was eager to get the word out, Åkerfeldt discusses, they wasted no time arranging photo sessions 'at a location in Ripley, just outside of Nottingham' and inviting journalists to listen to 'rough mixes' of the LP. Only he and Lindgren were there – and they were told that the pictures 'were for some guitar magazines only' – so López and Méndez weren't included in that batch of press shots. Afterwards, they joined the journalists; however, halfway into their listening session, Åkerfeldt got a call from his sister with terrible news: their grandmother (who gave him his first acoustic guitars and kick-started his interest in being a musician) was in critical condition after being in a car accident. He reminisces: 'I went outside for a 'cigarette', but really to weep. I tried to get myself together and go back to listen to the tracks with [them], but you know Opeth, at the time, wasn't really a priority in my train of thoughts'. The next morning, his sister phoned again to say that their grandmother had passed away, which is why he dedicated both *Deliverance* and *Damnation* to her.

Understandably, he wasn't in a happy mood during the ensuing 'one-off gig scheduled in the centre of Stockholm' or the full band photoshoot beforehand. Outside of that show (which likely occurred at the Shrine Club on 27 September), they didn't really take to the stage during this time, choosing instead to focus on finishing *Damnation* before embarking on a proper tour for *both* albums during the winter transition into 2003 and the subsequent summer season.

Like *Blackwater Park*, *Deliverance* sold a lot and received a ton of positive press. In fact, it earned Opeth their first Swedish Grammy in the 'Best Hard Rock' category; similarly, it peaked at #19 on *Billboard*'s Independent Albums chart and at #16 on the Heatseekers chart (demonstrating how they were getting bigger and bigger in America). In 2015, Åkerfeldt's original vision was fulfilled when *Deliverance* and *Damnation* were reissued together, with Wilson looking after the *Damnation* improvements while The Pineapple Thief's Bruce Soord oversaw *Deliverance*. Publications such as *PROG*, *Angry Metal Guy*, *PopMatters*, *AllMusic*, and *Progradar* praised both remixes (especially *Deliverance* since the original version – even by Opeth and Wilson's admission – didn't sound great).

Had they always been a shared sequence, *Deliverance* and *Damnation* would be Opeth's superlative record (or tremendously close to it). On its own, *Deliverance* is still way up there. Scarier and less welcoming than *Blackwater Park*, it requires more dedicated investment and investigation from the listener to completely comprehend. While there are scattered snapshots of beauty and solace – including one of the most gorgeous vocal harmonies you'll ever hear in its penultimate gem – *Deliverance* is an unforgivingly brutal ride. Gratefully, every second of it is spellbinding and inventive, making it, like most Opeth LPs, an out-and-out triumph.

'Wreath' (Åkerfeldt)

The album wastes no time establishing its demonic décor, with 'Wreath' living up to its title by having López's preliminary drum roll instigate a torrent of buzzsaw guitar chords alongside Åkerfeldt's unholy mandates. Like much of the record, it's an immensely barbaric and bleak passage that's kept enthralling because of how graciously spiteful it is. (In other words, its straightforwardness is offset by its captivating cruelty.)

Next, a distorted transition is backed by López's impeccable polyrhythms and pounding footwork, giving listeners a peek into how his playing and pervasiveness are upped on *Deliverance*. He really does steal the show throughout the record, peppering moderately unassuming movements with just the right amount of dexterity and flair. Meanwhile, Åkerfeldt's growls perpetuate utter godlessness around a penetrating guitar solo and Wilson's distanced and wraithlike textures.

A few more minutes of marginally nuanced – but persistently awesome – music carry us to a minor respite that highlights the power of López and Méndez's aforementioned cultural impact; an even fiercer solo explodes out of it, though, and is reinforced by rising guitar lines and stylish syncopation. Åkerfeldt's final howls are complemented by soft-spoken responses – 'Starting right back / Spiritual decay / (Still seeking) / Frozen in time / Mourn this departure / (All watching)' – and a jazzy acoustic interlude reminiscent of something from *Orchid* or *Morningrise*. It ends with a return to the start and an extra tricky transition into the brilliant title track.

'Deliverance' (Åkerfeldt)

It's a masterpiece of progressive death metal that rivals 'The Drapery Falls' as Opeth's most popular and representative opus. In a 2019 chat with *Kerrang!*, Åkerfeldt discloses that the tune is based on something that happened to Lindgren's girlfriend: 'She was having a ladies' night in with her friends and I think it was the ex-boyfriend of one of these ladies who turned up and he was high on something. He basically locked them in. He wouldn't let them leave the apartment and [he] started threatening them'. The man kept cutting himself, too; while the situation ended without anyone else being hurt, it inspired Åkerfeldt to write 'about that crazy kind of obsessive love where you want to own the other person and you can do whatever you want with them'. He also notes that because 'Deliverance' has so many riffs, he needed to name them all just to keep track, with *Destroy Erase Improve* by Meshuggah helping stimulate his writing.

For sure, its opening riff is among its best. Matched by shrill six-string accompaniment, jackhammer percussion, and engaging modulations, it's totally mesmerising and iconic. About a minute in, that fury dissipates into a gentle acoustic bypass with plaintive plucking, animated drumming, and smooth guitar overlays that evoke the start of *Still Life*. Åkerfeldt's meek desires – 'Tell me how / Your heart's in need / As I drown / You in the sea' – are disturbingly heartbroken but hostile. If not for the intruding gusts of terror in-between (boosted by Wilson's phantom theatrics), this part would fit fine on *Damnation*.

The caustic rage comes back in full force, with a quick pause providing unmistakable Opeth coolness. Then, the music dies down to give Åkerfeldt more supremacy as he screams, 'Face down beneath the waterline / Gazing into the deep'. A stunning solo takes charge before more incensed verses barrel into crudely demoralised guitar swipes and temptingly clean perceptions: 'The piercing sounds you make / Soaring higher, higher now'. After more transfixing trade-offs between that template and an irate alternative, López's clever drum fill incites an infectiously circular dose of biting catharsis ('The devil guides the way / Tells me what to say').

Åkerfeldt's high-pitched vocal garnish adds angelic depth prior to a final classy guitar solo, which then moves the track into its bouncily tranquil second-to-last section ('Deliverance / Thrown back at me'). It's a disquieting but elegant pathway that also hints at the unsettling loveliness of *Damnation*; however, it's speedily substituted for shimmering cymbals and suspenseful back-and-forth guitar notes that serve as a prelude to the song's ultimate victory.

If created by almost any other band, these four straight minutes of repetitious percussion (and adjacent instrumentation) would get tedious before long. But, this is Opeth we're talking about, so we're instead given four straight minutes of López ingeniously reinventing his methods every few measures. Although the cycle repeats ad nauseam, he – and Méndez, of course – add understated yet hypnotic alterations that keep it extraordinary. Frankly, their ability to make this closing portion *more* engrossing as it proceeds should be studied by every aspiring drummer and bassist. Naturally, Wilson's slowly reversed tones at the end become the cherry on top of what's already a flawless musical sundae.

'A Fair Judgement' (Åkerfeldt)

Because 'Wreath' and 'Deliverance' were so unremittingly violent, it only makes sense for Opeth to let us catch our breath with this majorly peaceful ode. Wilson's introductory piano chords (which anticipate Åkerfeldt's verses) are wonderfully sullen and paced, using what Åkerfeldt calls a 'telephone' or 'underwater' effect to enhance the eeriness of its looming misery. Once the full band kicks in, they produce a bewitching environment whose delicate and roomy backing is shrewdly contrasted by a domineering electric guitar lead that etches itself into your soul. Åkerfeldt's verdicts ('Losing sleep / In too deep / Fading sun / What have I done?') are emblematically crestfallen and attractive as well.

An imposing new progression acts as a compact corridor into a striking acoustic guitar arpeggio; its comparatively easy ascension and scratchy surface (as if it's being played on a worn vinyl record) gives it a lot of charisma. That muted feature makes the fuller segment that follows seem brighter and more luscious, especially when Wilson's falsetto is layered upon Åkerfeldt's sedative harmonies. The resultant guitar solo is very savoury, too, before it manoeuvres into a pile of relaxed acoustic fingerpicking and syncopation.

From there, the quartet takes a pleasingly chaotic route as an atypically fast guitar solo shreds over the mayhem. It's absolutely thrilling, sparking another stellar disparity when it abruptly dissolves into a harrowingly empty reiteration of Åkerfeldt's earliest statement (with only Wilson's piano chords supporting him). Despite slightly outstaying its welcome, the aggressively fatalistic outro successfully capitalises on the track's ever-changing attitude.

'For Absent Friends' (Åkerfeldt)

Taking its name from the second selection off Genesis' *Nursery Cryme*, 'For Absent Friends' is a remorseful and modest guitar ballad. Truthfully, there's even less to it than most of its cursory instrumental forebears, with only a few simple acoustic and electric structures intersecting. That's not a knock against it, though, because it's sufficiently touching and tasteful nonetheless, coming across like a pacifying appetiser to the despicable main dish that is 'Master's Apprentices'.

'Master's Apprentices' (Åkerfeldt)

The stampeding resentment that steers the LP's initial duo spearheads this one, too, with even Åkerfeldt's words – 'There is a voice calling for me / There is a light coming down on me / There is a doubt that is clearing' – bringing about arresting monotony. It's an exceptional example of how Opeth can make somewhat primitive arrangements consummately enticing. That said, 'Master's Apprentices' truly gets going around the two-minute mark, when some opulently peculiar guitar work generates a fresh offshoot that subtly links to the previous entry ('Movement for departed hope / Effect for absent friends').

All the while, the boys are sneakily building elation for the mid-section of the song, which easily ranks as a top-tier Opeth moment. A frolicking instrumental climb gives way to Åkerfeldt's entrancing echoes ('Soothing trace / Colours fade / And disappear'), only to be countered by additional tyranny before it comes back. This time, the outcome is downright euphoric, as acoustic guitar strums, lenient percussion, and anguished electric guitar wails lull you into a false sense of security. Åkerfeldt sings sympathetically, using his last line – 'Once I'm below / There's no turning back' – as a pivot into overwhelmingly saintly bellows. At the risk of sounding hyperbolic, he and Wilson deliver the most divine harmonies in the history of metal; no matter how many times you hear it, it never stops being entirely magnificent.

Inevitably, that splendour is briskly seized by a flood of nervous rhythms, prickly guitar work, and dejected hollers that neutralise any shred of lingering relief. It's an alarmingly spiky downfall that forces the composition – whose name comes from a late 1960s Australian hard rock ensemble – to climax with wide-ranging indignation amidst setting up *Deliverance*'s amazingly horrid finale.

'By the Pain I See in Others' (Åkerfeldt)

Once the intensifying 'telephone' effect wears off, 'By the Pain I See in Others' becomes a glaring candidate for Opeth's most grotesque gathering. Everyone's playing is pungent and disruptive (in a good way), and the off-kilter acoustic sweeps add a macabre undertone to Åkerfeldt's devilish instructions. His voice is uncomfortably phlegmy – so he sounds particularly inhuman – and the unyielding blast beats evoke the end of 'Deliverance'. It's quite a corrosive way to start, with some likeably chic guitar lines thrown in for good measure.

Suddenly, Wilson's ominously carnivalesque Mellotron intervals – played as a waltz and faintly foreshadowed at the end of 'Master's Apprentices' – tiptoe in for Åkerfeldt's folkie remarks: 'Outside in the park / The days move along / And nothing ever changes'. (In hindsight, this part also alludes to how Opeth will employ keyboards more regularly moving forward.) However, it's not long until the preceding belligerence arises once more, eventually converting into a spiral of complex instability that previews the more traditional prog rock leanings of *Ghost Reveries*. It's a beguilingly malevolent and ambitious trek that terminates with a stirring rupture of rescinding feedback.

Obviously, *Deliverance* has one more trick up its sleeve: a hidden sound collage that materialises after about 90 seconds of silence. Specifically, the spectral hodgepodge consists of two back masked – recorded backward and then played forward – slices from 'Master's Apprentices': the 'Soothing trance / Colours fade' and 'Fading away / And leaving / Long for sleep' verses. Not only does this give *Deliverance* an additional bit of frightening ingenuity, but it sees Opeth partaking in a popular music custom that dates back decades (to the Beatles' 'Paul is Dead' stunt, if not older).

Bonuses
Because the 'Making of *Deliverance* & *Damnation*' documentary is on *Lamentations: Live at Shepherd's Bush Empire 2003*, we'll wait until we get there to explore it. Beyond that, there are no extras for *Deliverance* as of now.

Damnation (2003)

Personnel:
Mikael Åkerfeldt: vocals, acoustic and electric guitars
Peter Lindgren: electric guitars
Martin López: drums, percussion
Martin Méndez: bass
Additional Personnel:
Steven Wilson: engineer, Grand piano, electric piano, Mellotron, backing vocals
Travis Smith: design, photography
Ken Seaney: photography
Rex Zachary: photography
Produced at Studio Fredman and Maestro Musik/Nacksving Studios in Gothenburg, Sweden, and at No Man's Land in Hemel Hempstead, England, July – October 2002 by Mikael Åkerfeldt and Steven Wilson.
Release date: 22 April 2003.
Highest chart places: UK: 181, USA: 192
Running time: 43:03
Current edition: 2015 Sony Music / Music for Nations CD/DVD digibook remix (with Deliverance)

Considering how many difficulties and oppositions the band faced as they made *Deliverance*, it's impossible not to marvel at how artistically, financially, and critically prosperous the finished product was. Even so, those assorted stressors – as well as the pressing desire to try something new and challenge themselves and their fans – meant that all involved were champing at the bit to begin focusing on the second half of the planned project. Therefore, they immediately got to work once they returned from the previously mentioned 'one-off gig' in Stockholm, doubling down on the material and tools they'd already been using while also relocating to Steven Wilson's No Man's Land home studio for additional vocal work in October 2002.

Thankfully, they managed to complete *Damnation* within the allotted time frame and achieve something far more outstanding than anyone could've foreseen. By homing in on their 1970s prog rock stimuli and dedicating themselves to fully exploiting their softer persona, they created a radiantly uncharacteristic but fruitful 'observation' that, as Wilson concludes in *Book of Opeth*, 'set a precedent for how Opeth is now'. Even when contrasted with the quartet's previous proclivity for astoundingly serene asides, the songwriting, production, and performances on *Damnation* reach a higher level of haunting exquisiteness. Likewise – and even with them abandoning their death metal slant for good after 2008's *Watershed* – it remains an awe-inspiring and mysterious anomaly in their catalogue. Truly, *Damnation* is a one-of-a-kind experience by which all other modern full-length metal excursions into gentler pastures must be measured.

Although Åkerfeldt was always in charge of Opeth, he continuously wanted his bandmates to be on board with his decisions, and that included the notion of doing an all-clean record. Gratefully, the other three members were as fascinated by the concept as he was. In *Book of Opeth*, Méndez ruminates that 'the idea of *Damnation* was really exciting' because it allowed him to 'explore different styles of music'; López concurs, commenting in the 'Making of *Deliverance & Damnation*' documentary that 'there's something special about playing those [soft] parts. They're peaceful moments, and I feel it when we do metal songs live. During those parts, I used to think, 'Fuck, I want to do this for a whole gig or whole album'. Chill down and play with feelings more than aggression'. That's exactly what *Damnation* permitted him to do (with the help of a different drum kit).

Of course, no one was more excited about – and relieved by – making *Damnation* than Åkerfeldt. After all, he'd exorcised many of the technical and creative hardships that befell *Deliverance*, and he had Wilson there from the start this time. He even judges the two albums with 'different eyes' because of how much more enjoyable making *Damnation* was, especially in terms of collaborating at No Man's Land. 'I got a hotel in central London, so Steve had to pick me up every day to go to the studio, which was located in his boy room at his parents' house. [It's] a really small wardrobe size room right next to the toilet. Anyway, it went great, and the album came out better than I'd dare to expect', he reveals.

While very confident in the completed record, Åkerfeldt's periodic unease about how well their milder material would go over with fans reared its head again (and not for nothing since this was an *entirely* soothing sequence). Even Farrow and the label were sceptical about how *Damnation* should be promoted, as he admits in *Book of Opeth*: 'It's always been the case ... that they're creating the music and I'm doing the marketing, putting the team together, creating the campaign around it and the rest – but they don't always make it simple'. Meanwhile, they'd scheduled a few interviews in Germany and France, which went well; upon coming back to Sweden, however, Åkerfeldt was struck with a 'terrible' sickness – general weakness, stomach problems, dizziness, etc. – that doctors couldn't diagnose. He concludes that it must've been a consequence of 'all the hard work and all the bad things that had happened lately'.

That's not to say that they were unable to play concerts in support of both *Damnation* and *Deliverance*; on the contrary, Åkerfeldt pushed through the pain as Opeth launched their largest tour yet in London and Athens, Greece. In fact, he says that those December 2002 shows were so good that they 'seemed to work as a cure for [his] illness'. Despite dealing with a prolonged cold and tour bus troubles along the way, Åkerfeldt and company had a great time playing around 200 more headlining shows, festivals, and the like (mostly in Europe and North America) between January 2003 and March 2004. Before it was all over, they'd shared the stage with several major artists, such as Lacuna Coil, DevilDriver, Moonspell, Iron Maiden, Sepultura, Lamb of God, Arch Enemy, and Metallica. They also made their first TV appearance (on Sweden's

TV4). While detailing every major incident would be unnecessarily exhaustive, there are three more major aspects of the *Deliverance/Damnation* tour that require elaboration: the addition of keyboardist Per Wiberg (effectively making *Damnation* Opeth's final album as an official quartet), the recording of Opeth's first concert film (*Lamentations: Live at Shepherd's Bush Empire 2003*), and the emergence of López's detrimental health concerns.

It would've been nonsensical to expect Wilson to accompany Opeth on their globe-trotting adventure – although he did reunite with them for a bit when Porcupine Tree co-headlined their summer 2003 North American stint to promote *In Absentia* – so finding a touring keyboardist was of utmost importance. Luckily, they didn't have to search too far or too long because Åkerfeldt knew the ideal person. He explains that he and Wiberg were already friends, adding, 'We were going to do a project together, just me and him, because I'd never worked with a keyboard player before and he was a bit of a mentor for me in many ways because he didn't come from the extreme metal background. He was a down-to-earth, cool guy'. Obviously, Wiberg was such a good fit that he ended up being asked to stay as a permanent member and expand their sonic possibilities on 2005's *Ghost Reveries*.

For certain performances, they'd play two sets – one acoustic and one heavy – and that was the case on 25 September 2003, when they stopped by Shepherd's Bush Empire in London. They played all of *Damnation* (with *Blackwater Park*'s 'Harvest' coming in-between 'Ending Credits' and 'Weakness') and then pulled out selected tunes from *Deliverance* and *Blackwater Park* (which makes sense since the LPs could be seen as a thematic and stylistic trio). Méndez notes that they 'only did two rehearsals' and 'were pretty nervous', while Farrow takes credit for suggesting the gig in the first place, deducing that it 'probably laid the foundations for the blueprint of the special event style concerts the band would do in the future'.

A less joyous occurrence would happen near the beginning of 2004, when Opeth were scheduled to play in Jordan. They were already facing trouble by planning to go without a crew (because of a fear of terrorist attacks), but before they could even leave, López called Åkerfeldt to say that he was unable to play due to severe anxiety. They cancelled the appearance and carried on, only to have López suffer more anxiety attacks while in Canada. Rather than abandon more shows, however, Opeth chose to send López home to recuperate while two new people – his drum technician and then Strapping Young Lad's Gene Hoglan – filled in. Fortunately, López returned by the time they got to Seattle, WA.

As exciting and flattering as it all was, touring eventually became as burdensome for Åkerfeldt as it was beneficial. '[It] wears you down so much [that] it's unbelievable, and it's so addictive that it's uncanny. When you're out, you long to get back home, and when you do, you can't wait to get out again', he reasons. No matter how fatiguing it got, Opeth couldn't help but bask in the fact that they were significantly closer to the 'ideal rock star life' Åkerfeldt envisioned when he first heard from Lee Barrett and Candlelight Records nearly a decade earlier.

The amount of accolades *Damnation* received had an equally gratifying effect. Most importantly, it saw them finally land on the *Billboard* 200 (at #192); it peaked at #181 on the UK Albums Chart as well, so it sold more than *Deliverance* and proved that Opeth's fanbase were quite open to their new experiment. At the time, professional reviewers were rightly ecstatic, too, and many retrospective writers said that they preferred it to *Deliverance* when they reassessed it as part of the 2015 double-disc reissue. In 2019, *Decibel* named it Opeth's third-best album, ruling that 'every tune ... delivers a memorable melody with a cool and crepuscular atmosphere'. Three years earlier, *Stereogum*'s Jonathan Dick called it 'an emotional wrecking ball' when he paired it with *Deliverance* as Opeth's fourth most noteworthy collection.

Perhaps *Damnation*'s greatest win is its ability to exude accessibility without forfeiting integrity or creativity. It gave innumerable diehard disciples – such as me – an introduction to Opeth via a monumental helping of their immaculate sensitive side. In turn, newcomers sought out the kinder parts of prior records, nurtured affection for the surrounding vehemence, and grew to adore *everything* Opeth had done. Along the same lines, it showed how receptive the metal community was to their favourite artists venturing down stranger paths (so it paved the way for some of Opeth's peers to try comparatively bold things further on down the line). Thus, its importance and merits cannot be overstated or brazenly dismissed, as its influence exceeds the boundaries of Opeth's discography. Even when judged as a self-contained effort, though, *Damnation* is just about perfect.

'Windowpane' (Åkerfeldt)
From start to finish, this lone single from *Damnation* is a celestial treat whose vintage glaze and sublime essence – like all of *Damnation* – transports listeners to a new plane of peacefulness. Even when compared to *any* of the band's earlier flashes of solitude, its velvety composure is devastatingly stupendous and graceful. The starting acoustic guitar arpeggios, coupled with Méndez and López's dapper accentuations, are enough to charm, but then Wilson's recurring Mellotron croons and Åkerfeldt's lonely commentary – 'Blank face in the windowpane / Made clear in seconds of light / Disappears and returns again / Counting hours, searching the night' – push its enchantments to the edge. Even his voice has newfound soulfulness and tenderness.

The masterful first electric guitar solo exemplifies another through-line of the record: the influence of classic progressive rock bands like Pink Floyd, The Moody Blues, and especially Camel. During the second verse, Wilson's high-pitched backing vocals add yet another indispensable element to the experience, and both the consequent melodic swing ('Inside plays a lullaby / Slurred voice over children cries') and its silky six-string bookends are just as scrumptious. Afterwards, López dishes out a glossy slice of syncopation as a segue into a handsomely gothic, perilous, and introspective instrumental precursor to the song's main guitar solo. Every note and timbre is immaculately chosen to underpin the regal grief of the track, which comes full circle at the end but with added apparitional frills reaching maximum impact and cementing 'Windowpane' as an untarnished work of art. (The official music features a negligibly shorter version played over footage of Opeth recording it, so there's not much to analyse about it.)

'In My Time of Need' (Åkerfeldt)
While not as multifaceted or imposing as the prior tune, 'In My Time of Need' is nonetheless another alluring examination of idyllic misfortune. The stilted and fatalistic nature of its verses is supported well by its gleaming guitar brushes and simple drumming, making the breezy resolve of its pre-chorus and folkier chorus quite refreshing by comparison. Similarly, the frenzied despair of the bridge – 'At times / The dark's fading slowly / But it never sustains' – adds an appreciated jolt of grisly urgency before some beachy slide guitar passes judgment on Åkerfeldt's insights. Lastly, Wilson's keyboard swirls become more commanding as the chorus caps off the piece with humble sadness.

'Death Whispered a Lullaby' (Åkerfeldt, Wilson)
Its overt narrative about death coming to claim someone conjures Blue Öyster Cult's seminal 'Don't Fear the Reaper'. Interestingly, it's the only inclusion co-written by Wilson, who – in *Book of Opeth* – says that he took on the duty because Åkerfeldt was so 'empty' and 'mentally exhausted' by the time they started working on it. Anyway, the opening acoustic guitar fingerwork is sort of like a fusion of how the last two tracks began, but with an emphasis on cryptic and cockeyed woodland depravity. Åkerfeldt's omniscient, fairy tale-like words mostly follow a traditional poetic rhyme scheme, and his timbre is richly regretful.

Startlingly, that rustic seclusion erupts into an energetic dirge punctuated by spunky guitar work, stress-free rhythms, and most importantly, dazzling harmonies from Åkerfeldt and Wilson. It's appealingly pastoral, providing a seemingly stable backdrop on which an almost otherworldly array of guitar notes roar animalistically. Its agony bleeds into the reprise of the song proper, only to come back at the end with even more hair-raising antagonism that cleverly depletes as the comforting 'Closure' sets in.

'Closure' (Åkerfeldt)
Åkerfeldt's stacked singing is luminously fragile and godlike at once, with tight acoustic guitar chords and fancy fingerpicking channelling Jethro Tull at the height of their prog rock reign. Once again, the unpretentious rhyme scheme of his lyrics (a/a/b/b) complements their forlorn eloquence, too. Next, an echoey electric guitar strum kicks off a tense and disorienting new pattern

as López and Méndez imaginatively cultivate magnetic psychedelic suspense. It's one of the coolest sections of *Damnation*, particularly because of how each timbre comes to a sudden, synchronised stop so that Åkerfeldt can return with another sombrely barren mini ballad ('Awaiting word on what's to come / In helpless prayers, a hope lives on'). As usual, Wilson's falsetto bolsters the beauty of Åkerfeldt's dense harmonies prior to 'Closure' transforming into a truly trippy jam full of fetching tribal percussion and a toweringly cursed guitar line. It's a positively flirtatious example of how *Damnation* charts paths never before attempted, and its unexpected cut-off – as if to prevent listeners from getting, well, closure – is an intrepid means of moving into the hopelessness that's about to arrive.

'Hope Leaves' (Åkerfeldt)
It's inarguably one of Opeth's greatest songs, as everything about it – such as the delicately mournful guitar work, the gut-wrenching nostalgic storytelling, and the emotionally wounded vocals – are ravishing. Even Wilson's sporadic electric piano intonations are vitally melancholic, showcasing how nailing the proper tone or effect can be just as important as the notes themselves. All along, López and Méndez offer an ideal support system by keeping the momentum going without distracting or trying to stand out. Like every other component, their playing is marvellously discreet but provocative. The midway detour, with its 'underwater' and feedback qualities, enhances the sense of isolation and wretchedness as well, providing an operative opposition to the cleanness of the returning verses. Needless to say, the rising chants at the end make the tune even more glorious.

'To Rid the Disease' (Åkerfeldt)
Embodying characteristics of both 'Benighted' from *Still Life* and 'Mordet i Grottan' by Sörskogen (a three-song collaboration between Åkerfeldt and Dan Swanö), 'To Rid the Disease' is instantly and ceaselessly traumatic. The main guitar loop conducts the jazzy rhythms and evocative call-and-response realisations with spherical seductiveness, leaving you defenceless against its hexing heartache. Behind it all, Méndez stands out more than usual with a springy bass line, and the subsequent combination of ornate instrumentation (including more ethereal Mellotron shells) and valiant melodies results in a splendid chorus.

Of course, it all builds eagerness for the stately guitar solo, which takes off with assertive tenacity and never loosens its grip as each note naturally glides into the next. It's efficient yet virtuosic and catchy, breaking away just as Wilson's disconsolate piano chords interject with secluded sorrow. Soon after, he's aided by López and Méndez's leisurely but dreary embellishments (which are then met by an uproar of dramatic guitars and keyboard). The pandemonium dies out discerningly, letting the track fade away with more chilling repentance, as if it's the score to the last scene of a staged tragedy.

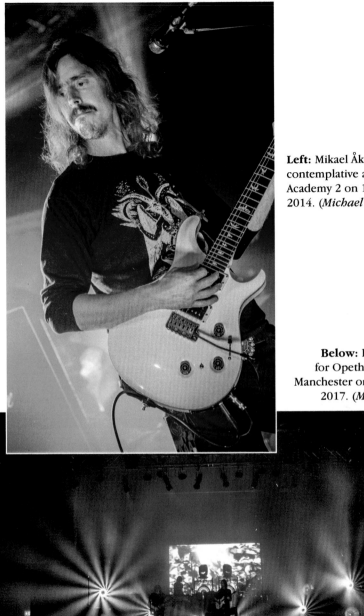

Left: Mikael Åkerfeldt looks contemplative at Manchester Academy 2 on 15 October, 2014. (*Michael Ainscoe*)

Below: Back and center for Opeth's gig at O2 Ritz Manchester on 15 November, 2017. (*Michael Ainscoe*)

Left: Opeth's debut LP, 1995's *Orchid*, finds this blooming flower signifying their blossoming career. (*Candlelight Records*)

Right: The look – and sound – of follow-up *Morningrise* LP was certainly gloomier yet more complex. (*Candlelight Records*)

Left: An evocative picture to represent their first conceptual opus, 1998's *My Arms, Your Hearse*. (*Candlelight Records*)

Right: 1999's *Still Life* is absolutely beautiful musically and visually. One of the best covers in all of metal. (*Peaceville Records*)

Left: Travis Smith's imagery embodies the bleak beauty of what many fans consider Opeth's greatest album to date, *Blackwater Park*. (*Music for Nations / Koch Records*)

Right: Like the songs it symbolizes, *Deliverance*'s appearance offers a perfectly dark complement to its lighter sibling, *Damnation*. (*Music for Nations / Koch Records*)

Left: A simple but effective flyer for Opeth's 3 April 2010 stop in Paris. (*Christophe Largeau*)

Right: Like numerous Opeth concert posters, this one is a work of art unto itself. (*Christophe Largeau*)

Right: You certainly know what you're in for with this matter-of-fact *Sorceress* show advertisement. (*Christophe Largeau*)

Left: See, *this* is an ingeniously subtle way to build upon an album's artwork to promote its corresponding tour. (*Christophe Largeau*)

Above: Gazing up at Opeth as they continue to dominate at Manchester Academy 2 on 15 October 2014. (*Michael Ainscoe*)

Below: A tilted Åkerfeldt pours his heart out at the very same show. (*Michael Ainscoe*)

Right: Meanwhile, Fredrik Åkesson exudes intensity as he provides backing vocals and vital guitarwork! (*Michael Ainscoe*)

Below: The always modest and measured Méndez gets bathed in green and blue lighting, too. (*Michael Ainscoe*)

Left: The brighter photography of *Damnation* helps ensure that hope never truly leaves the listener. (*Music for Nations / Koch Records*)

Right: It's only fitting that the immensely tasteful and gothic *Ghost Reveries* be characterized by such a classical and cryptic image. (*Roadrunner Records*)

Left: *Watershed* is definitely a polarizing record, yet it's nearly impossible not to love the symmetry and mystery of its cover. (*Roadrunner Records*)

Right: Smith and company truly outdid themselves with this colourful allegory. The metaphor of the falling heads is particularly effective. (*Roadrunner Records*)

Left: The main visual for *Pale Communion* wonderfully conveys that you're viewing and hearing a bona fide masterpiece. (*Roadrunner Records*)

Right: The skulls harken back to *Heritage*'s cover, and it's easily among Opeth's most striking, advanced and praiseworthy pieces of artwork. (*Moderbolaget Records / Nuclear Blast Records*)

Above: A golden sheen for Åkerfeldt's golden musicianship at the aforementioned O2 Ritz Manchester performance in November 2017. (*Michael Ainscoe*)

Below: All the while, blue lights illuminate like lasers as Méndez closes his eyes and gets into the zone. (*Michael Ainscoe*)

Above: Such a stunning glimpse at mastermind Åkerfeldt captivating each and every one of his countless apprentices at the same gig. (*Michael Ainscoe*)

Below: Back at Manchester Academy 2, with Åkerfeldt posing like a statue that's utterly enamored by his own craftsmanship. (*Michael Ainscoe*)

Left: In a way, *In Cauda Venenum*'s breathtaking main painting is the culmination of Smith's many past styles. (*Moderbolaget Records / Nuclear Blast Records*)

Right: They play all of *Damnation* here, so it's only logical that *Lamentations*' look implies that. (*Music for Nations / Koch Records*)

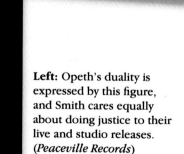

Left: Opeth's duality is expressed by this figure, and Smith cares equally about doing justice to their live and studio releases. (*Peaceville Records*)

Opeth

IN LIVE CONCERT AT THE ROYAL ALBERT HALL
"EVOLUTION XX – AN OPETH ANTHOLOGY"
COMPOSED BY MIKAEL ÅKERFELDT AND OPETH

**The Loyal Disharmonic Orchestra
Conducted by The Powers That Be**

Right: An almost perfect imitation of Deep Purple's *Concerto for Group and Orchestra* showcases a comparable level of prestige for this performance. (*Roadrunner Records*)

Left: The head motif returns to gorgeously insinuate that Opeth are now etched into Red Rocks Amphitheater's bountiful legacy. (*Nuclear Blast Records*)

Left: What an incredible line-up at San Francisco's The Warfield at the tail end of 2014. (*Daniel Cordova*)

Right: Opeth rather bizarrely stuck in a train toilet circa 1999. (*Jon Rosenthal and Simon Glacken*)

Far left: A stylish photo pass from *Pale Communion*'s European tour cycle. (*Michael Ainscoe*)

Left: Similarly, a photo pass from *Sorceress*' European tour cycle. In both cases, the contrasting colours are very effective. (*Michael Ainscoe*)

This page: A mishmash of ticket stubs from throughout the years. Oh, to have been there for all of these shows. (*Chris Conaton and Christophe Largeau*)

LE BATACLAN
GARMONBOZIA (350774/75)
PRESENTE
OPETH - CONCERT 20 ANS

samedi 03 avril 2010   18H30

Prix TTC : EUR 31,90   PLACEMENT LIBRE
Normal
Frais de location inclus
20091205/S02/B1048879607

06 01 35 58 20 / billetterie@garmonbozia-lec.com   GARMONBOZIA
lic. 1065607 & 1065608

OPETH

LUNDI 21 NOVEMBRE 2016 - 18H30
LE TRIANON - PARIS

36€ sur place

Billet n° 00094

LA LOCOMOTIVE
90, boulevard de Clichy
75018   PARIS

OPETH
+GUESTS
MARDI 13 SEPTEMBRE 2005   20H30

        PLACEMENT LIBRE

Prix TTC : EUR 22,00   Prix unique
(144,31FRF)   20050704/718/B0590371054

This is your ticket.
Present this entire page at the event.

PURCHASED BY VERONIQUE FRANK   SECTION GENADM ROW GA7   SEAT 9
ORDER NUMBER 10-29643 WES

DE1020L   GENADM GA7   9   A 17.50   KDE1020L
17.50   GA*STANDING ONLY*FCB02.50   CN 14360
9.50   HOUSE OF BLUES PRESENTS   VI 192
GENADM   OPETH   GENADM
VI 1X   WWW.HOUSEOFBLUES.COM   538ZIP
GA7 9   HOUSE OF BLUES SAN DIEGO   GA7
538AZIP   1055 5TH AVE / ALL AGES   A 17.50
2OCT11   THU OCT 20 2011 DRS 630PM   9

LA LOCOMOTIVE
90, boulevard de Clichy
75018   PARIS

OPETH
+ GUESTS
DIMANCHE 09 FEVRIER 2003   18H30

        PLACEMENT LIBRE

Prix TTC : EUR 18,70   Prix unique
(122,66FRF)   20030103/718/B035819895

HWL1017 GENADM GA7   84   EHWL1017
EVENT CODE SECTION,AISLE ROW,BOX SEAT ADMISSION   EVENT CODE
$ 0.00   GEN ADMISSION   C   0.00 COMP
$ CN 07819
GENADM   WAREHOUSE LIVE PRESENTS   GENADM
CA 4X   OPETH   CA501WHL
GA7 84   W/ SPECIAL GUESTS   GA7
HWL1912   WAREHOUSE LIVE BALLROOM   0.00
170CT8   813 SAINT EMANUEL ST   84
             FRI OCT 17 2008 DRS 7PM

HEIR APPARENT

GRAND CONJURATION

GODHEAD LAMENT

LOTUS EATER

HOPE LEAVES

DELIVERENCE

DEMON OF THE FALL

DRAPERY FALLS

Above: Quite the setlist for this 27 November 2008 appearance at Élysée Montmartre in Paris. (*Christophe Largeau*)

Right: Another great batch of tunes to replicate on stage – this time, at Paris' L'Olympia Bruno Coquatrix on 11 November 2019. (*Christophe Largeau*)

SVEKETS PRINS
LEPER AFFINITY
HJÄRTAT VET VAD
HARLEQUIN FOREST
NEPENTHE
MOON ABOVE
HOPE LEAVES
LOTUS EATER
ALLTING TAR SLUT

SORCERESS
DELIVERANCE

'Ending Credits' (Åkerfeldt)

After playing 'Ending Credits' at Shepherd's Bush Empire, Åkerfeldt jokes that it's 'totally ripped off from a band called Camel'; although it's refreshing to hear him point out his explicit stimuli, this instrumental departure does plenty to distinguish itself as an original and apropos farewell to *Damnation*. It starts off in the middle of things, with the clean guitar chords and playful percussion already underway as it becomes more audible. Resourcefully, López uses a hasty drum fill to transition into Åkerfeldt's softly solemn main motifs, which are backed by hearty syncopation and bass playing. In a way, it feels like the more polished and poised younger sibling of 'Epilogue' from *My Arms, Your Hearse*, and as you'd expect, the added guitar intervals and Mellotron varnishes increase its poignant longevity. Overall, it's a successfully slick and docile ode that symbolises how sophisticated and precise Opeth had become by this point.

'Weakness' (Åkerfeldt)

It's a chillingly vacant coda whose submerged keyboard aftershocks invoke Led Zeppelin's 'No Quarter' (as odd as that may be to suggest). Correspondingly, Åkerfeldt's ghostly decrees and overarching resonance – 'Lost you there / In a moment of truth / I trust you / Gave away the one and only heart / A gift to tear apart' – convey icy betrayal and purification from beyond the grave. Compounded by his submissive guitar work and unnerving phantasmal mantra ('Stain me / Save me / Take me to my home'), 'Weakness' is an astonishingly timid yet troubling postscript that's also a pretty parallel to the last moments of *Deliverance*'s 'By the Pain I See in Others'.

Bonuses

Because the 'Making of *Deliverance* & *Damnation*' documentary is on *Lamentations: Live at Shepherd's Bush Empire 2003*, we'll wait until we get there to explore it. Beyond that, there are no extras for *Damnation* as of now.

Ghost Reveries (2005)

Personnel:
Mikael Åkerfeldt: vocals, Mellotron, acoustic and electric guitars
Peter Lindgren: electric guitars
Martin López: drums, percussion
Martin Méndez: bass
Per Wiberg: Hammond organ, Mellotron, grand piano, Moog synthesizer
Additional Personnel:
Travis Smith: design, illustration, layout
Anthony Sorrento: band portraits
Jens Bogren: engineer, mixing
Rickard Bengtsson: recording
Anders Alexandersson: recording
Niklas Källgren: recording
Pontus Olsson: engineer, mixing on 'Soldier of Fortune' (bonus track)
Produced at Fascination Street Studios in Örebro, Sweden, March – June 2005 by
Opeth and Jens Bogren.
Release date: 29 August 2005.
Highest chart places: UK: 62, USA: 64
Running time: 66:46
Current edition: 2018 Music On Vinyl 2x vinyl reissue

Having fully realised their vision for *Deliverance* and *Damnation* (albeit not
as they'd originally intended, and not without facing some adversities), Opeth
were now doing better than ever – that is, aside from a few interpersonal
tribulations. Sadly, those conflicts persisted as the group got to work on their
eighth studio album; however, the period was also marked by at least two
positive, if controversial, developments – the official addition of Per Wiberg as
keyboardist and the move to Roadrunner Records – that further extended their
commercial and artistic potential. Therefore, the new quintet were primed
to produce their biggest record yet in more ways than one, and with the
decidedly progressive, staggeringly multilayered, and faultlessly balanced *Ghost
Reveries*, they absolutely did.

In contrast to their move from Peaceville Records to Music for Nations / Koch
a few years prior, Opeth weren't unhappy with their current representation.
Rather, Music for Nations closed in 2004, forcing the band to find a new place
to go. (Fortunately, the label relaunched prosperously in 2015 as a subsidiary of
Sony Music UK.) In *Book of Opeth*, Åkerfeldt recounts how he, Lindgren, and
Farrow 'went out on a shopping trip, meeting up with record labels around the
world', including Inside Out Music, Steamhammer/SPV, Century Media Records,
EMI, and even their current home, Nuclear Blast. Expectedly, they received a
few big offers and had a tough time picking where to go, but eventually, they
decided that signing with Roadrunner Records 'was the next logical step'.
Farrow remarks: '[W]e could see that [they] had the infrastructure. Although

the deal was actually £100,000 less than the biggest offer we had, we chose Roadrunner because I knew they would sell more albums than any other label, resulting in increased income streams in other areas, such as publishing, touring, and merchandising'.

Although the agreement was wonderful from a business standpoint, it rubbed some followers the wrong way since Roadrunner was perceived as being too mainstream (so fans felt that Opeth were 'selling out'). In his 2015 chat with *Metal Hammer*'s Dom Lawson – for Lawson's 'How Opeth Conjured Up Their Ghost Reveries' piece – Åkerfeldt reflects:

When we released 'The Grand Conjuration' as the first song from the album, people accused us of turning into a nu metal band! ... It's obviously bullshit. For me, Roadrunner wasn't the label of Slipknot and those kinds of bands. They were the label of Mercyful Fate, King Diamond, Suffocation and Pestilence – that kind of stuff. So it was a classic, legendary metal label. I really didn't expect any kind of backlash. It's not like we started making three-minute FM radio rock songs. We just went about our business as usual.

Clearly, he's correct, as *Ghost Reveries* saw Opeth progressing rather than regressing musically. Of course, the formal incorporation of Wiberg was the chief factor in that respect. He'd done a phenomenal job during the last tour for *Deliverance* and *Damnation* – and Åkerfeldt had become increasingly intrigued by the idea of using keyboards to develop their creative chemistry – so the choice to invite Wiberg aboard was a no-brainer. 'I was one of those guys who didn't like keyboards in the beginning, but since I got into the whole progressive rock thing, I started to appreciate and even love some of those sounds ... When we started playing with [Per], everybody said, 'Wow, we need him in the band'', Åkerfeldt comments in the 'Beyond *Ghost Reveries*' documentary. He also notes that Wiberg brought an 'energy injection' into the group dynamic and helped him 'see new ways to write these songs'.

Although Lindgren concurred with Åkerfeldt about Wiberg's input – 'He's the best musician in the band, and he's super professional when it comes to his playing and everything. I feel inspired when I see him play', he declares in the documentary – he continued to take a backseat role as they wrote and recorded *Ghost Reveries*. In *Book of Opeth*, Åkerfeldt recalls that Lindgren 'didn't participate' much; in fact, he only 'did one solo ... in the song 'Beneath the Mire'' because 'his confidence was just at an all-time low'. He also notes that Lindgren's behaviour during the ensuing tour – which we'll get to shortly – showed signs of disinterest and frustration: 'There were some fights. Peter was getting upset, slamming doors and yelling. He left the bus and travelled with other bands; it just got really bad'. (Lindgren would be replaced by Fredrik Åkesson by the time they began working on 2008's *Watershed*, so his tenure was quickly coming to an end.)

Woefully, López's struggles worsened as well, as Méndez reasons in *Book of Opeth*: '[He] wasn't in shape and I don't think Peter was in shape, playing-wise, either. As a band, you could feel that something was wrong in the atmosphere in the studio'. Åkerfeldt noticed that López went from being extremely reliable and passionate to being 'so inconsistent [that] it was unbelievable ... We had to punch him in all of the time because he didn't have any stamina; he just lost it'. Unsurprisingly, López's newfound fear of flying and other ailments impacted their 2005 touring, too, as Farrow admits: 'It was very difficult at the time. I'd be at home, and my phone would go at four in the morning with Mike telling me López has not got on the plane, and things like that'.

Hoglan still filled in on stage when López couldn't, and the writing on the wall – that López wouldn't be in Opeth for much longer – was becoming clearer by the day. It was around the summer of 2005 (during the 'Sounds of the Underground' tour) that the situation reached its climax, as López was sent home once again to recover because, as Lindgren puts it in the documentary, he 'wasn't fit to play' and even had trouble digesting food and maintaining a healthy weight. To be clear, he was still a member and his bandmates were affectionately pulling for him to get better and resume his role ASAP; however, that just wasn't happening, so Åkerfeldt began lamentably yet seriously searching for someone worthy of taking up the percussion mantle. Naturally, it didn't take long for him to find López's successor: Martin Axenrot.

Before digging more deeply into Opeth's next line-up change and concurrent touring cycle, let's backtrack a bit to explore the making of *Ghost Reveries*. For the first time in years, they not only had all of the songs written before heading into the studio (except for 'Beneath the Mire'), but they rehearsed for a few weeks beforehand as well. In *Book of Opeth*, Åkerfeldt states that writing the material was 'a good experience', explaining that he got over some preliminary 'writer's block' by 'returning the guitar to an open chord' and 'start[ing] from scratch with learning how to play the guitar'. This method yielded 'a lot of cool riffs', many of which originated as Åkerfeldt worked in his home studio amidst waiting for his then-wife, Anna, to give birth to their first child, Melinda. Even Wiberg noticed how Åkerfeldt's new approach – in conjunction with his own contributions – altered *Ghost Reveries*' direction: 'It wasn't a *major* difference, but it was big enough to generate a new vibe', he tells Lawson.

The band's commitment to preparation wasn't the only characteristic that harkened back to their earliest records, as *Ghost Reveries* is their first collection since *Still Life* to be at least partially conceptual. In 'Chapter X' of his Opeth journal entries, Åkerfeldt elucidates on the name and narrative of the LP, claiming that he came up with the title 'just like that' after deciding that *Ghost Reveries* sounded 'cooler' than *Ghost Letters*. Occult themes were intended, too, and influenced by Anna's collection of Satanist texts, with 'The Baying of the Hounds' and 'Ghost of Perdition' tying into those topics (whereas 'Isolation Years' didn't but was so good that Åkerfeldt chose to keep it anyway). Although the storyline isn't nearly as fleshed out or consistent as on *My Arms, Your*

Hearse and *Still Life*, allusions to a tale regarding a man feeling distressed after committing matricide are present.

To bring *Ghost Reveries* to life, Opeth decided to change locations and producers. In the documentary, Lindgren reveals that they wanted to try a new studio after spending almost a whole decade recording in Gothenburg, Sweden. 'We were talking about recording in Texas in the United States, and it's a great studio that we were looking at, but it's a lot easier to be close to home', he adds. Thus, they settled on Fascination Street Studios in Örebro, with the intention of bringing back Steven Wilson (who was interested in returning, too, but couldn't due to other commitments). At the suggestion of Jonas Renkse – who'd just worked with him on Katatonia's *Viva Emptiness* and, alongside bandmates Dan Swanö and Martin Axenrot, Bloodbath's *Nightmares Made Flesh* – they enlisted the equally capable but fledgling expertise of Jens Bogren.

In his interview with Lawson, Åkerfeldt boasts, 'We needed someone like that because of the state of the band', after which Wiberg concludes that having Bogren and Fascination Street Studios made the experience 'less stressful than previous recordings' because 'everything worked' and they had a 'hands-on' producer. However, saying that he was 'hands-on' is also a nice way of saying that Bogren was a bit of a taskmaster and stickler for the minutia of the process. Méndez laughs: 'We'd never had a producer like Jens before. We are perfectionists in a way, but he was *extremely* perfectionist. I did take after take after take'. Undoubtedly, Bogren's militaristic tactics paid off, as *Ghost Reveries* is a spotlessly fashioned accomplishment, leading Åkerfeldt – in *Book of Opeth* – to call him 'a fantastic engineer' who 'had the technical know-how to make every instrument sound great' and a 'sensibility for the sensitive side of music, which a lot of metal engineers and producers simply don't have'.

Once again, Travis Smith was to handle the artwork (with Anthony Sorrento providing the interior band portraits), which was created after the LP was done. At first, Åkerfeldt was looking for something in the vein of medieval woodcuts, but then he received 'the candle pictures' from Smith and was blown away. On Halloween 2006, a special edition of *Ghost Reveries* arrived that – among other things – contained new artwork, plus an extended booklet (featuring a letter from Åkerfeldt); an extra DVD with the documentary, the music video, a 5.1 surround sound mix of the record; and a cover of Deep Purple's 'Soldier of Fortune' as a bonus track.

As for promoting the record, they released 'The Grand Conjuration' as a single on 26 July 2005, with a music video (that features Hoglan instead of López, as well as a truncated version of the tune) premiering in early September. Curiously, *Ghost Reveries* also brought Opeth into the world of video games, as 'Ghost of Perdition' was included in 2008's *Saints Row 2* and 2010's *Rock Band 3* (albeit the following year). Likewise, 'The Grand Conjuration' made it into 2006's *Final Fight: Streetwise* and 2012's *Sleeping Dogs*.

Predictably, *Ghost Reveries* did quite well upon release, significantly outdoing all its predecessors by landing at #64 in the United States, #62 in the UK, and #9 in Sweden. In *Book of Opeth*, Farrow affirms that its immediate and sustained popularity led to it being performed in its entirety during Opeth's 25th-anniversary shows in 2015 (which marked the album's tenth anniversary, too). He continues:

> I suppose it took Opeth away from the underground and a bit more towards your average metal audience. When I first took on the band, the audience were all like 15-year-old boys with black t-shirts, and I've seen a real change. I don't even feel old at their gigs [because] the crowd is made up of vets, bald men, men with beards, all sorts of people; and one thing I did see after Ghost Reveries was a lot more girls in the audience – so that record really opened the band up to all walks of life and got them out of the niche they'd been in.

Virtually all the press reviews were immensely encouraging, too. For instance, *AllMusic*, *Blabbermouth*, *Drowned in Sound*, and *Kerrang!* gave it perfect scores, while *Pitchfork* surmised that it's a 'carefully crafted set of melodic progressive death-tinged metal' that makes 'Opeth's past releases feel like tiny sketchbooks for the present'. Once the dust settled, *Metal Hammer* named it the best album of 2005, and both *Loudwire* and *PopMatters* put it at the top of their lists of the best metal discs of the year. Many other publications felt similarly at the time and/or have since ranked *Ghost Reveries* highly in comparable tallies.

Circling back to the surrounding tour cycle and replacement of members, Åkerfeldt states in *Book of Opeth* that – as with Bogren – he reached out to Renske to see if he had any suggestions for a new drummer to take over for Hoglan and López (at least temporarily). Never one to disappoint, he suggested his current Bloodbath bandmate, Martin Axenrot. (Fascinatingly, the first Bloodbath sequence, 2002's *Resurrection Through Carnage*, was made by Renske, Nyström, Swanö, and Åkerfeldt; in-between that and 2004's *Nightmares Made Flesh*, Åkerfeldt was replaced by Peter Tägtgren and Axenrot was added.) In *Book of Opeth*, Åkerfeldt discloses: 'I met Axe at the Swedish Rock Festival and I was a bit drunk and quizzed him about drummers. When I asked who his favourite drummer was, the first name he said was Ian Paice [Deep Purple]. This was what I wanted to hear ... [and] I kind of knew it was going to work'. (In other accounts, Åkerfeldt states that Patrik Jensen of The Haunted recommended Axenrot – with whom he played in Witchery – so perhaps it was the endorsement of both he and Renske that sealed the deal.)

According to Axenrot (in *Book of Opeth*), his first gig with Opeth was in August 2005, and he was 'nervous' because they'd 'only rehearsed for one hour', but the set was actually '90 minutes longer' than expected. 'We jammed in front of 10,000 people or something, but it went okay, I guess. After that, there was a lot of touring. I'd never toured so much in my life. I think it was almost two years on tour' he smirks. Understandably, the group and López waited until absolutely necessary – 12 May 2006 – to officially announce Axenrot as Opeth's new drummer. Åkerfeldt tells Lawson: 'I'm very protective about members of the band. It's not until you're clutching at straws and nothing else can be done that you ever say, 'It's over'. But we were at that point with Lopez, so we had to find a new drummer'. As for López, he took time to heal before getting back to playing with black metal act Fifth To Infinity and – more importantly – the markedly successful and celebrated prog metal quintet Soen.

That undesirable yet unavoidable decision notwithstanding, the *Ghost Reveries* tour went exceedingly well. In the aforementioned journal entries, Åkerfeldt references being offered a spot in 2005's Ozzfest but declined because they would've had to pay to play. However, they rebounded by appearing at England's Download Festival, the Wacken Open Air festival, and the Netherlands Lowlands Festival during the summer of 2006. A few months later – between September and October – they played the main stage of the North American part of Gigantour (as did Lamb of God, Arch Enemy, and of course, Megadeth). Unquestionably, though, the chief performance from that period came on 9 November 2006, when they filmed a lengthy set at London's Camden Roundhouse for their second live release (and last release in general with Lindgren), *The Roundhouse Tapes*.

Despite retaining many of their most beloved and essential elements, *Ghost Reveries* logically comes across as the start of a new chapter in Opeth's history and musical trajectory. Sure, it restores their pre-*Damnation* hostile involvedness, but with far more density, vibrancy, and majesty than ever before. There's a newfound colourfulness, elegance, and grandeur to it all that – in hindsight – sees them leaving behind the desaturated bleakness of their past to predict the richly retro prog rock inclinations of their most recent works. In that way, *Ghost Reveries* is like their *A Trick of the Trail*: an ingenious middle ground between what they'd been and what they'd become.

'Ghost of Perdition' (Åkerfeldt)

This one clearly ties into Åkerfeldt's storyline about a man murdering his mother, and it's debatably *the* quintessential Opeth song because of how fluidly and intricately it marries their already extraordinary demeanours with superlatively vivid extravagances. In other words, it integrates their best attributes into a pleasurably decadent and dignified new context, giving you everything you could possibly want out of a progressive death metal masterwork (with an emphasis on 'prog').

The first few seconds alone are cunningly deceptive, lulling the listener in with gentle notes – as if it's carrying on *Damnation*'s solace – before pulling out the rug with a tirade of hellish impatience. The guttural guitar work is enormously compelling, and even with all of his personal plights, López manages to deliver an unblemished amount of quick-witted syncopation and straightforward anarchy. This is particularly true during the consequential juxtaposition of subdued implications ('Devil cracked the earthly shell / Foretold she was the one') and explosive reaction, wherein he guides the arrangement with addictive finesse before directing the track back to its brutal base ('Holding her down / Channelling darkness'). Although subtle, Wiberg's macabre varnish invaluably contributes to the imperially foreboding intensity.

Without warning, the composition becomes categorically blissful, with Åkerfeldt's climbing carol – 'Road into the dark unaware / Winding ever higher' – initiating lovely acoustic arpeggios and some of the best harmonies he's ever performed. (In the 'Beyond *Ghost Reveries*' documentary, he rightly gloats, 'I'm very happy with my vocals on [*Ghost Reveries*], especially my clean vocals. They sound like I actually can sing'.) The corresponding electric guitar solo is effectively emotive and refined, too. Then, crunchy riffs and López's polyrhythm astutely starts a new section – 'Darkness by her side / Spoke and passed her by' – that's attractively blunt and caustic, subsequently segueing into a sumptuous instrumental segment that's appropriately cut off by ghostly omniscience ('In time the hissing of her sanity / Faded out her voice and soiled her name').

From there, jackhammer percussion and more awesome guitar riffs assist Åkerfeldt's fiendish utterances of the title; afterwards, another irresistible wordless jam – decorated by Wiberg's angelic keys – sets up another heavenly annotation: 'To see a beloved son / In despair of what's to come'. In its wake, a fiery guitar solo summons more enticing musical vitriol, only to once again be swiftly offset by chaotic and cathartic call-backs. Finally, it rushes toward its last moments like a tornado of symphonic bedlam, fortifying 'Ghost of Perdition' as an intimidatingly complex and meticulously organised monster that can't help but engulf you in its brilliance.

'The Baying of the Hounds' (Åkerfeldt)

'The Baying of the Hounds' is famously inspired by the lyrics to Comus' 'Diana' (from 1971's *First Utterance*), and it's a superb showpiece for how well Opeth can seamlessly meld harsh and pacifistic dispositions. Its introductory revving is very cool, and Wiberg wastes no time supporting the lurid result with feudal punctuations and swelling gaiety. Cumulatively, it's like a sweltering dive into madness that only breaks when palmed guitar chords ferociously pivot into Åkerfeldt's riveting clean commandments: 'Everything you believed is a lie / Everyone you loved is a death burden. His harmonies are gorgeous, and the music follows him engrossingly.

The next portion is even more tremendous, as a skilful instrumental breakdown spirals into slight piano notes and an antsy beat to back Åkerfeldt's despondent and prophetic wallows ('Drown in the deep mire / With past desires / Beneath the mire / Drown desire now with you'). Before long, the captivating belligerence comes back, leading to a soaring guitar solo and dextrous display of acoustic guitar work and earthy percussion. It's like a warm but mildly worrying daydream that's speedily broken by Åkerfeldt's growl and the succeeding lawlessness. It scatters just in time to leave a few moments of respite before the LP resumes its ceremonious fury.

'Beneath the Mire' (Åkerfeldt)

López's prelude inventively cues a mixture of stilted six-string swipes and theatrically morose keyboard lines that combine into something resembling the soundtrack to a vintage vampire film. It's substantially hooky, too, before melting into a somewhat retro heavy metal score around the snarling verses. Obviously, that underpinning makes the transition into the decidedly catchy new passage – 'You'd cling to your pleasant hope / In its twisted fascination' – that much sleeker, especially with its initially double-tracked guitar solo.

The mellow movement into the middle of the song is daintily tactful, with Åkerfeldt's backing chants magnifying the sense of cultured remorse. After another exquisite guitar solo, some rapid acoustic fingerpicking shifts things into high gear via *Deliverance*-esque rhythmic abrasiveness and opulent but subjugated singing. That combativeness continues until the band launches into an awesome back-and-forth battle as gruff guitar riffs repeatedly jab at López's frisky drumming and Wiberg's eerie soundscapes. It dies down peacefully, yes, but also with an air of peculiarity that can only be rectified by the record's subsequent atonement.

'Atonement' (Åkerfeldt)

It's like a lost entry from *Damnation* that's draped in the mystical affluence of Led Zeppelin's 'Kashmir'. It's uncommonly relaxed, earthly, and carnal, with golden orchestral embellishments escorting easygoing percussion, reverberating organ wails, and tuneful guitar lines. Åkerfeldt's verses – which are emulated melodically by Wiberg's keys – are equally laid-back yet also a tinge wraithlike and menacing.

The rapturous opening instrumentation repeats around Åkerfeldt's surging outcry in-between verses, after which he returns with a second stanza ('Rising moon and my skin is peeling / Past undone / Suddenly, I can't justify / What I had become') that is open to interpretation. On the one hand, it could relate to the man coming to grips with the matricide, but it could just as easily be about a werewolf or something else.

For much of its duration, 'Atonement' sticks to a relatively repetitious and unassuming design, as even the outro maintains that underpinning (with Wiberg's tender piano ornaments and some spookily reversed timbres on top). However, it all changes about a minute before the end, when a guitar-driven coda (that's officially considered the 'Reverie' part of the next track, similar to what happened with 'Requiem' and 'The Apostle in Triumph' on *Orchid*) begins. It's extremely modest – just a few crunchy guitar chords surrounded by habitual keyboard echoes – yet also surreal and placating, so it's an ideal preamble for the artfully in-your-face 'Harlequin Forest'.

'Reverie/Harlequin Forest' (Åkerfeldt)

Yet again, López's adventurous musicianship steals the show throughout
the song, starting with his valiantly flamboyant chasing of some brittle guitar
work and Åkerfeldt's ardent singing (which perpetuates the LP's conceptual
continuity when he utters: 'Baying behind me / I hear the hounds'). It's
interwoven with nice guitar playing and a new and engaging vocal spin-off – 'A
trail of sickness / Leading to me' – before Åkerfeldt's roar signals impending
cataclysm. The arrangement manoeuvres around his grumbles expertly, giving
way to a merciful deviation ('Nocturnally helpless / And weak in the light')
whose sunlit drumming, strumming, and harmonic taps seem like a nobler
rendition of *Still Life*'s many acoustic mazes.

It's one of the most beautifully luscious blocks of *Ghost Reveries* – which is
truly saying something – with an impeccably bereaved guitar solo and more
dashing syncopation guiding the way to a heavier and ostensibly impromptu
reprise of Åkerfeldt's monologue ('It's all false pretension / Harlequin forest').
After a bit more instrumental grieving, another demonic shout prompts more
mesmerising savagery; it's deftly counteracted by a calming intervention
that's almost immediately thwarted by additional barbarity. Along the way,
Opeth foreshadow the labyrinthine rhythmic loop that will wrap things up;
it's not *quite* as chameleonic and entrancing as the analogous final minutes of
'Deliverance', but it's close, solidifying 'Reverie/Harlequin Forest' as a sneakily
temperamental beast.

'Hours of Wealth' (Åkerfeldt)

'Hours of Wealth' is eternally breathtakingly and majestic. It commences
with scrupulously knitted acoustic tapestries, transcendental organ coatings,
and poignant piano notes that submerge you in intoxicating refinement and
inner reflection. It's nearly too much to take, but then it ends abruptly to
make room for Åkerfeldt's measured soliloquy – 'Found a way / To rid myself
clean of pain' – and a few accompanying Mellotron tones. It's a charmingly
gloomy chasm that's made more impactful by his overlapping murmurs and
bluesy guitar solo. Like 'Atonement', it affords the audience a few minutes
of remedying downtime prior to the narcotic free-for-all that is the album's
penultimate selection.

'The Grand Conjuration' (Åkerfeldt)

It hits the ground running with a temptingly irregular clash of pouncing
rhythms, militant riffs, and spectral ambience. Shortly thereafter, it gets
sinisterly sparse as harmonious fingerpicking encourages Åkerfeldt to
courteously beckon his subject to submit ('Majesty / Faithful me / Pour yourself
/ Into me'). López's animated drum roll initiates a hurried switch toward
callous disarray, with Åkerfeldt barking 'The eyes of the devil / Fixed on his
sinners' on top of more caustic musicianship. Opeth stay with this seesaw
of aggression and meekness one more time – with Wiberg adorning the

second round with pained tonality – before an unwieldy guitar solo and more supernatural dissonance intensify the colossal delirium.

The band then moves into a more melodic coil that – despite dextrously hinting at a softer section to come – is no less destructive. Suddenly, that turmoil scatters so that Wiberg's fluid keyboard tones can ignite a downpour of even wackier depravity; it also pre-empts the return of the opening ruckus, which then surrounds more reassuring entrapment from Åkerfeldt ('Tell me why / Love subsides / In the light / Of your wishes') with indistinct ghostly mumbling as the music proceeds. The final couple of minutes see the group bolster this baroque debauchery before allowing it to fade away in a cloud of liberating tension.

Moving onto the music video, it was directed by Bill Yukich and features shots of the quintet (with Hoglan sitting in for López, as already mentioned) playing in a darkened room while illuminated by blue lights. In-between that footage are artsy shots of – among other things – a woman lying in bed with a malevolent nurse and a buff man wearing a Zorro-like mask as he burns photographs and integrates a man and a woman in their underwear. It's all suitably grim and ambiguous, coming across like censored clips from a modern 'torture porn' horror movie. The song itself is understandably abridged, but it retains much of the studio version's greatest elements.

'Isolation Years' (Åkerfeldt)

Perhaps the only track that's wholly unrelated to the matricide narrative, 'Isolation Years' closes *Ghost Reveries* with its briefest and most bittersweet journey. It grows gloriously from an amalgamation of bashful guitar work and scant drumming to include Åkerfeldt's heartrending poetry – 'There's a certain detail seen here / The pen must have slipped to the side / And left a stain / Next to his name / She knew he was gone' – and unbearably virtuous falsetto. It basically just repeats that template twice by the end; yet, that's all it needs to do to not only finish *Ghost Reveries* with lustrous salvation but demonstrate once again why Opeth are unequivocally matchless at constructing both diabolical and divine experiences.

Bonuses

The special edition digipak of *Ghost Reveries* is full of great stuff, such as the music video for 'The Grand Conjuration', a 5.1 surround sound mix of the LP, and insightful liner notes, photos, and the like. Its two best offerings, though, are its cover of Deep Purple's 'Soldier of Fortune' (formerly from 1974's *Stormbringer*) and the 40-minute 'Beyond *Ghost Reveries*' documentary. The former feels very much like a sibling to 'Patterns in the Ivy II' and 'Still Day Beneath the Sun' since it achieves a similar level of magnificent anguish. Åkerfeldt copies David Coverdale's phrasing exactly, baring his soul with each cleanly sung syllable as the rest of the band chaperon with touching Mellotron dustings, selfless rhythms, and thoughtful guitar work. Because of its heightened tranquillity, I dare say that it's better than the original.

'Beyond *Ghost Reveries*' follows the blueprint of past Opeth investigations by mixing one-on-one interviews with footage of them recording their parts, discussing their process, and fooling around a bit. That said, it's done more professionally, with better video and audio quality throughout, as well as more engaging editing and framing techniques (primarily, consistent use of split-screen to showcase what the members are discussing as they're discussing it). Best of all, Åkerfeldt is unquestionably honest as he confers how the material came to be; what he thinks works and doesn't work about it; and the state of López as a player and member. As usual, the biggest flaw is a lack of screen time for López, Méndez, and (now) Wiberg, but that doesn't prevent it from being a crucial watch for any Opeth devotee.

Watershed (2008)

Personnel:
Mikael Åkerfeldt: vocals, acoustic and electric guitars
Fredrik Åkesson: electric guitars
Martin Axenrot: drums, percussion
Martin Méndez: bass
Per Wiberg: Hammond organ, Mellotron, grand piano, electric piano
Additional Personnel:
Nathalie Lorichs: vocals on 'Coil'
Lisa Almberg: oboe, English horn
Christoffer Wadensten: flute
Karin Svensson: violin
Andreas Tengberg: cello
Travis Smith: artwork
Jens Bogren: engineer, recording, mixing
Mikhail Korge: recording
David Castillo: engineer
Johan Örnborg: engineer
Produced at Fascination Street Studios in Örebro, Sweden and Junkmail Studios in Stockholm, Sweden, November – December 2007 by Mikael Åkerfeldt and Jens Bogren.
Release date: 30 May 2008.
Highest chart places: UK: 34, USA: 23
Running time: 54:56
Current edition: 2018 Music On Vinyl 2x gold vinyl reissue

As both an exceptional musical statement and a testament to Opeth's capacity to push forward in the face of misfortune, *Ghost Reveries* was an undisputed triumph. After all, it infused their already top-notch formula with an extra dose of 1970s progressive rock stateliness, all the while ensuring that newcomer Wiberg earned his role and that the issues with Lindgren and López didn't impact the quality of the finished record. Knowingly or not, it was also the swan song for both veteran members, as they were replaced by Axenrot and Åkesson, respectively, by the time the group began sketching out their follow-up (and final album with death metal characteristics), *Watershed*.

Unsurprisingly, the duo instantly fit right in, thoroughly wielding their own specialities to enrich (rather than drastically amend) Opeth's cherished DNA. Along the same lines, *Watershed* picks up where *Ghost Reveries* left off in several ways, but somewhat paradoxically, it goes to stranger *and* more commercial places, too. In fact, it's the LP's moderate unevenness and lack of focus/cohesion that makes it a tad less victorious and vital than most of its predecessors. It's indisputably an excellent album – don't get me wrong – but it's their first since *Morningrise* to come across as merely a strong set of songs instead of as another profound work whose whole is greater than the sum of its parts.

As previously discussed, Lindgren's involvement and enthusiasm was steadily waning as the *Ghost Reveries* tour progressed, so it wasn't really a shock when he formally announced his departure on 17 May 2007. In his official declaration, he remarks that it while it was 'the toughest' decision he's ever had to make, he knows that it's 'the right one' because he 'simply lost some of the enthusiasm and inspiration needed to participate in a band that has grown from a few guys playing the music ... to a worldwide industry'. In *Book of Opeth*, he also admits, 'It was probably the touring that took its toll. I was married and we wanted to have kids, but I was never home, so we couldn't really ... It turned music from an obsession that I loved into more of a job'. Although he contemplated waiting 'for another album and another tour', he knew that – like all tough choices – it was best to make the move and deal with the aftermath ASAP (like ripping off a Band-Aid with one forceful pull, as the saying goes).

Lindgren played his last gigs with Opeth in mid-December 2006 – in Italy, alongside progressive/space rock troupe Amplifier – and went on to raise a family and work as an IT consultant. In *Book of Opeth*, he confesses that he and Åkerfeldt are still friends but aren't as close as they used to be; he also ponders how his life has changed over the last fifteen years or so, surmising: 'I wouldn't say I miss the life a lot, but I would love to do the occasional tour and maybe record half an album every now and then!'

As for his thoughts on *Watershed* and Åkesson, he told Jörgen Hellström (in a November 2008 conversation for Fanclub Sweden) that it was 'a weird feeling' to hear a new Opeth album that he hadn't worked on, but that once he wrapped his head around the songs, he thought they were 'damn good'. (Naturally, he felt similarly conflicted but proud when he first saw them in concert after he'd left.) In *Book of Opeth*, he says that Åkesson is 'a whizz on the guitar – a really good guitar player – [and] definitely better than I was!' Hence, Lindgren has never regretted his decision or felt anything other than happiness and hope for how Opeth continued without him.

Even though he could kind of see Lindgren's departure coming – and knew that it would be for the best – Åkerfeldt reasonably felt quite conflicted once he actually left. 'Even though I'm still in some kind of state of shock, I think it was a good thing for him personally and for the band ... Peter always loved the music, but I think his creative side needed more of an outlet ... People change and there's nothing one can ever do about that', Åkerfeldt writes earnestly in 'Chapter XI' of his Opeth journal passages. Whether or not Lindgren's parting was a benefit or detriment to Opeth's music is open to debate, but it's nice to know that both parties – he and Åkerfeldt – are comfortable with how things turned out.

In contrast to how the López/Axenrot switch was a moderately gradual process (since the group were hoping that López would make a full recovery at some point), the addition of Åkesson was much more immediate and urgent. Luckily, Åkerfeldt clarifies, he was the first and only choice upon Lindgren's exit.

In 'Chapter XI', he calls Åkesson 'a little bit of a legend in the Stockholm scene', and he remembers first meeting him 'in a small pub' in the area (where Åkesson was playing 'impressive' covers of some 'classic' metal tracks). In *Book of Opeth*, Méndez elaborates: 'When we'd done the Gigantour with Megadeth [in 2006], Fred was playing with Arch Enemy and he was hanging out with me and Mikael all of the time, so for a whole month we had a lot of fun with Fred and the chemistry was perfect already. So, when Peter left, Fred was our only option, as we knew how good he was as a guitarist and we knew he was a great guy'.

Fortuitously, the timing was ideal for Åkesson since he'd just been asked to step down as Arch Enemy's touring guitarist because founder Christopher Amott – who left in July 2005 – was returning. (Sadly, this means that Åkesson's only recording credit with Arch Enemy is 2006's *Live Apocalypse*, so he never appeared on a studio album.) In *Book of Opeth*, he muses that Opeth chose him because he 'could handle heavy touring, playing every night and all that'. He expounds:

> I was disappointed when I was asked to leave Arch Enemy ... but Opeth was a new challenge, playing such energetic material and long sets. There's more ups and downs in Opeth's music; it covers a lot more areas. That's not to say that I didn't enjoy my time in Arch Enemy. I did – it was a lot of fun – but everything happens for a reason, I guess. A couple of months after I left Arch Enemy, I was asked to join Opeth, and as we knew each other, it all happened very naturally; we got along really well right from the start.

He also mentions that before getting started on *Watershed*, he'd only played live with them once: at a gig in Finland (most likely the Joensuu Ilosaari Festival in mid-July 2007). Around the time of the album's release, he spoke with Mark Hensch of *Thrashpit* and explained his new role somewhat nonchalantly: 'I just do what I do. If I like what I'm hearing ... and the other guys like it too, then that's the first goal. Other than that, I think I like to add a bit of the rawness to the sound'. (Obviously, part of that 'rawness' comes from inspirations like AC/DC, KISS, Yngwie Malmsteen, and Ritchie Blackmore.) In the *Watershed* documentary – *The Rehearsal Tapes* – he credits Opeth with helping him develop 'a lot of [his] acoustic playing' and his rhythmic prowess. He also comments that many fans 'on the band's forum were afraid that [he] would overplay' because of his extreme metal background; fortunately, though, that's never been the case.

Of course, the rest of the band were equally excited about the new line-up (hell, *The Rehearsal Tapes* sees all of the members praising each other continually, and justifiably so). For instance, Méndez theorises (in *Book of Opeth*) that both Åkesson and Axenrot 'brought something new to the band ... especially playing live'. In his online diary for *Watershed*, Åkerfeldt writes that watching Axenrot play is 'a sheer joy' and that Åkesson 'took command right off the bat and really helped with everything'. Hence, whatever detriments came with the absences of López and Lindgren, it's clear that Axenrot and Åkesson rejuvenated Opeth into a happier and healthier musical family.

Because the quintet rapidly felt so connected and optimistic, the writing and recording processes for *Watershed* were very congenial. In *Book of Opeth*, Åkesson says that getting started so soon after he joined made him feel 'much more involved', adding, 'I just wanted to do the best that I could – I didn't leave the studio for the whole time we made [it]. Even though I don't play all of the guitar parts, I always like to know them'. Axenrot was just as 'hungry' to prove himself and contribute to new material, particularly after touring 'for two years for an album [he] didn't play on'. He also thinks back fondly on how they stayed at the studio and made dinner for themselves 'every evening'.

In the same chapter, Åkerfeldt confirms that making *Watershed* was 'a great recording, and a fast recording, too', as well as that they finally 'had fun again' because 'everything was just open, everybody was involved, [and] [they] were a band again, basically'. He'd had most of the songs written ahead of time, too, with a particular new influence – Scott Walker's 2006 LP, *The Drift* – having a big impact on his writing. He jokes: 'I pretty much shat myself [upon hearing it]! ... It had a profound effect on me. It's not my favourite Scott Walker record, but there was something about it; I'd never heard music like that before'. (It's also worth noting that for the first time, they brought in classical musicians instead of relying on synthetic imitations.)

Fascinatingly, Åkerfeldt was just as eager to validate himself to the newcomers as they were to him, leading to him 'step[ping] up' his game as a vocalist and guitarist. 'I wanted to keep them on their toes and have them playing material which was completely new and a stretch for them musically. I wanted to challenge them, but I felt that I was challenging myself by playing with them', he discloses. In his diary entries, he also shares a more personal reason for feeling positively about the time period: his ability to 'go home every weekend' and spend time with his family because of the improved recording schedule Jens Bogren designated. That freedom, Åkerfeldt admits, also required that he relinquish control a bit and stifle his need to 'have [his] finger in every fucking musical pie' that they were 'baking'.

In his interview with Hensch, Åkesson confirms that the cover art – once again a collaboration between Åkerfeldt and Travis Smith – is meant to paint 'a picture of total isolation'. He also suggests that the title falls in line with the collection acting as 'a fresh start' for Opeth. In his diary posts, Åkerfeldt sheds more light on the latter: 'My first title was 'Repulsion', but when I told Jonas (Katatonia), he started sending [me] mock covers with the Opeth logo and the green head from the 'Horrified' sleeve by the band Repulsion'. As for its themes, Åkerfeldt told Christopher Porter of the *Washington Post*: 'The lyrics are about my own experiences ... and how I've changed since I became a dad ... But it's not a fictional story like a generic concept record; it's not about a character'.

In keeping with tradition, the special edition of *Watershed* came with an alternative cover, three bonus tracks – the original 'Derelict Herds' and covers of Robin Trower's 'Bridge of Sighs' and Marie Fredriksson's 'Den ständiga resan' – a bonus DVD with a 5.1 surround sound mix of the record (sans extra songs), and *The Rehearsal Tapes*. (In his talk with Hensch, Åkesson reveals that they also recorded a version of Alice in Chains' 'Would?' but didn't want to include it.) Not to be outdone, the 180-gram double vinyl version came in gatefold packaging and included a CD copy of the album and a poster.

There's also a separate disc for 'Mellotron Heart', an alternate rendition of 'Porcelain Heart' that Åkerfeldt performs on mellotron and mini-Moog synthesizers. Its artwork mirrors the main image, but with the man and desk replaced with a mellotron. Fans who didn't get the disc itself could also get the track as a free digital download if they pre-ordered the LP. Like *Ghost Reveries*, *Watershed* took Opeth into the world of video games, too, by placing 'The Lotus Eater' in 2011's *Saints Row: The Third* and 'Heir Apparent' in 2015's *Rock Band 4*. (They also crafted a new tune, 'The Throat of Winter', for the *God of War: Blood & Metal* EP, which accompanied *God of War III*. It featured songs from Trivium, Dream Theater, Killswitch Engage, Taking Dawn, and Mutiny Within as well.)

By all accounts, the new quintet's first album together exceeded their expectations. 'I love *Watershed* and I'm really proud of the way it came out. It still has the death metal touch to it, but it went in some new directions in places, and some of them were quite extreme in a way', Åkesson rejoices in *Book of Opeth*. In his diary posts, Åkerfeldt praises how the LP goes for 'a very organic sound and something slightly dirtier than [*Ghost Reveries*]'. He presumes: 'At the end of the day, I know I am happy and that's what matters to me'. Even Steven Wilson showers *Watershed* – and Åkerfeldt – with praise in *Book of Opeth*:

> I remember listening to *Ghost Reveries* and thinking it was a very impressive piece of work, but I told Mike I thought that there wasn't any real sense of newness. It was possibly the most beautifully conceived and recorded version of what they'd been doing up to that point, but it hadn't broken any new ground, whereas *Watershed* was a breakthrough record for me ... That was the record where Mike had out-produced me; it was full of wacky and bizarre ideas and it seemed, at that point, that he was fearless ... Without wanting to sound pretentious, it was then that Mike started to become an artist.

Most critics were equally impressed, with outlets like *Rock Hard*, *PopMatters*, *Blender*, *IGN*, and even *The New York Times* giving it very high marks. *Metal Storm* awarded it 9.1/10, calling it 'another tour de force performance from Opeth', and the January/February 2009 issue of *Metal Edge* voted it the #1 album of 2008. Likewise, *Metal Hammer*'s Critic's Choice Top 50 named it the second-best album of the year (directly behind *Death Magnetic* by Metallica). On the sales end, *Watershed* outshone its predecessor by reaching #23 in America, #34 in the UK, and #7 in Sweden.

Deservedly, they toured the album for a while, which allowed Axenrot and Åkesson even more room to feel at home with Opeth. 'When we started rehearsing, it felt really good. We were really locked in together ... [and] I really had to learn Mike's style and dig deep into that, to start with, before my style began to blend in', he writes in *Book of Opeth*. Part of the process included a place in Mike Portnoy's Progressive Nation 2008 line-up (alongside 3, Between the Buried and Me, and headliner Dream Theater). They also appeared at Rock Sound Festival 2008, Peace & Love Festival 2008, Bloodstock 2008, and Download Festival 2009, as well as shared the stage with High on Fire, Baroness, Cynic, The Ocean, Bigelf, and uneXpect.

Just as the *Ghost Reveries* live cycle led to *The Roundhouse Tapes*, the *Watershed* era found them recording a show at London's most prestigious venue: The Royal Albert Hall. Filmed on 5 April 2010 – and released as *In Live Concert at the Royal Albert Hall* that September, with a cover that paid homage to Deep Purple's *Concerto for Group and Orchestra* – it was part of their 'Evolution XX: An Opeth Anthology' tour (designed to celebrate Opeth's 20th anniversary via a full performance of *Blackwater Park* and several other songs that were never played live). We'll dig into more precise details (such as Åkesson's guitar troubles) and analysis later in this book; suffice it to say now that it was a dream come true for Åkerfeldt. As he puts it in *Book of Opeth*: 'I remember, when we first met Andy [Farrow], he said that in 10 years we'd be playing the Royal Albert Hall and I was like, of course we are, of course we're playing the Albert Hall! But in 2010, we did play the Royal Albert Hall ... That's the nicest place that we've ever played, and it was amazing'.

Although he had a less enjoyable time due to being 'in the middle of divorcing [his] now ex-wife', Åkesson was blown away by the experience. 'The atmosphere in there was fantastic and the sound was powerful. People told us that we might have problems with the acoustics, but the soundman got it down perfectly. I was really happy that we played for almost three hours', he reminisced. Méndez concurs, citing it as 'a special thing' because it 'felt like a little bit of history' due to them being 'the first metal band to play there'. In fact, he confesses: 'It was the only time that, after a gig, Mike and I shook hands and said to each other, 'We did it''.

Indeed, they did. *Watershed* may not be as cohesive or substantial as most of its precursors – an opinion that many readers will disagree with, I'm sure, and for valid reasons – but it's a delightfully odd, varied, and riveting creation all the same. Rather than let the departures of Lindgren and López signal the end of the band, Åkerfeldt and company persevered with two outstanding new members and a newfound appreciation for, and dedication to, their craft. If nothing else, then, *Watershed* should be hailed as both a remarkable debut for Åkesson and Axenrot and a fitting – if unforeseen – farewell to the death metal mechanics that made Opeth so treasured in the first place.

'Coil' (Åkerfeldt)

It's an exercise in gorgeous simplicity, not to mention a wonderful welcome to *Watershed* and the *only* Opeth tune that has Åkerfeldt sharing lead vocal duties (he duets with Swedish singer Nathalie Lorichs, who was dating Axenrot at the time). Speaking with Hensch, Åkesson notes that the couple had an 'acoustic side project ... where she sings and he plays guitar. It's more of a singer-songwriter project with lots of folk tones to it'. Apparently, she got the opportunity after she and Axenrot played some demos for the group as they were eating 'a crawfish dinner at Mikael's house before [they] started recording *Watershed*'. Prior to that, Åkerfeldt 'never had the idea of doing female vocals', but he couldn't resist how elegantly Lorichs' voice complemented his own and suited the structure of the song. (In the documentary, he aptly likens it to 'a Nick Drake kind of thing'.)

It's one of Opeth's most basic compositions, consisting only of some humble acoustic guitar playing and supplementary orchestral timbres beneath Åkerfeldt and Lorichs reciting the same few verses. Even so, the combination makes a huge impression, as the reservedly moving instrumentation effortlessly assists the pair as they pour their hearts into poetic assertions of ill-fated romance: 'When you get out of here / When you leave me behind / You find that the years passed us by /And I can see you / Running through the fields of sorrow'. Both singers totally sell their lonesome fairy-tale wistfulness, and the ominous dissonance at the end cleverly prepares us for the looming doom ahead. (As Åkesson rightly deduces: 'The contrast between 'Coil' and 'Heir Apparent' is very beautiful and heavy'.)

'Heir Apparent' (Åkerfeldt)

According to Åkesson, this was going to be the opener before 'Coil' replaced it. While *Watershed* definitely benefits from that gentler preface, this one would've been an equally impactful way to start (for vastly different reasons, of course). It grows methodically, with slow percussion crashing around crunchy riffs that are imaginatively interrupted by Wiberg's isolated piano notes. Afterwards, it explodes with near thrash metal concentration as Axenrot's relentless pounding drives Åkerfeldt's oscillating brutality (which is enhanced by shadowy aftereffects). A swift drum fill introduces a tantalising new slice of violent intricacy whose stylishly piercing guitar solo gives way to a handsomely frightening recipe of gothic keyboards and unsettling acoustic fingerpicking.

It's a short-lived reprieve, however, as the contentiousness returns temporarily yet fully; from there, they embark on a jazzier and denser interlude that's undoubtedly among the best segments on the record. The remaining three minutes find Opeth smartly recycling prior portions with fresh ornamentations; that is, until they use noisy combustion to queue a pseudo instrumental epilogue that exudes tragedy and resentment. Like the dismal discord at the end of 'Coil', the final seconds of screeching provide a disconcerting bridge into the next track and a greater sense of flow for *Watershed* as a whole.

'The Lotus Eater' (Åkerfeldt)

In the documentary, Åkerfeldt says that 'The Lotus Eater' – whose title refers to a mythical Greek society that would eat lotus flowers and forgo their families and responsibilities in favour of remaining intoxicated and lethargic – is 'fucked up but interesting' and that it 'perfectly represents ... Opeth in 2008'. That's a fair way to describe it, to say the least, since it's among the most daring and diverse entries here.

Even his preliminary hums (complemented by horns) are rather atypical. Consequently, the song pursues a similar juxtaposition between dark and light phases as 'Heir Apparent', but with more playfulness and a firmer compromise of clean vocals and growling on top of the hectic backdrop. It's quite thrilling, especially when the guitar riffs surround Åkerfeldt's echoes before he sings, 'All those years caring for a liar / A benefit road is winding higher / You're a moth too close to the fire'. A vibrantly complex jam prompts both mayhem and calmness, with a blazing six-string solo resulting in a soothing intermission of forlorn guitar work and keyboard swirls.

As every fan knows, this passage ultimately births the coolest moment on *Watershed*, wherein anticipatory electric guitar strums and syncopation build suspense for Wiberg's hypnotically gaudy and retro prog rock counterpoints. It's an utterly enchanting and unexpected breakdown that can't help but make you smile (particularly if you're a fan of 1970s jazz fusion and/or Canterbury acts like Caravan, Soft Machine, and Hatfield and the North). Additional escalations – both guttural and melodic – follow, and 'The Lotus Eater' ends mysteriously as organ croons and ethereally indecipherable voices align. Naturally, Åkerfeldt's single sigh ties into the introductory hums, too, bringing the piece full circle.

'Burden' (Åkerfeldt)

Released as the third and final single from *Watershed* on 9 December 2008, 'Burden' is comparatively commercial for an Opeth tune. In fact, it sort of evokes early '90s alternative rock/metal while simultaneously channelling the 'big ballad[s]' of the mid-70s (as Åkerfeldt puts it in the documentary). Specifically, he divulges: 'There's a Scorpions song on the *In Trance* album called 'Living and Dying' that gave me my idea. It doesn't sound anything like it, but when I heard it, I knew I wanted it to sound like that. Overblown'. The parallels are actually closer than he may think since both rest on highly expressive guitar playing and exaggeratedly dejected singing.

As always, they knock it out of the park. Wiberg's starting piano motif is joined by wailing guitar notes and keys to set up Åkerfeldt's ravishing heartache. Before long, the emotional floodgates burst as compassionate rhythms and acoustic chords console Åkerfeldt as he eloquently belts out painful memories ('I, once upon a time / Carried a burden inside / I sung a last goodbye / A broken rhyme I'd underlined / There's an ocean of sorrow in you'). The music gets a bit heftier around the verses – with dazzling keyboard and guitar solos in-between the second and third ones – and the harmonies roughly halfway through are downright saintly. In standard 1970s rock fashion – for example, 'Reelin' in the Years' by Steely Dan – Åkerfeldt and Åkesson trade-off more repentant solos before uniting for particularly poignant punctuations.

Ordinarily, a composition like this would simply sustain that feeling of catharsis as it fades *out*; however, Opeth are no ordinary band, so instead, the two guitarists fade *in* an acoustic duet that gradually and skilfully detunes into a vindictive abstraction. It stops sharply so that Åkerfeldt's cackles can transform into purposefully monotonous and creepy tapping. It's one of several peculiar and audacious inclusions that – love it or hate it – makes *Watershed* commendably experimental.

The music video, directed by genre icon Lasse Hoile, shows the band playing the song on stage in-between cryptic shots of a man and woman seemingly separated, lost, and searching for each other. There's plenty of cryptic imagery and settings, too, and both their scenes and the band are basked in blue lighting to enhance the air of isolation and emptiness. Predictably, it uses a shorter version of the track – with the prelude and epilogue removed – and it does a great job of visually embodying the spirit of the track.

'Porcelain Heart' (Åkerfeldt, Åkesson)

It's the first single from *Watershed* – issued on 19 April 2008 and succeeded by 'Mellotron Heart' on 3 June – and the only composition co-written by another member (Åkesson). It sucks you in right away, with Axenrot's hasty syncopation cueing a thunderous array of dismay that's quickly suspended by haunting acoustic arpeggios, supportive piano notes, and Åkerfeldt's aching call-and-response: 'I lost all I had / (That April day) / I turn to my friends / (Nothing to say)'. Curiously, the track momentarily goes silent before the preceding heaviness returns, yielding an effective dynamic pattern that's elevated by Axenrot's potent fills and extra guitar squeals upon the acoustic refrain. It's an alluring example of how Opeth routinely add extra spice to repeated arrangements.

Instead of reciting the same heavy movement once more, a subtle but enthralling electric guitar riff creeps out of the shadows to launch a comparatively persuasive new one; joined by Åkerfeldt's deep and mournful bellows, it's an immensely arresting outcome. Then, it all dies away so that a soothing guitar lick can bring about the most purely devastating section on the record, during which more acoustic accentuations pursue Åkerfeldt's high-pitched misery ('Icy roads beneath my feet / Led me through wastelands of deceit'). In-between verses, classical resonances augment his grief, and 'Porcelain Heart' wraps up with the previous entanglement of vigorous instrumentation and solemn chanting. It's phenomenal.

Logically, Hoile's video is like the darker sibling of the one for 'Burden'. It, too, intercuts footage of the group playing (in a house this time) around footage of people walking around alone or getting – shall we say – cosy with each other. However, it's far more sexualised and ghoulish, as if it's directed by David Fincher or Tim Burton. During the quieter parts, Åkerfeldt sits alone and plays acoustic guitar, which is a nice touch. Like 'Burden', it's undeniably one of Opeth's best music videos (not that there's a lot of competition, mind you).

'Hessian Peel' (Åkerfeldt)

In discussing the LP with Porter, Åkerfeldt concedes that this one – as well as 'Hex Omega' – is influenced by 'a [former] girlfriend who committed suicide' while he was in the studio. He continues:

> She had a son who was the same age as my oldest daughter, so it was a pretty big source of inspiration ... We weren't in touch anymore. We were together for a couple of months, and I always kept track of what she was doing and that she became a mother. But when we were together, she always had really deep problems. I think she was on Lithium and she was very depressed; she was always like that. I always heard what was happening with her because my mother and her mother were friends – they worked at the same place ... And there was never any good news, but when I heard she had her kid, I was really happy about that and hoping that she'd pull together, if not for herself then for her kid. Next thing you know, she was dead. She was a very complex person.

That framework surely makes the tastefully folkie start of 'Hessian Peel' more meaningful (namely, Åkerfeldt's soulful initial inquiry: 'Will their children cry / When their mother dies? / And in the autumn of their lives / Will they feel the same?'). The score is pleasantly nostalgic and malleable, exuberantly changing course around an alarmingly reversed snippet of that opening stanza. Wiberg's comforting layer is an essential attribute here, and Åkerfeldt's ensuing sentiments are heartily harrowing. The subsequent electric guitar riff amplifies the sonic misfortune prior to more acoustic fingerpicking, synths, and piano chords inciting wicked outbursts.

This environment, paired with a bit more vocal manipulation, conjures 'By the Pain I See in Others' from *Deliverance* and the coarse weirdness of Walker's *The Drift*. The symphonic quirkiness that follows is magnetic – especially with the destructive descent that interrupts it – and the last couple of minutes are as petrifyingly strange as anything else the group has done. In spite of its minimalism, the avant-garde climax (comprised of a grotesque collage of sound effects that transitions into and bass and keyboard thumps) is severely disturbing.

'Hex Omega' (Åkerfeldt)

The album closes with this musical and thematic colleague to 'Hessian Peel', whose feverish front seems like a shinier excerpt from *My Arms, Your Hearse* or *Still Life*. Intuitively, Wiberg's silky veneer counters the enveloping upheaval well and acts as peaceful footing for Åkerfeldt's glum decrees (for which Wiberg also delivers backing vocals). The rest of the textures thrive around them, leading to a constant ebb and flow between the two musical personalities that are capped off by a satisfyingly haphazard electric guitar solo.

All of a sudden, the frenzy evaporates so that Wiberg's desolate and taut keyboard progression can take the spotlight. It shrewdly provokes a more sluggish reprise of Åkerfeldt's verses, only to be obstructed by a beefier outro that concludes discreetly with a prolonged organ chord. All in all, 'Hex Omega' is the least intriguing part of *Watershed*, but it's a decent enough way to finish both the sequence itself and the death metal part of Opeth's career (at least for now).

Bonuses

Divided into five chapters – 'Prologue', 'From Another Planet', 'The Lotus Eater', 'The Junkmail Studios', and 'Epilogue' – Fredrik Odefjärd's *The Rehearsal Tapes* is, to a certain degree, lacklustre. In a nutshell, it's not very insightful in terms of the songwriting or recording sessions for *Watershed*. Rather, it's a mostly laidback and unfocused hangout session with the band that centres too much on them complimenting each other and joking around. That's certainly entertaining, and it humanises the quintet a bit, but fans looking for a more significant examination of their creative and professional sides during this period may walk away frustrated.

Gratefully, the ancillary songs fare better. For instance, 'Mellotron Heart' is emptier and eerier – almost to the point of seeming like a lost part of *In Cauda Venenum* – and includes alternate vocals from Åkerfeldt. Some of the singing on 'Porcelain Heart' is replaced by more instrumentation as well, and near the end, his organic percussion makes for another attractive change. In general, it's a sizeably altered interpretation.

In his *Watershed* diary entries, Åkerfeldt claims that 'Derelict Herds' has some of his best lyrics, and while that's debatable, they're definitely among his clearest and most direct. With a supernatural cadence, he utters: 'Someone died for looking too far / While I was asleep in my house / A child was killed, I heard it from a friend / A war raged in a distant land / Caused me to linger on a piece of text'. Meanwhile, enticingly repetitive percussion and multifaceted guitar riffs create a dramatically menacing atmosphere that harkens back to the ghastly heavy metal of the 1970s. There's also an abrupt change halfway through that finds Åkerfeldt screaming as horrifically as ever over an appropriately corrosive soundtrack. Honestly, it would've been more at home on *Blackwater Park* or *Deliverance*, if anywhere, and despite not being a true hidden gem, it's pretty damn good.

Similarly, the trio of covers they did around this time are very interesting. First, 'Bridge of Sighs' – originally from Robin Trower's 1974 LP of the same name – is almost a minute longer than Trower's studio version. It replaces his chimes with gusts of wind and otherworldly pings, but other than that, it mirrors the original closely (including the tone of the guitar and Åkerfeldt's deep singing). It's a tad smoother and less arid, yes, but not by much, so it's mainly just an enjoyable emulation.

The same can be said for 'Den ständiga resan' (which translates to 'The constant journey') and 'Would?' (which, again, isn't part of *Watershed* at all but was recorded at the same time, so it should be explored). The former cut comes from Fredriksson's 1994 record of the same name, and while Opeth play it in a different key and lower register (and without any symphonic embellishment), it follows the same path. (Fascinatingly, the acoustic strums are virtually identical to those in 'To Bid You Farewell', so it's almost certain that her tune was a direct influence). As for their reimaging of the finale of Alice in Chains' second album – 1992's *Dirt* – it's expectedly more polished and less grungy, yet it develops their blueprint quite intimately otherwise. Åkerfeldt's voice doesn't capture Layne Staley's grittiness, but he's more melodic and welcoming, so it's kind of a fair swap. The playing is equally sophisticated but authentic, so it feels as much like an Opeth track as it does the work of another artist.

Heritage (2011)

Personnel:
Mikael Åkerfeldt: vocals, acoustic and electric guitars, Mellotron, grand piano, sound effects
Fredrik Åkesson: electric guitars, acoustic guitar on 'Pyre' (bonus track)
Martin Axenrot: drums, percussion, photography (exclusive booklet)
Martin Méndez: bass guitar, upright bass
Per Wiberg: Hammond B3, Mellotron, grand piano, Rhodes piano
Additional Personnel:
Alex Acuña: percussion on 'Famine'
Björn J:son Lindh: flute on 'Famine'
Joakim Svalberg: grand piano on 'Heritage'
Charlie Dodd: sound effects on 'Häxprocess'
Travis Smith: art direction
Sandra Artigas: photography
Paul Barker: concept, design (exclusive booklet)
Christer Lorichs: concept, design, photography (exclusive booklet)
Jasper Schuurmans: project coordinator
Janne Hansson: engineer
Steven Wilson: vocal engineer, effects engineer, mixing
Produced at Atlantis Studios in Stockholm, Sweden, Junkmail Studios in Stockholm, Sweden, No Man's Land in Hemel Hempstead, England and Abbey Road Studios in London, England, January – March 2011 by Mikael Åkerfeldt.
Release date: 13 September 2011.
Highest chart places: UK: 22, USA: 19
Running time: 56:47
Current edition: 2013 Roadrunner Records 2x clear vinyl repress

Rarely, if ever, has a metal band transformed its sound as significantly and bravely as Opeth did with 2011's *Heritage*. True, it upholds their trademark tricky aggression and folkish serenity in spots, but its complete abandonment of their death metal roots – and complete embrace of both the accessible and the avant-garde jazz fusion/prog rock lenses they'd only hinted at previously – make it an astonishingly drastic and divisive overhaul. That revised aesthetic, in conjunction with the fact that it's Wiberg's final outing (and keyboardist Joakim Svalberg's first, albeit unofficially and almost trivially), means that *Heritage* is easily one of Opeth's most important and laudable 'observations'.

Unfortunately – though understandably – the end result is a double-edged sword. For all of its admirable shakeups and explorations, the record too often comes across like a series of unusually meandering and drawn-out demos and detours. There are praiseworthy *ideas* scattered around – and every track is agreeable to an extent – but only a handful of them wholly realise their promise and match the weightiness, allure, and care (in terms of balancing depth with duration) that Opeth had long since perfected. To use a possibly clunky metaphor, it's like Opeth were learning to ride a bike with training wheels: they're irrefutably determined and honourably courageous, yet they're also perpetually unsteady and unsure, only occasionally moving with ample confidence and planning. Those detriments aside, *Heritage* is a largely likeable album that sees the group figuratively dipping their toes into a majorly new stylistic pond before fully – and flawlessly – diving in with 2014's *Pale Communion*.

Of course, *Heritage* didn't begin as the launching point for a majorly new version of Opeth; it began as an extension of their preceding two collections. You see, Åkerfeldt started penning new stuff around the time of the Royal Albert Hall show, but soon found that he wasn't satisfied with what he had. 'I wrote a few songs that were like a continuation of *Watershed* [and *Ghost Reveries*], but I couldn't feel it; it was as if I wrote the songs but was kind of lying to myself, saying to myself I thought they were good, when really I didn't', he discloses in *Book of Opeth*. Despite being highly convinced that they'd done all they could with 'that sound' and 'couldn't take it any further' or improve upon it, he needed a second opinion to be absolutely sure; therefore, he played his untitled recordings for Méndez, who – luckily – came to the same conclusion. In 'The Making of *Heritage*: A Documentary', Méndez clarifies: 'When I first heard the demos as Mike's place, during a party, I said, 'If that's going to be the next Opeth album, I will be disappointed. We need to do something different and explore other kinds of music that we want to play and listen to''. (Interestingly, Åkesson loved those initial recordings, but he obviously respected Åkerfeldt's choice to change gears, too.) With the invaluable bassist backing him up, Åkerfeldt deleted what he had – never to be recovered – and set out to discover what he *really* wanted to create.

Before continuing with that, it should be mentioned that in a 2011 chat with Chad Bowar of *About Entertainment*, Åkerfeldt admits that he'd also become 'a bit discouraged with the contemporary metal scene' in general and wanted to 'break away from it even more'. He adds: 'I just couldn't see myself writing another album in the same vein as the last couple of records'. In his lengthy conversation with the YouTube channel *FaceCulture* (from the same year), he also addresses newfound concerns with his growling that led to the decision: 'The problems I had with my screams I was unaware of until I heard the Albert Hall. I sounded a bit strange. Then, when I was doing shows with Bloodbath, I felt like I had a sore throat after I sang'. At the time, however, he didn't swear off returning to his beloved belligerence at some point, expounding, 'I'm not saying that we won't do death vocals anymore, but I don't feel like they're me as much as they were ten years ago'. Now, ten years – and three more LPs – *later*, it appears less and less likely that Opeth will ever return to their former fiendishness (for better or worse).

Even Steven Wilson saw Åkerfeldt's resolution as inevitable, as he avows in *Book of Opeth*: 'I knew that Mike was feeling less and less comfortable with writing metal music because he was no longer listening to it, and it was something that didn't really interest him a great deal'. Ultimately, he says, 'it was, again, a sign of an artist growing'. As any diehard fan knows – and as alluded to earlier – *Heritage*'s final form didn't come out of nowhere; there'd been traces of it in Opeth's music ever since *Orchid* first introduced them to the world. In fact, Åkerfeldt professed when the record was announced, he'd been 'building up to write for and participate on an album like this' since he was 19.

Happily, it didn't take long for him to start fulfilling that dream once he discarded those unsuitable *Watershed*-esque fragments; specifically, he soon sketched out the foundation of 'The Lines in My Hand' (a composition 'so weird' that it immediately set the course for the rest of the record). '[I]t just gave me a straight road, to do whatever the hell I wanted with the other songs, and so it became an album that's all over the place', he gloats. It was only natural for him to check with Méndez about the new direction, too; as anticipated, he was totally on board, cheering, 'What the hell? What is this? I love it!' Mercifully, even Åkesson eventually grew accustomed to and proud of Åkerfeldt's reworked vision: '[W]e are lucky enough to have the privilege of being able to freak out more than other bands can do ... Mike is the pilot, the director, and it's always interesting to see what's going to happen next', he smirks.

In addition to Åkerfeldt's regular genre stimuli, the album is expressly inspired – to varying degrees – by Swedish rock ensemble The Hives, Swedish pianist Jan Johansson, Ronnie James Dio, Magma, and Swedish folk music. Although it was engineered and/or mixed by Janne Hannson and Steven Wilson – making his return after nearly a decade – *Heritage* is the first Opeth record entirely overseen by Åkerfeldt. Clearly, his increased role required a change in approach, as he breaks down in *Book of Opeth*: 'We were talking about recording live in the studio, but that plan was scrapped because I wanted to be a producer and overview the whole recording, and you can't jump between acoustic guitars and electric guitars in real time – they have to be done separately. So in the end we recorded the drums and bass ... live in the studio [for the first time since *Orchid*] to get that live vibe'. (It should also be recognised that the LP was mastered by Peter Mew at Abbey Road Studios. His prior work on records like the Pretty Things' *S.F. Sorrow* and Pink Floyd's *Ummagumma* – as well as the studio's esteemed history – made Åkerfeldt feel like 'a kid in a candy store looking for footprints that could've belonged to Paul McCartney or Pink Floyd').

In order to get the most faithful textures and moods possible, the band used a few veteran tools and guest players, too. 'Everything was old. The microphones were used back in the Abba days of [Atlantis] studio. The same with the amps. We used an old Marshall 800 and cranked it up. There's no editing or trickery', Åkerfeldt told Bowar. Meanwhile, Méndez was pushed almost completely out of his comfort zone by playing upright bass for the first time; he later called the experience 'a [cool] challenge'. Furthermore, Åkerfeldt brought in Peruvian-American drummer Alex Acuña (Weather Report,

Koinonia, Chick Corea, Joni Mitchell) and Swedish flautist Björn Jason Lindh to add eccentric flair to *Heritage*'s seventh track, 'Famine'. In the documentary, Åkesson remarks that both men did a superb job making the tune sound even more 'evil', while Méndez says that meeting Acuña was 'really special' because he'd 'been listening to his work for years'. Combined, those attributes definitely give the record an efficient (and almost contradictory) sense of pulsating immorality and earthly solace.

Lamentably, the *Heritage* sessions also recalled the past in one negative way: the spiralling disinterest and subsequent dismissal of Wiberg. As Åkerfeldt tells it (in *Book of Opeth*), Wiberg was arguably more overtly apathetic and uninvolved than Lindgren was only a few years prior: 'Per is a lovely, lovely guy, but he never really wanted to say that he was in the band ... I was worried, and I was heartbroken ... that he didn't really want to be part of the gang'. Delving deeper, Åkerfeldt states that while everyone else would be at the studio 'regardless of who was recording' to show 'support' and be 'part of the team', Wiberg was routinely absent. 'He showed up for a few lunches, and didn't really say much, other than complaining that we weren't recording live, and when Axe suggested that we set up and do it – just to test Per – he didn't know the songs ... Whenever Per did show up, everyone else left because he came in like a dark cloud', he reflects. Åkerfeldt even wrote Wiberg an email to ask if he was planning to leave anyway, and Wiberg said, 'Yes'. On 7 April 2011, Opeth formally proclaimed that Wiberg was 'relieved of his duties ... as part of a mutual decision with the band'.

It seems like Wiberg's firing – once *Heritage* was more or less finished – shocked no one (including Farrow, who reveals: 'He'd done a few things on tour where he'd forgotten his passport, and things like that'). Nevertheless, the group was once again in the untimely position of having to find a new member ASAP. Thankfully, Åkesson knew just the guy: Joakim Svalberg. They'd met way back in 1994 when they each auditioned for – and then were accepted into – a Stockholm music school. In *Book of Opeth*, Svalberg reminisces: 'By that point, Fred had already established himself as a guitarist due to his work with Talisman, and I was some way behind him in terms of career achievements'. Despite not having seen each other in several years, Svalberg made a large enough impression for Åkesson to call him and see if he was interested in the new position. Svalberg confesses that he was 'aware' of Opeth but 'had never really listened to them' and 'didn't have any idea what it was all about' prior to their conversation.

Trusting Åkesson's judgment, Åkerfeldt invited Svalberg to go for a drink, consequently finding himself intrigued by Svalberg's preference for 'rock, prog rock, fusion, jazz, and that sort of thing' over death metal. Similarly, Svalberg was taken aback by Åkerfeldt's songwriting, lyrics, and musicianship. Obviously, they got on quite well personally, but Åkerfeldt still needed to verify Svalberg's musical compatibility, so he asked him to come to the studio and play on the LP's 'impossible' opening title track. 'Playing a grand piano is very sensitive',

Åkerfeldt stipulates, so the fact that Svalberg was able to lay down the piece in only a few takes made it 'a great audition'. Méndez adds that he was actually 'the first to work with him' and that Svalberg was 'really professional'. 'We practised the song about ten times and he kept asking for one more – he kept me there for about five hours!' Méndez rejoices.

Svalberg wasn't just a terrific replacement for Wiberg instrumentally, but vocally as well. 'His voice probably fits my voice better than Per's voice, so in that sense, it's even better', Åkerfeldt told Bowar. Likewise, Åkesson declares in the documentary: 'He's got a good sense of rhythm, and he's a good singer. The first time I heard him play was when he was in the studio, recording the title track. He didn't seem nervous; he nailed it, pretty much, with the perfect time of emotion'. Naturally, Svalberg didn't become an official member that easily or that quickly, though; Åkerfeldt still wanted to use the *Heritage* tour – which we'll get to momentarily – as a means of 'trying each other out' to see if Opeth could indeed help Svalberg attain his 'dream ... to be part of a collective'.

In the past, the group hadn't publicly poured salt into the wound regarding interpersonal conflicts and key line-up shifts, yet the cover of *Heritage* – which depicts Wiberg's head literally falling from the Opeth family tree like a rotten apple – changed that. In his *FaceCulture* discussion, Åkerfeldt says that the artwork is 'based on the band, with the roots going down to hell symbolising our past. The occult death metal, and the tree now flourishing and taking in other influences, and everybody wants a piece of us ... We wanted to have the band on the sleeve, and [Per's] no longer in the band. How do you solve that? [By insinuating that] he's too ripe'. (Hence why Wiberg's head will end up on the ground, alongside the skulls of other past members.) Reportedly, the nine stars represent Opeth's previous nine studio records, but as for the burning city in the background, Åkerfeldt acknowledges that he doesn't know what it means because it's just something he 'woke up with one day'. In the *Heritage* documentary, he remembers instructing Travis Smith to aim for something akin to Bruegel's *The Triumph of Death* and the Beatles' *Yellow Submarine*, concluding that the finished imagery (like the music it represents) is consciously controversial – and 'funny' – with 'more colours than [they've] ever had and more of a psychedelic vibe'.

As usual, *Heritage* was made available in several formats. Outside of the standard CD offering, there was a double vinyl LP version; an exclusive CD/DVD digipack pre-order version (with a *Heritage* coin and autographed 'The Making of *Heritage*' booklet); a special edition CD/DVD digipack (with two bonus songs – 'Pyre' and 'Face in the Snow' – as well as the documentary and a 5.1 surround mix of the sequence); and 12' box set that includes all of those extras and a limited edition set of Opeth postcards.

Beyond relying on the typical marketing techniques, Åkerfeldt and Wilson ingeniously promoted the record as being part of a thematic/stylistic trilogy rounded out by Wilson's second solo LP, *Grace for Drowning* (distributed two weeks after *Heritage*), and their relatively abstract self-titled debut LP as Storm Corrosion (distributed on 7 May 2012). Unsurprisingly, they'd worked on the latter collection while working on their own albums, and although it was ready to go in September 2011, they decided to postpone it so that they could properly promote the other two LPs. Because we're concentrating solely on Opeth's catalogue, we won't get into the nuts and bolts of either outside project other than to say that visually and musically, there are certainly enough connections to unify the three releases as individual segments of a single puzzle.

Commercially and critically, *Heritage* was adequately prosperous. It maintained Opeth's album-by-album ascent in the UK, US, and Swedish charts – outselling its predecessors – and did comparably well in Denmark, Australia, Germany, France, Norway, and Poland, among other key areas. Reasonably, physical and digital magazines such as *Revolver*, *BBC Music*, *The Guardian*, *The Quietus*, and *Rolling Stone* gave it positive write-ups, whereas *Drowned in Sound*, *Q*, *Uncut*, and *Sputnikmusic* were less keen. Either way, practically all reviewers at least respected, if not loved, the quintet's revamped characteristics. It was even nominated for the Album of the Year award by *PROG* (yet it's also been positioned as one of Opeth's weakest collections in more recent record rankings by *Loudwire*, *The Pit*, *Decibel*, *PopMatters*, *Stereogum*, and *The Prog Report*). Evidently, the professional consensus has always been that *Heritage* merits more applause for its objective boldness than for its overarching quality.

No matter how conflicted the press were about it, however, their reactions paled in comparison to how many of Opeth's most fanatical followers were outspokenly scornful toward the group's latest compilation. Granted, Åkerfeldt was prepared for *some* level of backlash, but not the indisputably startling and inexcusable vitriol he and his bandmates wound up receiving. 'I think people are dying for us to say that it was a mistake, but that's never going to happen ... I knew it was going to cause some ripples on the water, but I didn't expect that I would get threats. I think it's a bit fucked up that death metal fans embraced a soft record like *Damnation* but not *Heritage*, which is at times really heavy, gloomy and fast', he ponders in *Book of Opeth*, and he's absolutely right.

They even tried to ease audiences into the new material during the North American and European *Heritage* concert cycles – where they played with Katatonia, Ghost, Mastodon, and Pain of Salvation – by incorporating some older classics into their on-stage itinerary. Nevertheless, they dealt with an absurd amount of audible, visible, and even physical pushback. Speaking to *PROG*'s Dave Everley in October 2017, Åkerfeldt explains: 'We were hitting places where they were a bit loud in voicing in their opinions in the middle of the show. People started complaining and screaming and leaving during the show. And people started to challenge me to fights onstage. At this one show, this guy threw down his glove. He was challenging me to a duel ... I had him thrown out'.

Rationally, Åkerfeldt entered the tour (which, he clarifies, 'started before the album came out') on edge anyway since it marked the introductions of Wiberg's replacement and an untested method of performance. (He was also hesitant to do more growling since it may've hurt his voice.) In *Book of Opeth*, he illustrates:

> All of the songs in the set list were brand new or songs from the past that were never played before; there was a drum solo, there was all sorts of improvisation, [and] there were acoustic bits; we even played a song that we'd recorded for a game ['The Throat of Winter'], which was very obscure. Stepping on stage that first night – we were in Massachusetts at a metal festival with real metal bands – and doing this weird set was very daunting ... I was also worried about whether I was going to strain my voice if I was doing the screams because those new songs were much, much harder to sing than any of the older clean stuff I had done.

Thankfully, Åkesson asserts, it wasn't *too* long before their crowds became calmer and more accepting of what Opeth were doing. Méndez even states that the risky and tumultuous experience ultimately proved beneficial for all involved because they 'started to get all sorts of [new] people' interested in Opeth, such as folks of 'different ages' and 'non-metal fans'. Looking back, Åkerfeldt relishes how the group 'grew' afterwards, adding that they 'became a better band musically', with both Åkesson and Svalberg singing more.

For Svalberg, his first live journey with the band was eye-opening and invigorating in multiple ways. Despite being a newcomer unexpectedly receiving a crash course in how spiteful Opeth fans can be – particularly in America – he has mostly fond memories of the experience. 'When I played those first summer festivals with Opeth, it was the first time I had played death metal, and we played a lot of the really heavy stuff. I immediately liked it, but it took a lot of digging into that environment', he discloses in *Book of Opeth*. He also cheers at the on-stage chemistry between them, as well as how the 'diversity' and difficulty of the material meant that he really had to 'be on [his] toes ... to get the songs right'. Of course, Åkerfeldt was just as enthusiastic about Svalberg's commitment, declaring, 'Touring with the brand new line-up was great ... [Joakim] was so excited and that makes everybody else a bit more excited, too'.

In retrospect, and paradoxically, *Heritage* is both a high point and low point in Opeth's discography. On the one hand, it found them heroically throwing caution to the wind with one of the most unapologetically radical stylistic changes a metal band has ever made. (Even if there was truly no other path forward – and by Åkerfeldt's own admission, there wasn't – it was nonetheless an extraordinarily dicey and creditable move.) However, that doesn't save the finished product from being chiefly empty, aimless, and underwhelming, with only a few glimpses of distinction amidst the novel yet negligible rubble. It's not a *bad* album, per se, but it is one that far too infrequently lives up to its potential. Luckily, hindsight also allows *Heritage* to be viewed as a necessary stepping-stone toward the intimidatingly excellent *Pale Communion*.

'Heritage' (Åkerfeldt)

Svalberg instantly proves himself with this short but sweet wordless preface (which, Åkerfeldt told *FaceCulture*, literally alludes to their 'musical heritage' of Swedish folk music). Its mournful elegance and melodic precision keep it engaging even if it's also emblematic of *Heritage*'s aforementioned tendency to extend ideas beyond their value. In other words, more could be done in the time allotted – or the piece could be even shorter – but that's really just a nit-pick in this case. Plus, Méndez's patient upright bass notes provide ideal accompaniment. (Structurally, 'Heritage' also set a precedent for Opeth albums to begin with a prologue, which 2016's *Sorceress* and 2019's *In Cauda Venenum* – but not *Pale Communion* – followed.)

'The Devil's Orchard' (Åkerfeldt)

It's easily the most developed, pleasurable, and forward-thinking track here, as its full-bodied intricacy and speed most explicitly pinpoint to where Opeth would go next. It was the first single released from the LP, too, premiering at *Stereogum* on 26 July 2011 (with a music video arriving on 23 September). As for its meaning, Åkerfeldt claims that it's about 'the collapse of civilization ... and religion in a certain way', as well as the 'the feeling of being robbed'.

That helps explain why he so passionately sings, 'God is dead!' during the catchy chorus. Stepping back a bit, its instigating influx of wild rhythms and guitar riffs – alongside intermittent keyboard whirls and church bells – is awesomely retro, summoning the tempo-shifting coolness of Black Sabbath, Deep Purple, and King Crimson. It's nearly impossible not to get sucked into it both musically and vocally, and that's before the second chorus runs into an exquisitely jazzy, tasteful, and gothic interlude whose subtle decorations demonstrate the brighter and quirkier trajectory Opeth were now embarking on. In every way, it's a masterful exercise in sophisticated strangeness.

After a brief return to the previous animosity (wherein Åkerfeldt soulfully bellows, 'In the corner of my eye / Demon fades from the hole', although certain websites – and the official booklet – state: 'In the corner of my eye / You are tearing flesh from bone'), Wiberg's carnivalesque keyboard murmur prompts another steadfast statement: 'Led the blind / In search to find / A pathway to the sun'. All the while, Axenrot's hyper syncopation leads the charge skilfully, paving the way for a shrieking, classic rock-esque guitar solo to bring the track to its climax. As the exhilaration dies down, Åkerfeldt repeats the chorus' key phrase with echoey falsetto as Wiberg's piano notes imitate his intonation. It's an essential respite from the vivid chaos, not to mention a chilling coda for the record's shining moment.

As for the video, it was directed by photographer Phil Mucci and presents a macabre mixture of live-action and animation (as well as a mixture of colour and B&W). It seemingly captures a woman diving from a building into hell as Satan takes control of her city. There's a lot of abstract imagery, too, such as kaleidoscope filters and cosmic double exposures. It's pretty cool, and it definitely embodies the cryptic extravagances of the song itself.

'I Feel the Dark' (Åkerfeldt)

In the official documentary, Åkerfeldt says that it was supposed to start *Heritage*, but Steven Wilson advised him to use 'The Devil's Orchard' instead. It was a wise decision since that tune makes a much more urgent and stark impact, whereas the tenderly brooding 'I Feel the Dark' works best right here.

The acoustic guitar work is particularly sublime throughout, as is Åkerfeldt's singing. (In fact, many magazines rightly acknowledged how tremendous his clean vocals are on the entire LP, pointing out that no matter how missed they may be, his growls simply wouldn't have worked with this material.) The score builds smartly, too, with light rhythms, psychedelically reverberating electric guitar lines, cascading synths, and other ghostly surfaces ornamenting the graceful first half.

Suddenly, the creamy groove dissipates into a simple, ethereal loop as Åkerfeldt distressingly whispers, 'A flaking wish inside'. Then, the arrangement temporarily surges into vibrant outrage, dials back for gentler acoustic arpeggios, and then erupts again into flashy madness. The interplay between the acoustic and electric guitars, in addition to Åkerfeldt's overlapping vocals, is magnificent, finally resolving into a slightly amended reprise of the deliciously delicate beginning.

'Slither' (Åkerfeldt)

It was the second and last single released from the album (on 21 November 2011), and as Åkerfeldt explained to YouTube channel *The House of Zazz* in September 2011, it was a deliberate homage to one of his biggest inspirations:

> 'Slither' was a tribute to Dio, and I came up with it and thought, 'This sounds a little bit like 'Kill the King''. It had the working title of 'Kill the Queen', which I wrote initially as a gimmick. But, as I was such a big fan of his and he passed – he was one of the most important hard rock vocalists in my life, and he's been on some of the most important records. When he died, it was like a family member died. It's not necessarily an original song — at least by my standards — it's [just] a tribute to him.

True to his intention, it barrels along with the robust feistiness of Dio's finest tracks and the all-encompassing spectrum of 1970s heavy metal. As such, it's sensibly blunt and basic – well, at least for Opeth – with razor-sharp guitar work, keyboard roars, and agitated percussion sturdily guiding

Åkerfeldt's vehement verses. The swift guitar solo two minutes in is predictably astounding, and there are a handful of habitually complicated twists and turns as the ending draws near. The mounting acoustic postscript is a nice touch as well, with Åkerfeldt and Åkesson's fingerpicking counterpoints resulting in a handsomely rustic, though also overly prolonged, outcome.

'Nepenthe' (Åkerfeldt)

Åkerfeldt got the title (which means 'medicine for sorrow') from a record label he supported, and Méndez states that he liked the tune right away because of its 'jazzy sound'. It's ruminative but off-kilter, with a decisively stiff ascending melody and allusively minimalistic outline that marks a prominent instance of Opeth's gutsy reinvention not necessarily spawning a riveting consequence. Frankly, it's commendable but lifeless, at least until Wiberg storms in with a dissonant riff that kicks off dizzying guitar freak-outs and some spirited rhythms. Sadly, the continual tug of war between that hecticness and the surrounding stillness is monotonous and wobbly, lacking Opeth's hallmark poise and wonderment. Hence, 'Nepenthe' is a primary example of why *Heritage* is sometimes underdeveloped yet exceedingly indulgent.

'Häxprocess' (Åkerfeldt)

Translated to 'witch process', it's one of Åkerfeldt's favourite songs on *Heritage* because of its 'melancholic feel', 'drive', and 'emotional' ending. Its warm and almost freeform introduction is undeniably absorbing, with successfully irregular start/stop pacing and artful intersections of timbres birthing a compelling run-up to Åkerfeldt's downtrodden and isolated commencement. His lyrics are especially poetic ('A lifeline in a drop of blood / A dying wish to shun a god / Sought a dream inside the light / Finally relieved from plight'), and the adjacent acoustic guitar and Rhodes piano garnishes are subtly gorgeous.

The spectral background voices enhance the mood, too, and help create an air of sombre beauty before an onslaught of challenging acoustic patterns activates a livelier and lovelier deviation. The quintet truly play with luxurious finesse and harmony here, and Åkerfeldt's singing is divinely pained. About two-thirds of the way through, a sparser and sadder transition takes over whose richly unaffected guitar solo and evocatively faint piano notes offer an awe-inspiringly tragic send-off. Overall, 'Häxprocess' could be a smidge more lucid and less disjointed, but each passage is supremely striking in its own ways.

'Famine' (Åkerfeldt)

According to Åkerfeldt (in the documentary), the preliminary flute scales were literally recorded as Lindh 'was tuning and walking up to the microphone'; blended with Acuña's percussion and the wraithlike sound effects, it makes for an extremely unnerving and unorthodox opening. Touchingly, it's rapidly cut off by morbid piano chords, howling electric guitar tones, and Åkerfeldt's stirring laments: 'I can't see your face / And I can't breathe your air / So I wonder why / I get cold inside / When I hear your name'. The hollowness around his deep voice and the scarce instrumentation is as powerful as any audible component.

Of course, things get more energised after that, with frantic rhythms, spicy guitar work, and hollering keys embracing Åkerfeldt's fuller delivery. The blistering midsection jam soon dissolves into another quiet segment (bringing back Acuña's sprightly tapping in the process) and then into an even fiercer detour highlighted by gruff guitar riffs and Lindh's domineering woodwind wallops. From there, a mellower and more impressionistic underpinning traces Åkerfeldt's hearty closing outlook – 'Become a ghost in perpetual void / And neglect all reasons why' – until the previous hostility returns. As Wiberg's final devilish note rings out, withered piano chords sneak in and join with paranormal hues to generate a gratifyingly terrifying outro.

As with 'Häxprocess', 'Famine' lets its harsh tonal variations get in the way of its fluidity and concentration, but not to the degree of diminishing its immersive vivacity and pathos.

'The Lines in My Hand' (Åkerfeldt)
Åkerfeldt fittingly described it to *FaceCulture* as 'a cross between a band called Captain Beyond' and – particularly in regard to the track's drumbeat – The Hives. It's charmingly festive, focused, and folksy, with buoyant rhythms; majestic keyboard and guitar embroideries; and a central melody that demands you sing along. Wiberg's multi-layered pastoral segue into the brawnier next portion ('The writings on the wall depict a truth that no one sees') is sleek, too.

It produces an appealingly frisky whirlwind of musicianship that fuels a tenser outburst from Åkerfeldt: 'Burning voice of insanity / Nothing is the same / Barren lands for the idle man / Find all the lines in your hand'. All along, the arrangement stampedes with unrelenting passion, never letting up or giving the listener a moment to catch their breath. It's calculatingly and captivatingly intense, as Åkerfeldt justly celebrates in *Book of Opeth*: 'There is no more energetic music that we've made, as far as I am concerned than the ending minute or two of 'The Lines in My Hand''. For sure, it's hard not to be blown away by it.

'Folklore' (Åkerfeldt)
From its gradual growth and melodic sheen to its eventual punchy dominance and cyclical entrapments, this one – purposely or not – owes a lot to 'Hårgalåten' by Kebnekajse. The secluded electric guitar preamble is mischievously shadowy before it astutely converts into the song's lead riff and triggers everything else. Once 'Folklore' really gets going, it's a funky and smooth voyage underscored by murky verses, soft acoustic plucks, slick electric guitar licks, and Méndez's characteristic flexibility (among other bewitching elements). Its hooky ethos is heavily predictive of *In Cauda Venenum* as well.

Before long, that spellbinding formula is countered by a fabulously deserted space of demoralised acoustic arpeggios and piano notes; with the help of Axenrot and Méndez's conducting partnership, the morose void hurriedly detonates into an ambush of wounded guitar work, mediaeval keyboard coatings, and bleak predicaments ('Lost control and called your name / Left a home in the pouring rain / In a sea of guilt and shame / Will we sustain?'). Åkerfeldt's doubled phrasing adds heartrending dignity, and the concluding guitar part is nearly as moving despite its circular simplicity.

'Marrow of the Earth' (Åkerfeldt)

Like 'Heritage', 'Marrow of the Earth' is a modest but useful endcap that gives *Heritage* a stronger sense of profundity and wholeness. (It also foreshadows Opeth's ability to bring *Sorceress* full circle with an epilogue.) It's lengthier and more elaborate than the title track, though, with an elegantly remorseful synthesis of acoustic and electric guitar themes being adorned by pensive rhythms by the end. As with some preceding compositions, the whole thing could be either more advanced or more concise, but what's here is undoubtedly advantageous.

Bonuses

All special editions of *Heritage* come with two discarded yet amiable tunes: 'Pyre' and 'Face in the Snow'. 'Pyre' – which was co-written by Åkesson – is suitably jazzy, colourful, and straightforward, with desirable melodies (especially the chorus) and playing (especially the synths, percussion, and fancy acoustic guitar solo near the end). Admittedly, it's a bit stagnant, too, because it basically grooves along the same template all the way, essentially running its premise into the ground by the time it's done.

It's good for what it is, though, and so is 'Face in the Snow'. It's a relatively slow ballad that largely consists of Åkerfeldt's singing soulfully over nominal drumming, sullen guitar strums, and bulging keyboard varnishes. It's definitely not on par with 'Patterns in the Ivy II' or 'Windowpane', but it's persuasive and refined enough to hold your attention until it's over. Also, it's interesting how its narrative ('I see a face in the snow / Inside my head a voice calls for me / I see your face in the snow / And outside the sun is too far away to feel') arouses the lovelorn saga of *Still Life*.

Luckily, the hour-long 'Making of *Heritage*' (directed by Åkerfeldt and co-edited by Tom Grimshaw, who also worked on *The Roundhouse Tapes*) is likely their top documentary thus far. For one thing, Åkerfeldt is humble and humorous throughout it, giving viewers a tour of his home studio and even a sample of an early version of 'Pyre' amidst a comparatively mature, humanizing, and educational look at the creation of the record. Obviously, the other members pop up from time to time to share their methods and goals, and their fresh reactions to the departure of Wiberg (who is absent from the entire film) is particularly sobering. Above all else, the video shows

Opeth as a resolute yet rambunctious and unpretentious team who are committed to their new sound while also being aware of how segregating it will be for fans.

Pale Communion (2014)

Personnel:
Mikael Åkerfeldt: vocals, lead guitars, engineer, art direction
Fredrik Åkesson: lead guitars, backing vocals
Martin Axenrot: drums, percussion
Martin Méndez: bass
Joakim Svalberg: keyboards, piano, backing vocals
Additional Personnel:
Dave Stewart: string arrangements
Travis Smith: artwork
Tom Dalgety: engineer
Janne Hansson: engineer
Steven Wilson: mixing, engineer, backing vocals
Colin Bradburne: recording on 'Solitude' and 'Var Kommer Barnen In' (bonus tracks)
João Paulo Da Costa Dias: recording on 'Solitude' and 'Var Kommer Barnen In' (bonus tracks)
Produced at Rockfield Studios in Monmouth, Wales, Atlantis Studios in Stockholm, Sweden, Junkmail Studios in Stockholm, Sweden, Angel Studios in London, England, and No Man's Land in Hemel Hempstead, England, early 2014 by Mikael Åkerfeldt and Tom Dalgety.
Release date: 26 August 2014.
Highest chart places: UK: 14, USA: 19
Running time: 56:00
Current edition: 2018 Roadrunner Records 2x clear vinyl

In many ways, Opeth entered the 2010s in the most audaciously polarising way possible. Not only were they forced to announce yet another major change in personnel (exchanging Wiberg for Svalberg), but they'd unashamedly swapped out numerous trademarks in favour of following an intensely different route. As a result, *Heritage* sold enormously well but was far from universally accepted by fans and critics. That dichotomy wasn't totally unwarranted considering that *Heritage* comes off as a majorly satisfying and respectable – yet cumulatively uneven and apprehensive – initiation into the quintet's modern persona. Really, it was like the group's second debut record, succumbing to the simultaneous pros and cons of many first efforts by only hinting at the greatness that, hopefully, would be wholly attained with its more reliable, developed, and secure successor.

Even so, few people (inside or outside of Opeth) could've envisioned just how big of a leap they'd make with *Pale Communion*. Improving upon everything that worked about its forebear (and rejecting everything that didn't), the eight-track tour de force is an unequivocally brilliant capitalisation of what Åkerfeldt wanted to accomplish with his revised muses and musical ambitions. From beginning to end, it radiates marvellous songwriting, engrossingly luscious arrangements (both fiery and fragile), and perhaps the most immaculately unpredictable but cohesive flow of *any* Opeth 'observation'. Honestly – and at the risk of slightly spoiling my main thoughts on *Sorceress* and *In Cauda Venenum* – they've yet to surpass themselves when it comes to this approach. Thus, *Pale Communion* is not just Opeth's superlative effort in this style, but – at the equal risk of provoking the wrath of countless readers – it's also a clear contender for Opeth's best album to date.

Although the troupe were resilient in making *Heritage* precisely what they wanted it to be (regardless of any volatile aftermath that might arise), that doesn't mean that its downright confrontational reception played no part in shaping *Pale Communion*. In *Book of Opeth*, Åkerfeldt specifies that *Heritage* signified the first time that Opeth 'had really got a lot of shit from both fans and journalists', leading him to say to himself: "OK, let's try again. Let's make it a bit more polished so these stupid fuckers can finally understand what we're trying to do' So, [it] is a bit more polished. The music on there is kind of going for the throat. It's cool music that closes in on the UK and Italian prog scenes'. He also differentiates the two LPs by stating that he 'put more emphasis' on 'strong, almost-sing-along-y-type of melodies' here, clarifying: 'Most of the songs aren't as schizophrenic and all-over-the-place as the songs on *Heritage* ... *Pale Communion* is more focused, streamlined, and linear'. Gratefully, Åkesson indicates, the rest of the band were on board with Åkerfeldt's methodologies.

In the past, Åkerfeldt had trouble coming up with new material, but that wasn't the case this time since he'd begun writing the songs in August 2012 and essentially finished all of them by the end of the *Heritage* tour. Once again, he drew stylistic ideas from a wide array of older artists – David Crosby, Scott Walker, and (obviously) Goblin – and wrote by himself. In fact, Åkesson confessed to *Stereogum*'s Justin Norton in August 2014, 'When [Mike's] writing, he tends to be very isolated, especially on this album. He's a bit of a lone wolf when it comes to that ... I was recording a lot of ideas ... and he liked them, but on these songs – the sequence just worked. We didn't get to experiment with more'.

That's reasonable considering that Åkerfeldt gave his bandmates fairly advanced home demos (with vocals that didn't really require any re-dos or updates); plus, he was 'going through a hard time' in his private life – this was around the time of his divorce from Anna, after all – and he needed to exorcise his inner turmoil with the tunes. In July 2014, he told *Invisible Oranges* that he's proud of *Pale Communion*'s songwriting because it's so personal, adding, 'Lyrics became a thing that I wanted to relate back to myself, to get more comfortable singing stuff that I know ... I have a tendency to worry a lot. Sometimes I create an alternate future in my head of something that could happen, and when I do, it's something quite bleak ... Many of the lyrics are based on those worries'.

Just like 'The Lines in My Hand' established the direction of *Heritage* as a whole, so too did 'Faith in Others' of *Pale Communion*. (It's a bit ironic, then, that it's both the first track written and the last one sequenced.) In a July 2014 video conversation with *The Pit*, Åkerfeldt elaborates: 'Musically, we didn't really have any plans. Eventually, once I had written the first song, I figured maybe we should do something more melodic this time ... [so that] it might be easier to get into than *Heritage* or some of the earlier records'. In *Book of Opeth*, he mentions that 'Faith in Others' also led to them implementing 'a musical ingredient' that they'd never incorporated in as much depth before: orchestral strings. (He also told *Decibel* that *Storm Corrosion*'s blending of avant-garde and classical elements 'made [him] realise what a massive difference it can mean to incorporate the real shit' rather than 'synthetic sounds or effects'.)

At first, Opeth wanted to return fully to Atlantis Studios, but Andy Farrow felt that doing so would be too expensive given *Pale Communion*'s relatively demanding cost, so he suggested the legendary Rockfield Studios in Wales instead. Luckily, moving there meant that Åkerfeldt could still uphold his tradition of using locales with musically significant backgrounds because – as he divulged to *Metal Assault* in March 2014 – it's where 'many of [his] favourite bands recorded' (such as Queen, Black Sabbath, Judas Priest, and Rush). The other major reason was that he knew that *Pale Communion* would require such a professional and sophisticated setting to get right, as he wanted to transition from *Heritage*'s early '70s kind of production to a 'late '70s and early '80s' model. '[It's] beautiful – in the middle of nowhere, some moors and nothing around, completely quiet, just sheep and cattle ... It was perfect, a 20-minute walk into Monmouthshire where there were a couple of pubs, a couple of restaurants', he says of the place in *Book of Opeth*. (To be clear, minor parts of the LP were worked on elsewhere, but for all intents and purposes, Rockfield Studios was where they literally lived, breathed, and birthed *Pale Communion*.)

With the right spot picked out, it was time to find the right person to assist Åkerfeldt as co-producer and lead engineer. Yet again, Farrow had the answer: Tom Dalgety, a proven master of his craft who – despite not really having a history with metal artists – was familiar with the studio and whose 'references were old references' in that 'he liked old records but had the know-how with new technology', as Åkerfeldt puts it. Indubitably, Dalgety was an integral part of the process, not the least of which is because he helped keep things on track in case Opeth got a little too inebriated. 'I was drunk all the time and so were the other guys. We bought insane amounts of red wine and beer and just sat there and enjoyed ourselves. It was like a part, but everybody was focused; it was just like a holiday, which is a paradox because we were working long, long hours but just drinking wine and having a good time', Åkerfeldt concedes in *Book of Opeth*.

Another reason why completing *Pale Communion* was such a positive experience is that they'd rehearsed a lot beforehand and recorded it in less than fourteen days (which was possible in part because they'd used digital

technology instead of tape). 'Everybody knew their stuff really well before we
went into the studio – I don't think the band had been that efficient before',
Åkesson reflects. In particular, Axenrot and Méndez worked on their parts
together in Barcelona – where Méndez also resides – for about two weeks
beforehand and then laid down their layers live so that everything else could
be tallied on top afterwards (just as they'd done on *Heritage*).

Really, the only complication came from the studio's Hammond organ
breaking down after 'someone who had been recording before [them]
dropped it' (according to Svalberg in *Book of Opeth*), forcing them to
return to Atlantis Studios for a little bit to get those parts done. Fortunately,
Svalberg had an easy time knocking out his contributions, and he was even
able to come up with 'several parts' that weren't contained in Åkerfeldt's
demos. That setback – as well as a few strange occurrences regarding
ghostly sights and sounds that harkened back to the recording of *Still Life* –
notwithstanding, the group had a superb time making the record. 'I would
say it was probably my best recording experience because the band was in
such great shape and everybody was happy with the songs. We were on fire,
to be honest; it was magical', Åkerfeldt contemplates.

Oddly enough, it was the album title that ended up being the most elusive
element. Originally, the sequence was going to be called *Nux Vomica*, but
an embarrassing realisation – recounted in a 2014 video interview with
Roadrunner Records – convinced Åkerfeldt to reconsider. As the story goes, he
liked its symbolism (the term refers to 'a medicine for people who are ill-willed
and overly sensitive to light and sound. And irate people who get irritated
quickly and are searching for fights'); however, he soon learned that 'the
side effects ... [involve] erection problems and constipation'. He continues:
'I figured that's gonna be the first question in interviews and I thought it was
maybe not a good title after all'. Eventually, he confessed to *The Pit*, he basically
'came up' with *Pale Communion* as 'something that tied the lyrical concept
between the songs together' (like 'a form of diary' rather than narratively) and
'sounded cool and looked good on paper'.

Logically, Travis Smith was brought back to work with Åkerfeldt on the
album's artwork; although its three central portraits are evocative and lovely –
they're meant to represent 'a story through life' and *not* act as an homage to
ELP's *Pictures at an Exhibition*, Åkerfeldt clarified to *Invisible Oranges* – it's
the Latin text beneath them that's even more eye-catching. The left painting
quotes 17th-century Swedish statesman Axel Oxenstierna ('Don't you know,
my son, with how little wisdom the world is governed?'); the middle picture
quotes ancient Roman-African playwright Publius Terentius Afer ('In these
days friends are won through flattery, the truth gives birth to hate'); and the
right panel quotes ancient Roman poet Marcus Valerius Martialis ('He grieves
truly who grieves without a witness'). It's unknown why the pair chose these
specific phrases, but it's easy enough to presume connections between their
sentiments and Åkerfeldt's songwriting.

As for special editions, the grandest assemblage is the limited-edition deluxe box set that comes in a 7' foil-stamped double slipcase and comes with three 7' records (for 'Cusp of 'Eternity' and two bonus tunes – 'Solitude' and 'Var Kommer Barnen In' – both of which were recorded live at Stockholm Sodra Teatern in April 2012). There are also CD and Blu-ray (5.1 mix) versions of *Pale Communion* in the same gatefold jacket; a slim booklet with lyrics and credits, and a download code for all of the songs (including the two extras). It's a must-own package for fans.

Disappointingly, the release of *Pale Communion* was pushed back two months, from 17 June to 26 August. In an official statement, Åkerfeldt confirmed the delay, explaining that 'several circumstances prevented the band from delivering essential tools to Roadrunner in time' that were 'needed to set up the album release properly'. (In his *Stereogum* piece, Norton speculates that the postponement arose from 'the band's brilliant-but-unpredictable frontman [being] too consumed with writing and recording new music to address such details as album art and promotional stills'.) Therefore, the group and the label 'mutually decide[d]' to resolve the 'schedule conflicts' by moving it to the end of summer. Happily, many Opeth devotees (professional writers and casual listeners alike) felt that it was undoubtedly worth the wait.

Once the LP finally hit store shelves, Méndez mentions in *Book of Opeth*, 'the reaction ... was easier on [Opeth] than it was after *Heritage* ... it was as if [fans] understood the new sound and they realised it wasn't going to change'. Indeed, *Pale Communion* sold as well – if not better in a few territories – than its immediate predecessors, and it earned a lot of love from outlets such as *Classic Rock Magazine*, *Alternative Press*, *Record Collector*, and *Kerrang!* (Yes, other key publications – namely, *Pitchfork* and *Revolver* – were far more mocking, but the majority of write-ups embraced it.) Writing for *AllMusic*, Thom Jurek correctly concludes: 'Though they readily display numerous musical influences here, ultimately Opeth sound like no one but themselves. This set is a massive leap forward, not only in terms of style but also in its instrumental and performance acumen; it is nearly unlimited in its creativity'.

The ensuing touring cycle was a huge deal not just because of *Pale Communion*, but also because it commemorated the tenth anniversary of *Ghost Reveries* and the twenty-fifth anniversary of Opeth. Intermittently, they were on the road from June 2014 to November 2015, stopping by Download Festival, Hellfest, Getaway Rock Festival, the Sweden Rock Festival, Bloodstock Festival, and both the Wacken and Vagos Open Air festivals as they touched down all over the world (such as in Poland, Italy, Prague, Austria, Germany, England, France, Spain, Scotland, Greece, Japan, and North America). Along the way, they shared the stage with metal titans like Alcest, Black Sabbath, Rob Zombie, Avenged Sevenfold, Within Temptation, Soilwork, Caligula's Horse, Gojira, and In Flames. Sensibly, they prioritised *Pale Communion* for most of their live trek, with later concerts showcasing *Ghost Reveries* in its entirety alongside a career-spanning set of songs.

Prior to all of that, though, Åkerfeldt received further validation for how far Opeth had come by being asked to curate – and appear at – Roadburn 2014 (which was held that April in the Netherlands). In March 2014, he chatted with *Metal Injection* co-founder Robert Pasbani and broke down his process for putting it together:

> They basically just gave me a budget and I had an open choice of what type of bands I wanted to pursue. It was a bit of a headache. I've never done anything like that before, you know, reaching out to bands and offering money. It was fun; my tastes are a bit different than the 'normal' Roadburn punter. It'll be an invasion of old guys. I went for some of the bands that I thought could fit the bill anyway, like Magma from France. They're intense.

In summation, the event featured over three dozen more acts, including Candlemass, Änglagård, Comus, Elephant 9, Napalm Death, Yob, The Vintage Caravan, Loop, and Crowbar.

Speaking of Opeth's legacy at this point (in *Book of Opeth*), Farrow rightly claims: 'They kind of downplay how good they are musically, and also, as a person, Mike's definitely very down to earth, very friendly, and he doesn't have a sense of entitlement whatsoever ... Opeth are so into it, they rehearse every day and the passion is there for the music'. Similarly, Steven Wilson – who, unsurprisingly, came back to help with *Pale Communion* – reckons: 'The important thing is that you are constantly fascinated by what [musicians] will do next, and you get that with Opeth's records'. Actually, Wilson admits, Åkerfeldt is the only person with whom he kind of feels an artistic jealousy. He rationalises: 'Every time I hear what he's done, it feels like he's raised the bar and I have to go away and try and do something to match it. I love him as a friend and completely respect him, and we push each other in a very good way. There's almost a competition there to keep raising the bar, and he's done that again with *Pale Communion*'.

Internally, both the newest and oldest members of Opeth are eager to dig into why they've endured for so long. Svalberg raves: 'There are many reasons for the band's continued success. For me, the key point is the amount [and variety] of emotion in the music ... I have to pinch myself sometimes when I think about how lucky I am to be involved in this music, and I think I could go on playing it forever'. As for Åkerfeldt, he's just as enthused: 'I never want to quit playing music, and I'm currently playing music with four other guys who I admire and I love – and they're friends of mine and they're fantastic musicians and they're into the music that I'm writing, so why the hell should I stop playing with these guys?'. That said, he's also grounded and earnest about whether or not he's happy with Opeth's current popularity:

> I would love for us to get some type of a Rush status, to eventually be one of those bands who never rely on singles, never had radio play and videos but to

still sell out gigs whenever we come to town; play a nice big venue with lots of people there. I wouldn't mind staying at this level where we are now forever, that's fine too. I never had any aspirations to become the biggest band on the planet, I just want to have fun and keep being creative.

If any Opeth studio collection deserved to propel them further into the mainstream spotlight – and if any collection demonstrated a wonderful fusion of imagination and thrill – it's *Pale Communion*. It's truly the quintet's definitive exploration of this sort of sound, bursting with gripping hooks, effervescent craftsmanship, and ceaselessly inventive and dynamic elasticity. Sure, naysayers who refuse to accept Opeth's new direction on principle will always disparage it, but those who welcome the change will almost certainly find it flawless. Simply put, *Pale Communion* is a masterpiece that rivals *every* other Opeth record and ranks as one of the greatest albums of its kind and of its era.

'Eternal Rains Will Come' (Åkerfeldt)

It's covered in 1970s Italian prog rock flamboyance, which is one of many reasons why it's debatably the group's best opening track. The initial combination of spooky croons, diabolical yet measured keyboard strikes, sinister guitar licks, and rowdy rhythms is hypnotically dynamic and imaginative; frankly, it harnesses a level of vibrant spiritedness that was rarely, if ever, found on *Heritage*, and it does a great job of fully demonstrating what Svalberg can bring to the Opeth table.

Cleverly, that unruliness melts into a brief moment of relief – consisting of cyclical piano notes, synth overlays, and despondent guitar patterns – before picking back up to provide an overwhelmingly attractive prog/folk/jazz rock base for one of the most infectiously rewarding melodies Åkerfeldt has ever sung. His words (such as 'Eternal rains will come / We should say goodbye / And suffer on our own / As all our thoughts were wrong' and 'And when the flood comes to drown us / There is nothing we can do') allude to some sort of Biblical apocalypse, such as the story of Noah's ark or the *Book of Revelation*. The pathos in his voice, as well as the sheer splendour of the vocal harmonies, help sell the gravity of the situation, and the accentuated keyboard and acoustic guitar sweeps that complement each lyric are the cherries on top of an already exquisite sundae.

The creeping guitar solo that storms in around two-thirds of the way through is enchantingly woeful as well, and the peacefully nihilistic bridge that follows the second chorus ('Here it comes / Our death comes / And in my sleep / I can't forget') is a highly impactful divergence. The consequent instrumental flare-up – led by Svalberg – is an amazing display of their total devotion to their post-*Watershed* recipe, and just when you think it's over, the quintet return for a hasty postscript ('Reaching for the surface / I see you') that firmly puts the nail in the song's seductively destitute coffin. From start to finish, 'Eternal Rains Will Come' is incredible.

'Cusp of Eternity' (Åkerfeldt)

Arising out of its forebear's synthy ashes with ominously icy six-string oscillations, 'Cusp of Eternity' was released on 3 June 2014 as the only single from *Pale Communion*. (It was also made available as an iTunes pre-order bonus.) It's the most commercial and traditionally organised tune of the bunch, not to mention its most blatant bridge to *Sorceress'* comparatively accessible itinerary. Nonetheless, its place as the weakest part of the LP is really just a testament to the quality of what surrounds it since there's still plenty to like.

It marches along at a brisk pace, with entrancingly mechanical riffs and rhythms assisting Åkerfeldt's expressive narrative. The gothic roars and eerie effects encircling the verses are the real highlights here, and no matter how unlikely, it's fun to think that one of his lines – 'And she turns around to stare at a scene from her memory' – is meant as a nod to his friends in Dream Theater. The ghastly and extremely complex breakdowns halfway in and near the end, respectively, are cool touches, too, with the latter subtly – and unintentionally – foreshadowing the chorus of 2016's 'The Wilde Flowers'. Other than that, there's not much more to say about 'Cusp of Eternity'. It's fairly blunt and basic compared to the rest of the record, but it's still a considerably pleasing and appropriate inclusion.

'Moon Above, Sun Below' (Åkerfeldt)

'Moon Above, Sun Below' is basically a musical stew containing numerous portions of other songs that would've worked well as their own fully developed tracks. When pooled together, they serve as a dazzlingly condensed overview of every temperament and trick *Pale Communion* has to offer. Embarking with a malevolent drone, shifty syncopation, belligerent guitar work, and a key keyboard riff, Åkerfeldt sings accusatorially about the deceitful behaviour of his adversary before diving into the titular ritualistic chant. It's already a spellbindingly wicked environment, and he's never conveyed such gruffness with his clean vocals before. Anyone complaining about Opeth going 'soft' or 'safe' after *Watershed* need only hear this first segment to see how hellish they can still be.

A dense and forceful transition introduces regal acoustic arpeggios, mellow guitar lines, and angelically gloomy comprehensions (with heartbreaking harmonies): 'I'm always waiting for you before I sleep / There is no comfort in the distance that we keep'. Without warning, drums and synths kick in to take us to a new, more hostile phase fleshed out by a scorching guitar solo; then, multiple voices shout, 'Voices of despair is a familiar friendship / A society in your head holds the code of destruction' before another beautifully glum acoustic ballad takes over. It's reminiscent of the *Still Life* and *Blackwater Park* era, but with a modern Opeth sense of golden stylishness.

Otherworldly ambience and whispers shift the song onto more menacing terrain, with Svalberg's threatening keys and Axenrot's unbalanced percussion enveloping Åkerfeldt's vindictive echoes ('There is no help in the wake of our needs / There is no help to dispel the pain') and mediaeval blow-ups. It's concurrently foreboding, soothing, and wholly dramatic, as if listeners are engulfed in a smothering cacophony of ominous opulence. Its catastrophic finality is cemented once he defeatedly cries, 'Only circles on the water' as the arrangement prolongs its mesmeric devastation, leaving behind a piano-based coda as a sample of lingering solace. It's a bittersweet ending to what's unquestionably one of Opeth's most multifaceted, ambitious, and impressive compositions ever.

'Elysian Woes' (Åkerfeldt)
The title refers to distress and the afterlife, and it's a suitably dour yet heavenly journey that affords listeners a momentary reprieve after the intensity of the preceding tracks. The dual acoustic guitar motif that opens it is lovingly grief-stricken, as are Åkerfeldt's vulnerably sung feelings ('What is left when the morning comes / Is the memory of a future / And when my plight is done / There is nothing left to hold onto'). The high-pitched backing vocals and additional timbres intersect magnificently to yield an utterly breathtaking instrumental passage for the next two minutes or so. Eventually, acoustic guitar chords prompt more verses – aided by a dreamily celestial backdrop – that in turn make way for dissonant guitar notes and forsaken moans around Åkerfeldt's last decree: 'I don't want to bare my scars for you'. It's a stunning ode that, thankfully, is but the first of two harrowingly gentle gems on *Pale Communion*.

'Goblin' (Åkerfeldt)
Obviously, this one is majorly inspired by the 1970s Italian progressive rock band of the same name (so it would probably fit as the score for a Dario Argento movie). In the aforementioned *Stereogum* interview, Åkerfeldt explains: 'I've liked them for some time now. I came across them through record collecting ... I started buying the horror film soundtracks and pretty much loved everything. Their sound is like *Dirty Harry*. The musicianship is really good, and the songs are good – it's just cool'. He also reveals that 'Goblin' began 'as a jam on tour in North America for soundcheck. After a few days, people were humming the riffs in the corridors, and we'd just been jamming it. I figured I should finish it and we ended [up] with this tribute'.

That was a wise decision, given how delightfully quirky and exhilarating it became. Beginning with stilted guitar notes alongside jazzy keyboard patterns and percussion, it's instantly hip and captivating. The ways in which it detaches from that core set-up to both discover heartier flights of fancy and build momentum over already established themes and through-lines is continuously stimulating and intriguing, too, illustrating once more how energised, resourceful, and compatible the new line-up is. It's an expertly crafted slice of instrumental prog rock/jazz fusion.

'River' (Åkerfeldt)

In *Book of Opeth*, Åkerfeldt connects 'River' to the friendly folk luxuries of Crosby, Stills, Nash and Young, conceding that while he never 'deliberately wanted to make [Opeth] sound country', that's what happened here 'because of the harmony vocals'. He also links it to 'Harvest' because of the '¾ beats', and he cites it as one of his favourite tracks on *Pale Communion*. To his credit, it does seem like an idyllic sibling to the *Blackwater Park* ballad – at least at first – due to its hurriedly descending arpeggios, vigorously harmonious melody, and hospitable lyricism ('Show me a sign / Of the troubles in your heart / Spare me your lies / And tell me that you're mine'). It's some of the most blissful singing the band has ever recorded, and the corresponding musicianship – including the victorious guitar solo – is impeccably restrained and jovial.

That cheerfulness doesn't last long, though, as an unhappier movement appears and sees Svalberg's desolate chords augmenting Åkerfeldt's solemn declaration: 'In light of all things to come / Why do you despair? / Because when you have no one / No one would care / So don't care'. Afterwards, a melody that strongly evokes 'Godhead's Lament' from *Still Life* ('Thought I could not leave this place on this imminent day') is played by keyboard and acoustic guitar simultaneously prior to more succulent layers being added to another verse.

Startlingly, 'River' erupts into a boisterous jam full of eccentric polyphony; it's arguably the most zanily intricate section of the entire LP – particularly with all of the back-and-forth electric guitar trade-offs – and it's totally enthralling. Svalberg, Méndez, and Axenrot maintain order as much as possible as Åkerfeldt and Åkesson do battle with classic rock panache; according to Åkerfeldt, people told him that it 'sounded a bit ... like Dire Straits', and they're not wrong. Finally, the band unites for a collaborative blitz that's tantalisingly technical and erratic, dispelling temporarily for Åkerfeldt's spectral proclamation ('Can't see / Can't feel / You run / I long') before resuming with extra gusto. It's an exceptionally fervent and meticulous climax to another outstanding song.

'Voice of Treason' (Åkerfeldt)

Ghostly bells and bellows pre-empt its thunderously mystical personality, which – because of its celebratory strings and rhythms, and in the wake of 'Atonement' from *Ghost Reveries* – kind of comes across like Opeth's second take on Led Zeppelin's 'Kashmir'. The synchronisation of rock music and orchestration also recalls The Moody Blues' *Days of Future Passed*, and it shrouds Åkerfeldt's relatively simple – yet still commanding – melodies remarkably well.

Before long, a peculiar keyboard structure plays over acoustic guitar strums and other potent textures, signalling an abrupt and affective musical redesign as Åkerfeldt yells: 'Have you ever had the feeling / Of a sorrow inside?' Knowing

111

what Åkerfeldt was going through and thinking about during this time makes it wholeheartedly authentic, and the shift from that fury into the frailty of the last moments (when he dejectedly asks, 'Have you given up? Is winter hiding in your heart?' over subdued electric piano chords) is emotionally crushing. Of course, the sudden swelling of strings afterwards is an enticing addendum as well, nurturing anticipation for what's ...

'Faith in Others' (Åkerfeldt)

Indisputably among the group's most splendidly agonising pieces, 'Faith in Others'. It's Åkerfeldt's other favourite track from the record, and in *Book of Opeth*, he spells out how it originated from him 'fooling around with the synthetic strings' on his computer: 'I was just testing out to see if they even sounded real and, of course, it didn't sound like real strings, but through testing, I had this arrangement – I had the kind of chord structure for what was going to end up as the song'.

It's unshakeable proof that some of the most noteworthy music of all time can be born out of happy accidents. The starting blend of remorseful drumming, blossoming strings, and imitated woodwinds alone is profoundly poignant, almost overpowering the listener with its prospering heartache. Likewise, Åkerfeldt's upset remarks – which are modified to sound like he's a spirit, or perhaps like he's bringing back *Deliverance*'s 'telephone' or 'underwater' effect – are equally painful. Next, it all vanishes so that Svalberg's plaintive piano chords and other delicately sympathetic embellishments can encourage a tenderer recognition: 'A written decree of our loss / And we carried no faith in the cross / And the cold years are coming / For the victims of a longing'. It's a chillingly touching segment that masterfully moves (via a cosy guitar lick) into suffocating instrumental anguish and bereaved verbal hums before another set of verses.

Piano notes and plucked acoustic guitar intervals accompany Åkerfeldt's emotionally exhausted assertions ('Asleep in the rain / A child once again / And the ghost in my head / Has forgiven me / Lifted his curse upon me'). Following an overflow of interlocking guitar work and piano complements that conjure the ending of 'Burden' from *Watershed*, 'Faith in Others' fades away with an extra dose of falsetto croons and classical misfortune. It's a spectacular finale to a virtually faultless album.

Bonuses

Aside from all of its other goodies, the real draw of the deluxe box set is the presence of the two live cover songs: 'Solitude' and 'Var Kommer Barnen In'. The first came from Black Sabbath's third studio sequence, 1971's *Master of Reality*; as expected, Opeth's version essentially emulates the original as closely as possible when it comes to its classily cheerless pacing, singing, and timbres, with the only real differences being a bit more fancy guitar work throughout and a bit less of Black Sabbath's passive spirituality.

Unsurprisingly, 'Var Kommer Barnen In' – taken from Swedish pop/rock troupe Hansson de Wolfe United's second LP, 1981's *Existens-maximum* – falls into the same category. It's just as patient, brooding, and dynamic, but with a slight emphasis on condensed gruffness over the original's breezier vibe and organic production. In other words, Opeth's rendition will appeal more to hard rock and metal fans, while Hansson de Wolfe United's will appease fans of synth rock and world music. Neither track is vital, but both are agreeably accurate yet idiosyncratic homages.

Sorceress (2016)

Personnel:

Mikael Åkerfeldt: vocals, acoustic and electric guitars

Fredrik Åkesson: acoustic and electric guitars, backing vocals

Martin Axenrot: drums, percussion

Martin Méndez: bass

Joakim Svalberg: Hammond C3 Organ, Mellotron, Fender Rhodes 88, Harpsichord, Grand piano, Moog synthesizer, percussion, backing vocals

Additional Personnel:

Will Malone: string arrangements

Pascale Marie Vickery: spoken words on 'Persephone' and 'Persephone (Slight Return)'

Travis Smith: artwork

Tom Dalgety: engineer, mixing

Produced at Rockfield Studios in Monmouth, Wales, RAK Studios in Stockholm, Sweden, Junkmail Studios in Stockholm, Sweden, Psalms Studios in Bath, England, May 2016 by Mikael Åkerfeldt and Tom Dalgety.

Release date: 30 September 2016.

Highest chart places: UK: 11, USA: 24

Running time: 56:35

Current edition: 2020 Nuclear Blast 2x clear/green/red/yellow/blue splatter German vinyl limited edition reissue

Although *Pale Communion* faced opposition from some people, it was generally more welcomed than *Heritage*, and it's easy to see why. Beyond being a vastly superior album, it was a firm doubling down of the quintet's reworked vision. Therefore, cynics knew that no matter how they felt about it, *this* was what Åkerfeldt and company want to do (so they could either get on board or leave the Opeth camp; there's no room for uncertainty). As such, the band was even more self-assured in creating *Sorceress*, an album that – in *Book of Opeth* – Åkesson keenly surmises 'stands on its own' despite being 'connected stylistically' to its two precursors as a part of 'a new era'. Indeed, this third entry in Opeth's contemporary canon is fundamentally a hodgepodge of *Pale Communion*'s primed durability and *Heritage*'s experimental bizarreness. It doesn't reach the highs of the former, but it also doesn't succumb to the lows of the latter; instead, it sits securely in-between them as a mostly excellent endeavour that's marginally held back by some formulaic preferences and middling moments.

As usual, Opeth stumbled upon some interesting developments in the lead-up to *Sorceress*. Namely, their contract with Roadrunner Records had expired, so they decided to sign a licensing deal with Nuclear Blast – who tried to get them a decade prior, before *Ghost Reveries* came out – *and* start their own imprint, Moderbolaget (which translates to 'Mother label'). 'We are working almost identically to how we worked with the record labels before, when we were under a record contract', Åkerfeldt explained to *Billboard*'s Christa Titus in September 2016. They'd been thinking about starting one for years, he later told *Prog Sphere*, as a way to potentially 'do side projects or solo projects, or reissues of [their] own records, or even [sign] up other bands in the future'. To date, however, Moderbolaget has only issued other Opeth collections, including *In Cauda Venenum* and *Garden of the Titans*.

To honour their twenty-fifth anniversary, Opeth partnered with Northern Monk Brew Co. to launch two kinds of beer: the staggeringly alcoholic 'XXV Anniversary Imperial Stout' – limited to around 1,700 bottles – and the modestly intoxicating (and shrewdly titled) 'Communion Pale Ale'. Seeing as how dozens of other rock and metal artists have also created their own drinks, as well as much Opeth like to imbibe as they work, this collaboration was a no-brainer. The same can be said about *Deliverance* and *Damnation* finally being released together via a special box set. It featured new artwork from Travis Smith; new liner notes from Åkerfeldt and *PROG*'s Jerry Ewing; and new mixes from Steven Wilson (who handled *Damnation*) and Bruce Soord (who handled *Deliverance*).

Clearly, the band had their hands full with other activities between the end of 2014 and the start of 2016, yet they remained immensely focused on the follow-up to *Pale Communion* the whole time. In fact, Åkerfeldt wrote it in about six months – with no material being rejected – and intended it to be their most diverse batch of songs yet. Although it's undeniably tied to the two LPs that precede it musically, Åkerfeldt specifies in *Book of Opeth*, it's not linked thematically (nor is it a concept album in the traditional sense). He also doesn't view *Sorceress* as their conclusively best work: 'I don't think it's a better record than *Pale Communion* or the ones before it, [but] it's kind of the last one in a trilogy you could say'.

What *does* distinguish its subject matter, however, is that it's a 'happy record' penned in the aftermath of him suffering 'many years of ... personal issues' like 'divorce and a relationship that didn't work out'. He elaborates: 'I was really happy with everything in my life. It's not a happy-sounding record at all, but that's where I was, personally'. Méndez also noticed how the project 'kind of helped [Åkerfeldt]' and 'was good for him psychologically'. In his September 2016 conversation with *The Quietus'* Dan Franklin, Åkerfeldt confirms that none of his lyrics here are directly 'autobiographical in any way'; that said, he told *PROG*'s Polly Glass around the same time, they are 'mainly personal'. While he didn't intentionally write about his past troubles, they ended up tangentially influencing how he focused on 'the negative emotions you can get with a positive feeling like love: paranoia, insecurity, anger, jealously, hate even ... Love is like a mental disease, which everybody kind of wants to catch. It's crazy when you think about it'.

Åkerfeldt also leaned purposefully into his hard rock tendencies as he wrote, in part because he wanted to accommodate the rest of the group's strengths and preferences (especially Axenrot's). In an October 2016 chat with *Metal*

Injection's Riley Rowe, Åkesson praises the LP's heaviness, adding: 'I would say this one is in a way more direct. It's still quite an intricate album and has a lot of freaked out parts, but some of the songs are more easy to get into'. Nevertheless, Åkerfeldt makes clear in the above-mentioned *Prog Sphere* exposé, *Sorceress* expectedly 'jump[s] between genres a lot'. Obviously, he was also inspired by Jethro Tull releases like 1971's *Aqualung* and 1979's *Stormwatch*, as well as John Coltrane and the Mahavishnu Orchestra.

Despite 'The Wilde Flowers' being the first song written, it wasn't chosen as the opener because (as he remarks in *Book of Opeth*), Åkerfeldt had a very deliberate plan in mind for the sequencing: 'I wanted those naysayers who loved us in the past to check us out, even if it was to dismiss us again. I wanted them to stay with the record a bit longer'. So, he ensured that it 'starts off heavy and then ... goes strange in the middle and up to the end' in order to 'lure people in'. It's an effective strategy, for sure, as is bookending the set with succinct instrumentals – 'Persephone' and 'Persephone (Slight Return)', respectively – as he did with *Heritage*.

Naturally, they returned to Rockfield Studios and engineer/co-producer Tom Dalgety to give *Sorceress* the same kind of spark as *Pale Communion* (as well as record it in a comparably short amount of time: twelve days). Furthermore, Dalgety took over mixing duties from Steven Wilson (who, despite not being directly involved this time around, still impacted the LP in another significant way, as we'll see soon). Reflecting on Dalgety's additional role, Åkerfeldt said to *Prog Sphere*: 'We can speak freely, and he knows what we mean, you know, if we are looking for a specific sound ... it's very pleasant to work with him that way and we became good friends in the process'.

Outside of that – and alongside the hard rock nature of the arrangements – the only other notable aspect of *Sorceress*'s recording to point out is Åkerfeldt's growing comfort and adaptability in mirroring classic rock vocalists like Paul Rodgers and David Coverdale. 'You have to bear in mind that I never identified with being a singer. I never wanted to be a singer ... I know I won't arrive at a place where I feel I am as good as them, but it helps me to advance to work towards a goal musically that is completely out of my league. It really helps me to develop, I think', he confessed to Franklin. By all accounts, then, making *Sorceress* was a fast, fluid, and restorative exercise.

While the sounds of the sequence are definitely its greatest assets, the artwork is terrific, too. According to Titus, Åkerfeldt is a fan of Scottish hard rock ensemble Nazareth – whose 1973's LP, *Loud 'n' Proud*, features a peacock – yet 'he's not sure why a picture of the bird sitting on a mound of carnage popped into his head long before he started writing *Sorceress*'. Even so, the end result fulfilled two desires at once: his need for something 'beautiful and disgusting at the same time' and his need for 'collective narcissism' in likening Opeth to 'this beautiful peacock ... laying everything to waste'.

Predictably, they released a special box set of the LP that contained a two-CD digipak with bonus tracks, a double vinyl set of all the material (coloured rosewood) with a gatefold cover, a multichannel DVD of the proper album, a 12' signed photo card, a 12' foldout poster, and parchment paper. There was also a pink vinyl version whose proceeds were donated to Gilda's Club NYC, a charity founded in honour of late comedian Gilda Rudner (who passed away from ovarian cancer in 1989). Other vinyl options included blue, orange, and mint pearl colour variants.

In terms of commercial sales and critical reviews, *Sorceress* fared about as well as *Pale Communion*, with *The Guardian, Kerrang!, PopMatters, Exclaim!*, and *Metal Injection* singing its praises. Even more gratifyingly (at least to Åkerfeldt), fans really began warming up to their latest aesthetic. When asked by *Rolling Stone*'s Steve Smith if their devotees are showing enthusiasm for the new material during concerts, Åkerfeldt answers, 'I think so ... it seems like people are starting to accept what we're doing now, and possibly even starting to like it'. Similarly, he tells *Prog Sphere*: 'There's people yelling out for the new songs when we play, which is [the] first time that has ever happened when we put out a new record, and been touring for the new record'.

The *Sorceress* touring cycle – where they played and/or co-headlined alongside The Gentle Storm, Caligula's Horse, Magma, iamthemorning, Trivium, Anathema, The Sword, and many other acts at events such as Be Prog! My Friend 2016, Caroline Rebellion 2017, and Download Festival 2017 – was perhaps their biggest one yet. As validating as that was, however, some members were really starting to feel fatigued from the hustle and bustle of continuous live performance. 'It's a slightly different set-up now, you don't want to burn yourself out or squeeze everything out of your fans either. You want to keep them hungry and be sure you're not burning the candle at both ends', Åkesson ponders in *Book of Opeth*. Conversing with *Ghost Cult Magazine* in October 2016, Åkerfeldt is even more honest about such gripes: 'I'm not going to lie, there are a lot of days when I don't want to be on tour. It's just a fact. It sounds bad, but it's the truth. I miss my kids. I miss my girlfriend. I miss that part of my life while on the road, and those are the most important things in life to me'. Nonetheless, he's almost always rejuvenated once he steps out on stage and sees the eager crowds ready to rock out to the band's every note and word.

Among the myriad performances were three special shows – at Radio City Music Hall in New York City, the Sydney Opera House in Australia, and the SSE Wembley Arena in London – at which Opeth once again treated attendees to two separate sets. The first was compiled from a mixture of older and newer stuff, while the second exclusively highlighted *Damnation* and *Deliverance*. It was also during this time (specifically, on 11 May 2017) that they appeared at Red Rocks Amphitheatre in Colorado to record what would become their newest concert film, 2018's *Garden of the Titans*. They were accompanied by Gojira and The Devin Townsend Project, and in *Book of Opeth*, Åkerfeldt reflects that he 'wasn't so happy with the show' because the freezing temperature made it 'really difficult for us to play'. To his astonishment, though, he found that it sounded and looked 'great' when he finally found the nerve to look over what was captured.

As any Townsend fan knows, the Canadian virtuoso is enormously outgoing and charming on stage, so it's no real shock to learn that some of his charisma and courage rubbed off on Åkerfeldt several years prior. As Åkerfeldt reminiscences with Franklin, he and Townsend played together during the 2005 Sounds of the Underground tour and became close after discovering that they had so much in common. Even so, Åkerfeldt admits to envying how Townsend could be so extroverted and hilarious and fearless on stage and then become so pensive and modest afterwards:

> He transformed, yet he didn't, if you know what I mean ... I never knew how to talk to a crowd before ... But after meeting Devin, I gradually started talking about what we had for dinner or whatever it was ... not only did the crowd seem to like it but I relaxed once I talked to them like they were friends. It was very helpful to me as a frontman ... That really helped me to calm down and ultimately perform better. And since then, I'm not as nervous when I go onstage, or for a few minutes I'm nervous, but after the first time, I say something to the crowd, I calm down.

Undoubtedly, Åkerfeldt's spontaneous banter has since become a beloved staple of Opeth concerts, and the *Sorceress* tour greatly benefited from it. Regarding the album itself, again, it is a minor step down from its predecessor, but that was almost guaranteed to be the case considering how phenomenal *Pale Communion* turned out. (In other words, it was practically impossible to make such exquisite lightning strike twice.) In every way, *Sorceress* is the natural and highly satisfying continuation of their post-*Watershed* trajectory, with its mightiest inclusions ranking alongside Opeth's top-tier creations. Even at its most lacklustre, clichéd, and snug, it's still very good, and thankfully, it would be bested by the band's more temptingly ghoulish and unified last 'observation' (for now), *In Cauda Venenum*.

'Persephone' (Åkerfeldt)

It's titled after the daughter of Zeus, who became the wife of Hades and the queen of the Underworld. Åkerfeldt claims (in his talk with Franklin) that he got the name from a track off Kula Shaker's 2007 LP, *Strangefolk*, adding, 'I wasn't too into Greek mythology or anything like that, so I had to look it up. It stuck in my head that it was a nice little story, and it could make this album feel like a concept record, framing it the way I did with the intro and the outro. The reason being that some of the lyrical content dealt with tragic love, in a way'.

Certainly, the concise Spanish guitar instrumental prelude is enjoyably sentimental and tasteful but also rather simple and repetitive. It works well enough for establishing a mood, though, and Svalberg's accompaniment is adequately impactful. Lastly, Pascale Marie Vickery's speech – 'A beloved name inside my heart / A fleeting glance became the start / A missing word I am still awaiting / A wretched deception, I am creating' – is wistfully cryptic, elegant, and astutely predictive of *Sorceress*' ninth tune.

'Sorceress' (Åkerfeldt)
In an October 2016 video interview for Nuclear Blast Records, Åkerfeldt rightfully forecasts that *Sorceress*' first single 'sounds American and it'll go down well in America' because he has 'an American accent [on it] ... which was not intentional. Singing with a deeper voice'. Likewise, he deduces (in his August 2016 track by track guide with *Metal Hammer*'s Dom Lawson) that it's 'very heavy, almost stupid meat and potatoes. I think it sounds like you're about to be beaten up'.

That is an apt assessment of the piece since it's more or less a groovy, psychedelic bit of grisly hard rock excess. There are some fusion elements at the start, too, with the bass and electric guitar riding the same swaggering riffs around the shuffling percussion. It's sufficiently appealing but also kind of generic and rudimentary, and that only becomes truer once Opeth settle into their mechanically scratchy verses. It's performed well and holds your attention, but that's about it. Luckily, the midsection juxtaposition of frail guitar arpeggios and irregular outbursts is a tad more enticing, as is the subsequent segment ('Empty vessel / Drained of hope'). The multidimensional conclusion (that's 'very influenced by Abba') is desirable, too, but it doesn't save 'Sorceress' from being merely decent overall.

'The Wilde Flowers' (Åkerfeldt)
Regrettably, the album's third single – initially known as 'Jethro One' and 'nicked from an Aerosmith song ... called 'Mia'', according to Åkerfeldt – is only somewhat less average because it follows an analogously standard classic rock/metal path. It's named after a short-lived 1960s Canterbury band whose members went on to form pioneering acts such as Camel, Caravan, and Soft Machine. Expectedly, then, some of that mellow charm is here, but so is an abundance of run-of-the-mill aggression.

The stiff first few minutes are definitely demanding from a technical standpoint (with some engaging keyboard curiosities fluttering around), yet they also feel like something the quintet could've written and recorded in their sleep. That said, the vocal harmonies and hallucinogenic jamming are powerful attributes, and the restful detour about two-thirds of the way through – with its ornamental harp strums and falsetto warbles – is incontestably lovely. Of course, it quickly explodes into a frenzied finale that can't help but make you smile despite its conventionality.

'Will O the Wisp' (Åkerfeldt)
This second single from *Sorceress* was overtly influenced by Jethro Tull's 'Dun Ringill', which Åkerfeldt first heard when Steven Wilson insisted that he check

out 1979's *Stormwatch*. Upon hearing it, he decided that he 'wanted to do a song with [his] capo really high' to make 'the guitar sound glittery' and complement his 'simple, catchy vocal melody'. (He also states that 'Will O the Wisp' has a 'positive vibe to it, but the lyrics are really, really dark'.)

It's easily among Opeth's greatest acoustic dirges, with extremely touching chord progressions, melancholic synths, and concerned syncopation aiding Åkerfeldt's demoralised verses. He sings with riveting conviction as well, delivering each lyric with richly cautionary warmth to enhance the composition's bucolic gravitas. It culminates in a gorgeous post-chorus – 'And you can never find the satisfaction / When you can't outgrow your false distractions' – and some bluesy guitar solos that bolster the tune's peerless grandeur.

'Chrysalis' (Åkerfeldt)

Originally called 'Shuffle', it's another 'meat and potatoes heavy rock song' – as Åkerfeldt appropriately puts it – whose early playful bombast evokes *Ghost Reveries* and *Watershed*. Both Akesson and Svalberg decorate the landscape with zesty theatrics and duelling solos as Méndez and Axenrot equally play their asses off (to put it crudely). The chorus is exceedingly hooky and luscious, too. Those delights notwithstanding, it's the eventual transition into the song's quieter movement that's absolutely beguiling. Seamlessly, Opeth's showy panic dissipates into a steady beat, a dreary guitar solo, and woeful acoustic guitar arpeggios as Åkerfeldt's unveils his pure, multilayered murmurs: 'Leave it all behind you / There is comfort in giving up'. It's surely *Sorceress*' superlative moment and one of Opeth's finest passages so far.

'Sorceress 2' (Åkerfeldt)

It's intentionally a 'very nice, calm, [and] fragile piece of music' for which Åkerfeldt had 'no aspirations to have the drums kick in or anything like that'. Unfortunately, that plainness is the track's biggest detriment. Yes, it's eloquently sung and played – the acoustic fingerpicking and soulful Mellotron cascades go together well, and the lyrical couplets are poetically enigmatic – but there's just not much to latch onto in any area (or much more to say about it). Honestly, it's one of Opeth's most inoffensively disposable efforts.

'The Seventh Sojourn' (Åkerfeldt)

Gratefully, *Sorceress* is redeemed by this titular tribute (which was nicknamed 'Jethro Two') to The Moody Blues' eighth studio record. It's scored by Will Malone (Black Sabbath, Iron Maiden, Todd Rundgren), whom Åkerfeldt initially emailed with another goal (as he explained to *Prog Sphere*): '[T]he intention was, in the beginning, to ask him about his solo records basically. But I felt a bit stupid doing that, so I kinda threw it in if he would be interested in scoring strings for a song. And at the time, I didn't even have the song, I was just wondering if he would be interested in working with us. And he said yes'.

Furthermore, the tune's most distinctive characteristic – its Eastern qualities – was 'inspired by the band Family', Åkerfeldt affirmed to Lawson. 'They have a song on their [*Family*] *Entertainment* record called 'Summer '67' ... so I wanted to do something like that', he boasted.

The outcome is a dignified and dramatic marriage between two mindsets, as its stately palette and raga posture contrast well with the group's emblematic melodic unease. Put another way, it's easy to imagine that 'The Seventh Sojourn' is really a customarily Asian adaption of an already existing Opeth piece (making you wish that they'd employ other outside cultural aesthetics into their usual strange brews). As for the saintly addendum, it seems deviously incongruous at first, but it actually fits ingeniously with the previous atmosphere.

'Strange Brew' (Åkerfeldt, Åkesson)

'That song was a long time in the making' – Åkerfeldt mused with Franklin – because it involved Akesson coming up with 'the verse – that soft thing that starts the song' and then Åkerfeldt 'dismantling his demo' and building it back up with 'this [crazy] keyboard lick'. All the while, he was conscious of how 'it's always a bit sensitive when you're working with something which somebody else wrote', and together (while speaking to Lawson), they compare it to Led Zeppelin, Mahavishnu Orchestra, and (obviously) Cream.

It's a fascinating musical alliance, with its sparsely threatening preliminary piano hymn neatly mutating – via cleanly contemplative guitar licks – into a fabulously sinful jazz fusion storm. Afterward, the instrumentation dies down to give Åkerfeldt's croaky croons ('There is a chasm between you and me / You have no face, no body, no words to speak') more attention, only to then pick back up with a blazing jam. The song becomes more riotously melodious prior to reprising the introductory meditation, which then leads into a last batch of caustic thoughts: 'A voice through the rain / Tells me I'm here / A glance from a veil / Brings me to tears'. All in all, it's one of the LP's most aspiringly sundry selections

'A Fleeting Glance' (Åkerfeldt)

It's a sunny and frolicsome – but also marginally serious – acoustic voyage that Åkerfeldt claims is 'one of [his] favourite' Opeth songs. He justly surmises: 'It's very British sounding. It reminds me of Queen and Porcupine Tree and Pink Floyd'. Frankly, it sounds like something that might accompany a feudal court jester as he performs for his royal overlords. Åkerfeldt's high-pitched assertions and harmonies are commanding yet quirky, and the harpsichord backing (a first for Opeth) intensifies that vivid oddness.

Soon, the rest of the team chimes in with befittingly leisurely rhythms, mannered keyboard chords, and terse guitar work that discerningly incites Åkerfeldt's fetching vocal counterpoints: 'A fleeting glance again (tells me everything) / Took a chance in vain (drown to a futile idea)'. On that note, both the singing and lyricism are tremendously sophisticated throughout the composition, and all the components work in concord to generate one of Opeth's most radiant choruses ('But it's fading away from my mind / There's another 'me' waiting behind'). The adjacent guitar solos are sensational as well, capping off one of the group's best tracks of the 2010s.

'Era' (Åkerfeldt)
This fourth and final single from *Sorceress* kicks off cleverly with a foretelling snippet of 'Persephone (Slight Return)' before booming keyboard notes and guitar riffs convert it into what Åkerfeldt deems 'a catchy '80s heavy metal song' that's 'really fucking difficult to play'. Indeed, it charges forward with pressing medieval haste, wasting no time dishing out urgently abrasive musicianship and distraught rhymes that recall the apocalyptic devastation of 'Eternal Rains Will Come'. Along the way, Svalberg implements a brief pattern that also relates to the album's epilogue, and central hook – 'The end of an era / One starts anew / You know the devil / He lives in you' – is irresistibly stylish. The remaining portion is briskly and dextrously alluring, too, with a piercing guitar solo that gets your adrenaline pumping.

Markus Hofko's music video (which was nominated for 'Video of the Year' at the 2017 Progressive Music Awards but lost to King Crimson's 'Heroes') appears to draw from Hayao Miyazaki's 2001 animated masterpiece, *Spirited Away*. In it, a boy is guided into the afterlife by a figure cloaked in black who wears a white mask. The duo walks along a divine desert until they find a passageway into an infernal wasteland dominated by fiendish creatures and abstract imagery. Eventually, they're surrounded by buried statues of the band – perhaps an homage to the poem 'Ozymandias' by Percy Bysshe Shelly – and the boy returns to the desert, where he puts on the mask. It's an imaginative representation, for sure.

'Persephone (Slight Return)' (Åkerfeldt)
The title is a blatant wink at Jimi Hendrix's 'Voodoo Child (Slight Return)', and Åkerfeldt clarifies that meant to signify how 'the sorceress has calmed down and stopped being vicious'. It emerges from the last percussive eruption of 'Era' and presents a movingly imperial piano outro underneath Vickery's concluding elegy, 'The years went by with disquieting grace / A past obsession sunk without a trace / I moved into winter and found my home / As my boiling blood had turned into chrome'. As with 'Marrow of the Earth' on *Heritage*, it grants *Sorceress* a greater sense of value and permanence.

Bonuses
Swankier editions of *Sorceress* come with two new songs: 'The Ward' and 'Spring MCMLXXIV'. Åkerfeldt professed to Lawson that Opeth 'had a little bit more fun with them, so to speak. They became a bit more experimental and it didn't matter so much what style they were'. Specifically, 'The Ward'

is a light and romantic ballad that 'glanc[es] over to jazz music and [has] a Uriah Heep type of chorus'. It has the quaint classiness of a 1960s lounge act or piano bar performance, too, with its calmingly introspective verses and six-string accentuations being offset by gutsy acoustic guitar thrums and wordless outcries that channel 'Era'. Conversely, 'Spring MCMLXXIV' (whose title *isn't* a nod to Åkerfeldt's birthday of 17 April 1974) is similarly easygoing and congenial but with a brawnier and spacier blues/folk foundation in the vein of Procol Harum, Hawkwind, and Traffic. Both inclusions – as well as the modestly beautified and/or slowed down renditions of 'Cusp of Eternity', 'Voice of Treason', and 'The Drapery Falls' that they recorded with the Plovdiv Philharmonic Orchestra in Bulgaria in September 2015 – are worthwhile but not essential.

In Cauda Venenum (2019)

Personnel:

Mikael Åkerfeldt: vocals, acoustic and electric guitars, ramblings, spoken words, string arrangements, mixing

Fredrik Åkesson: lead and rhythm guitars, backing vocals, whistles, coughs

Martin Axenrot: drums, percussion

Martin Méndez: bass

Joakim Svalberg: keyboards, backing vocals

Additional Personnel:

Dave Stewart: string arrangements

Alva Åkesson/Ahlberg: spoken words

Bruno K. Öijer: spoken words

Klara Rönnqvist Fors: spoken words

Melinda Åkerfeldt: spoken words

Mirjam Åkerfeldt: spoken words

Olof Palme: spoken words

Tora Ahlberg: spoken words

Travis Smith: artwork

Stefan Boman: engineer, effects, mixing

Tom Jondelius: studio assistant

Produced at Park Studios in Stockholm, Sweden, Junkmail Studios in Stockholm, Sweden, and Angel Studios in London, England, November 2018 – March 2019 by Mikael Åkerfeldt, Stefan Boman, and Dave Stewart.

Release date: 27 September 2019.

Highest chart places: UK: 13, USA: 59

Running time: 67:57

Current edition: 2021 Northeast Steel Industry 2x blue/white swirl Japanese vinyl limited edition

Because *In Cauda Venenum* is the most recent Opeth album – fashioned without any significant band drama or developments – there's less to discuss regarding its creation or lasting impact. By and large, it picks up where *Sorceress* left off musically, so it's very much the fourth chapter of the group's current stylistic phase. Having said that, it is deliberately baroque, perverse, and distinguishing, with Åkerfeldt keeping his creative purposes and processes closer to the chest. Consequently, it's a more invitingly mysterious and perpetually succulent affair in several ways, and the fact that it prompted Åkerfeldt to step outside of his comfort zone and record entirely in Swedish (for the first time) is probably its standout feat. If not for *Pale Communion*, *In Cauda Venenum* would unmistakably be Opeth's best work since *Watershed* over a decade earlier.

In *Book of Opeth*, Åkesson comments: 'There's something so magical about *In Cauda Venenum*. We were fully in control of our powers in channelling Mikael's writing ... The goal was to make an epic album and every song had to be as epic as possible'. While Åkerfeldt had always been in charge of the band's direction, he wrote *Sorceress* with the other members' musical preferences in mind. That wasn't really the case here, as he prioritised his own interests above all else. 'I got to write music that I felt was important. For *Sorceress* – which is a really good record – I felt I catered to what the other guys ... wanted ... That was cool, but I didn't want any kind of basic heavy metal on this record. I wanted something more elaborate [and] complex without sounding complex. I wanted it to be sing-along and melodic, but not gimmicky', he explains in the official press release.

In fact, he was so determined to devote his entire attention to writing that he made sure Opeth took a sabbatical from playing live following the last concert cycle. While the rest of the gang thought he was just spending time with his family and relaxing, he started working on the record in secret around the end of 2017. In a formal video interview with Nuclear Blast Records, he breaks down how the process kind of kicked off accidentally, citing his unexpected urge to write in Swedish (which arose as he was driving his kids to school one morning) as the catalyst:

We'd just come off a tour for the *Sorceress* record and I was planning on taking a long break. I don't know why I went down to the studio; usually, I'd leave it and not go there until I'm really working on a record or new music. I'm not there between tours. I'm there all the time when I'm writing and then I'm gone, pretty much. I didn't really start until I came up with the idea of doing a record in Swedish. I didn't necessarily feel that it was a new way for me to have my lyrics come across – I didn't particularly think about the lyrics. It was just the idea of Swedish lyrics that I could write music to. From then until autumn of 2018, I wrote most of the material and recorded demos in my own studio. I made a good-sounding demo and sequenced them in the right order. I couldn't stop writing, so I had more songs than we could fit on the record. Thirteen songs, I think.

Despite questioning whether or not fans would respond well to *In Cauda Venenum* being in Swedish – which is why he eventually chose to offer an English alternative even though he sees the Swedish option as the 'main' version – he stuck to his guns and proceeded without really checking to see what his bandmates thought. For him, his native language simply allowed him to sing indirectly or vaguely about isolation, politics, and mental health in a more 'contemporary' and blunt way, as well as prevented him from 'hid[ing] behind beautiful words' like he'd done in the past.

Suddenly re-energised by the new course of action, he still held to tradition by composing the music *before* any official lyrics. By the end, he'd written more material than ever before, resulting in at least three extra tracks (only one of which, 'Cirkelns Riktning', was ever released as far as I can tell). In terms of inspirations and objectives, Åkerfeldt told *Flood Magazine*'s Dan

Epstein, he looked to Queen, Kate Bush, Mozart, and Scott Walker. He expounds:

> I went down to my home studio to restring a guitar, and I ended up starting to write music. And I had, quite quickly, some nice ideas, and I was having such a good time that I just continued. But I didn't really tell anyone until I was about halfway through; I didn't want management to go, 'Ooh, you have a new one on the way? OK, let's start booking dates for the studio and the tour and the press trip!' I didn't want that. I just wanted to sit there and have a good time. So, I waited until I thought, 'OK, I want to record this', and then I told management, and we started looking at studios.

Originally, they planned to go with producer/engineer David Castillo at Ghost Ward Recordings. However, as mentioned in the press release, a dinner conversation with Ghost mastermind Tobias Forge led to Åkerfeldt seeking out Park Studios (which is only '15 minutes' from where he lives) instead. So, he 'called up Stefan [Boman]', who was more than happy to invite the group over and oversee production. Åkerfeldt mentions that Boman's work with pop bands – expressly, 1990s shoegaze troupe Kent – also played a part in his choice. 'I like to work with people from a different genre; otherwise, you stay in your comfort zone, and it'll end up sounding comfortable. I wanted uncomfortable a little bit, and a new input'. Obviously, they struck up a lucrative alliance since *In Cauda Venenum* is certainly more strange, sumptuous, opaque, and emotive than *Sorceress*.

Åkesson reveals in *Book of Opeth* that he dealt with 'several chest pains' and 'a small heart infraction' amidst the recording process. The group didn't want to 'talk about it at the time, during promotion, because [they] didn't want it to take over'. Happily, he was able to go to the hospital and get stents put in before it became too severe. 'It was seriously scary, man, but it does run in my family and I guess life on the road might have something to do with it, too', he ponders. Since then, he's 'changed' [his] lifestyle' and put in extra effort to take better care of himself.

Regarding the title and imagery of *In Cauda Venenum*, Åkerfeldt knew early on that he 'wanted a Latin title ... that would work for both versions'. After trying to adapt many of his own phrases to the language (to no avail), he stumbled upon the term 'In Cauda Venenum' – roughly translated to 'The Poison is in the Tail' – and knew that he'd found the right moniker. 'It means 'There's a nasty or unpleasant surprise at the end', which I liked, and it connected with the artwork that we already had. Before I came up with the title, we had a band drawing where the five of us have our heads on a scorpion tail. It's quite a coincidence', he muses in the Nuclear Blast Records discussion.

Going further into he and Travis Smith's visual designs, Åkerfeldt states that the 'original plan was to have a big yard with a castle in the centre and then a garden with trees cut like [Opeth]'. That didn't pan out, so the pair settled on 'a big house with the five windows' (each one displaying an Opeth member) to embody their 'safe place' as a 'sanctuary for ... old heavy metal guys'. They even managed to bring manager Andy Farrow in as the 'little pissing fountain boy' – which Farrow loved – and Åkerfeldt is particularly proud of how the artwork stretches out to expose that the house is 'actually standing on the tongue of a demon' that's 'ready to swallow' the quintet.

Justifiably, many publications showered the record with acclaim, including *Consequence of Sound*, *NME*, *PopMatters*, and *The Quietus*. Famously, *Wall of Sound* gave it a perfect score, arguing that it's 'a masterclass in musical composition' and 'perhaps the best album' they've made since *Ghost Reveries*. At the end of 2019, *Loudwire*, *Rolling Stone*, and several *Metal Hammer* writers named it one of the best metal album of the year as well. Luckily, they were able to tour *In Cauda Venenum* for a handful of months (alongside acts such as The Vintage Caravan, Alcest, Graveyard, YOB, and Meshuggah) before COVID-19 forced them to stop in early March 2020. They were scheduled to resume their concert run during June 2021's Graspop Metal Meeting, but that was postponed. Hopefully, Opeth will be able to get back out there in 2022.

Even with comparably few live chances to advertise *In Cauda Venenum*, Opeth's latest collection has made a hefty impression. It significantly improves upon its nearest precursor in multiple areas, leading to a thoroughly captivating, resourceful, and valuable artistic statement. 'That's the beauty of Opeth: you never know what's going to happen and you never know where and how it's going to happen', Méndez concludes in *Book of Opeth*. Like virtually every album before it, *In Cauda Venenum* is a superb testament to the staggering malleability, wonder, and trustworthiness that Opeth's catalogue has shown since *Orchid* triggered their reign over twenty-five years ago. There's no telling where the Swedish icons will go next, but there's no doubt that it, too, will see them harvest greatness as only they could.

'Garden of Earthly Delights/Livets Trädgård' (Åkerfeldt)

It's a very suspenseful and ominous prologue, with the space between its evolving gothic choir making the listener feel uneasy yet unable to turn away. Then, wavering tones, ascending piano notes, and miscellaneous organic sounds (such as bells, footsteps, whistling, and kids' voices) slither in to boost the golden dread. At the end, a child innocently says, 'För det om man slutar tänka / Då blir man död' ('Because if you stop thinking / Then you will be dead'). It's the disturbing final detail of a track that completely ensconces you into its sinister location by previewing *In Cauda Venenum*'s prevailing creepiness.

'Dignity/Svekets Prins' (Åkerfeldt)

In the Nuclear Blast Records interview, Åkerfeldt specifies that this second single is also 'the first real song on the record, and the last one [he] finished. It represents the record'. It also features a speech from Olof Palme, a former

Prime Minister of Sweden whose 1986 murder was never solved. Åkerfeldt continues: 'I knew it would be the opening track and it needed something to pull the listener in. I found a New Year's speech from 1969 ... and what he was saying was a bit fleeting, if you know what I mean ... He was talking about concerns with the change of a year. People might feel melancholy or stressed about the future. I could relate to it to some extent'. It's also worth noting that the Swedish title actually translates to something like 'The Prince of Treason', but Åkerfeldt felt that that would be 'too gimmicky', so he chose 'Dignity' instead.

It breaks out of 'Garden of Earthly Delights' with a fusion of tortured vocal harmonies and fiery instrumentation – crossing guitar lines, shuffling rhythms, intimidating keys – that offset Palme's candidly delivered speech. A blistering guitar solo and additional musical shake-ups suggest weightier things to come. Before they do, though, cyclical acoustic arpeggios escort Åkerfeldt's mild description ('Prince of lies is on his knees / Holy rites, spreading the disease'). His voice is much higher than usual, so he's definitely stretching his range in a new way, and the classical garnishes that follow improve the score's deep and alarming serenity.

Abruptly, that enchanting lullaby is totally interrupted by a ferocious influx of riffs and roars – 'Can we dictate life with dignity? / Foul agenda, corrupt in secrecy / Oh, no, no, no, no, no' – that's awesomely engrossing. The next section ('Congratulations to the five men of affairs / There was a purpose with this life') purifies melodically and musically before Åkerfeldt's multilayered warning ('He's waiting for darkness / Opens the door / He's slithering') leads a tastefully corrosive backing. It disperses into an acoustic coda that juxtaposes Åkerfeldt's falsetto wallowing with the maniacal laughter of several spectres, furthering endowing the LP with unrelenting otherworldliness.

The official visualiser (posted to YouTube roughly a month before the LP arrived) is a trippy and abstract cartoon that swiftly shuffles from one location to the next. For instance, viewers enter a clown's mouth and then watch a politician speak on a TV that's floating in space. From there, miscellaneous depictions of piety, corruption, and persecution are given, properly conveying some of the sentiments that Åkerfeldt had in mind when he wrote the tune.

'Heart in Hand/Hjärtat Vet Vad Handen Gör' (Åkerfeldt)

The first single from *In Cauda Venenum*, 'Heart in Hand' was written about the 'contradictions', 'double standards', and 'hypocrites' that surround modern society and politics (as Åkerfeldt professed to *Billboard*'s Christa Titus back in 2019). It beings with a two-way conversation – 'Det är för bedrövligt. Usch! / Vem fan är du?', or 'It's too deplorable. Yuk! / Who the hell are you?' – and then explodes into a tirade of trudging intricacy and resolutely disconcerted verses and choruses for its first half. It's a comparatively simple and monotonous set-up, but it's compelling enough.

Thankfully, it gets more delectable once the messily psychotropic jam kicks in, momentarily resolving into what Åkerfeldt considers 'the nostalgic ending'. '[It] basically [goes] back to my childhood. When you don't have any concerns or worries. You don't know. You're just detached from the adult world, playing with the toys in your room', he contemplates in the Nuclear Blast Records feature. Certainly, it's a sweetly ruminative passage with a curious effect on his voice. Of course, he starts off by sneakily referencing the Beatles' 'Help!' as well ('When I was young / So, so much younger than today').

The song's visualiser – which arrived about two months before the album and animates the album art with engaging camera angles, close-ups, and the like – is a novel way to experience what Åkerfeldt rightly calls a 'rather rocking little thing' whose 'happy mistake' – Méndez's bass breaking down and subsequently 'humming real bad' throughout the tune – is among its 'best part[s]'.

'Next of Kin/De Närmast Sörjande' (Åkerfeldt)
The unified ghostly chants provide a mesmerising way to begin, and the juxtaposition of considerate reflections and densely beaming antagonism is skilfully done. Its winding rhythms and strings make it seem like a far more cataclysmic and colonial offshoot of 'The Seventh Sojourn', too, and the acoustic interludes are an inventive way to break up the persistent upheaval. The final lyrical segment ('Am I the last one of my kind / Who's afraid of dying?') is enormously gripping, giving way to about another minute of sunnily explosive instrumentation. It's a significant highlight of *In Cauda Venenum* that never loosens its grip.

'Lovelorn Crime/Minnets Yta' (Åkerfeldt)
Because it's another centrepiece piano ode, 'Lovelorn Crime' immediately exists as a kindred spirit to 'Burden' from *Watershed*. It's not *quite* as resonant or unique, but it's attractive all the same, with Åkerfeldt's singing regularly rotating between authoritative might and endearing meekness. Meanwhile, the arrangement chases his fluctuating attitude with pertinent quantities of zealousness and tenderness. The sizzling guitar solo capitalises on the piece's overarching misery as well, and the piano chords at the end are faintly haunting and not easily forgotten.

'Charlatan' (Åkerfeldt)
The title track from *Sorceress* contains the following lines: 'You're a charlatan / You get everything you wish'. So, this one could be a spiritual successor to that, not only for its lyrical link but also because of its unyielding combativeness. Rhythmically, it's remarkably twisted and appetising, with Svalberg's discordant zigzags acting as the unsettling icing on the cake. Honestly, Åkerfeldt's melodies are suitable and pleasing, but they're nothing special, and they'd definitely feel blander without the surrounding musical madness. After an extended instrumental freak-out, the song dies down so that strings, keyboard

notes, and eventually choral wailings can envelop a conversation between a woman and girl that's far too long to quote and transcribe here. Suffice it to say that it's among the most arresting parts of the record.

'Universal Truth/Ingen Sanning Är Allas' (Åkerfeldt)

It's both the first ballad written for *In Cauda Venenum* and the most juicily secretive and unpredictable. It jumps back and forth between countrified majesty and noble chaos, with each drastic reversion signifying the band's growing adeptness at balancing subdued tunefulness and uninhibited flights of symphonic fancy. There's an unparalleled level of craftsmanship and gracefulness to these initial minutes, with a killer guitar solo and virtuous harmonies kicking it into overdrive.

Then, a few seconds of silence are broken by a brand-new acoustic speech – 'Time won't heal any wounds you bear / A set few years of your life are stolen' – that's made more daunting once the strings and sound effects come in. They segue into another set of verses and choruses that are brighter and lighter than the opening ones, permitting 'Universal Truth' to come full circle with an added dose of heavenly precision. It's wonderful.

The animated music video was directed by Jess Cope, so it's no surprise that its unmistakably similar to the ones he did for Steven Wilson's 'The Raven that Refused to Sing', Storm Corrosion's 'Drag Ropes', and Skyharbor's 'Patience' (among others). Switching between blue, red, and beige colour palettes, it portrays a man contemplating suicide and fixating on a past love as he grows old and lonely. It's as handsomely grim as the song itself, making it a terrific supplement to it.

'The Garroter/Banemannen' (Åkerfeldt)

'The Garroter' begins with a rugged acoustic soliloquy that bleeds into a bittersweet piano hymn prior to revealing itself as a menacingly jazzy treat. Svalberg's steers with a modestly devilish motif that serves as the underbelly for Åkerfeldt's mounting melodies. His every word is backed by terse strings, looming percussion, and/or other eclectic textures – such as horns and clean guitar sweeps – that develop into an overpoweringly nightmarish milieu. It's too calculated and effective to be improvisational, but it seems substantially freeform and flexible, too. It's even brilliant narratively due to Åkerfeldt's foreboding and measured omniscience – 'The beautiful people / Look down from ruby vantage points / While in the gutter / Starvation invites us to join' – and his method of mumbling alongside the closing guitar solo (in addition to the final diffusion of notes) adds more jazzy authenticity.

'Continuum/Kontinuerlig Drift' (Åkerfeldt)

This penultimate jewel glides in with nail-biting syncopation, rustic acoustic guitar chords, and repentant insights ('Empty house and empty pockets / There's an echo in the hall / I keep your picture in a locket / In the past we had it all'). Other evocative hues chime in to add vibrancy and intrigue, and the arrangement hangs for a bit as a man utters: 'Det är bara en ny dag / Inget särskilt har hänt' ('It's just a new day / Nothing special has happened').

It's already a fairly rocky mood, and the uproariously weather-beaten chorus deepens the track's retro sturdiness. The ensuing moments of angelic respite and far-out musicianship are a grand contrast, and naturally, the agitated guitar solo that appears afterwards is astounding. In typical fashion, the chorus comes back again; however, it's swiftly swallowed up by a godly storm of acoustic arpeggios, synthy veneers, and high-pitched yowls that adorn one of Åkerfeldt's most cherishable melodies ('The river of time flows on / Blind and ruthless'). It's a ravishing wrap-up whose melancholic percussive reprise smoothly pivots into ...

'All Things Will Pass/Allting Tar Slut' (Åkerfeldt)

... *In Cauda Venenum*'s toweringly mournful and supple farewell, 'All Things Will Pass'. A cowering guitar lick and murky piano taps sneak in as Axenrot's drumming fades away; it's not long until he returns, though, ushering in an oscillating torrent of indignancy and despair. It's a characteristically marvellous distinction between severe and sympathetic demeanours that cunningly lays the groundwork for the rapturous ending. Before it gets there, another instance of echoey drumming cues a bewitchingly impassioned call-and-response – 'Your silver voice in my throat / Potion without an antidote' – that's supported by subjugated piano patterns. It gives way to the aforementioned finale ('If everything ends / Is it worth it to turn back home again?') which is as potent and transfixing as it is wholly cathartic and absolute. Unquestionably, it's one of Opeth's greatest album closers, increasing anticipation for whatever the successor to *In Cauda Venenum* turns out to be.

Bonuses

Although Åkerfeldt has stated that there are three bonus songs for the LP, the only one to be released at the time of this writing is 'Cirkelns Riktning' ('The Circle's Direction'). It was published as part of *Decibel*'s 'Flexi Series' on 2 October 2019 (and subsequently featured in the November 2019 print issue). No one in Opeth has given any background information on the track, and as you'd expect, it's sung in Swedish. It kicks off powerfully, with carnivalistic guitar and keyboard riffs orbiting around surging rhythms and outraged singing. The pre-chorus and chorus are a tad more tolerant, yet they're still significantly irate. Halfway in, a shredding guitar solo is accompanied by a grimmer base, yet it's then countered by a serenely whimsical acoustic intermission that distinctly harkens back to the most prestigious 1970s progressive folk acts. Then, the heaviness returns until the end, fortifying 'Cirkelns Riktning' as an extremely fitting B-side to *In Cauda Venenum*. Let's hope that its two leftover siblings see the light of day ASAP.

Roundup – Live/Video, Compilation, and Extra Tracks

Live/Video

While Opeth have been reliably prolific when it comes to crafting *studio* albums, their live output has been much more limited. In fact, they've only put out four concerts so far, starting with the exceptional *Lamentations: Live at Shepherd's Bush Empire 2003*. Filmed on 25 September 2003 – and released almost exactly two months later by Music for Nations / Koch, with a slim pamphlet that includes a heartfelt introduction by Dom Lawson – it's the band's first official offering with Wiberg. Clocking in at just over two hours (and comprised of a light set followed by a heavy set), it begins intimately and suspensefully, with multiple camera angles showcasing the classily arranged stage – featuring blue, green, and white lighting alongside a black and gold Opeth banner – and excited crowd.

It's not long before the fresh-faced troupe take the stage and run through *Damnation* in its entirety. (Oddly enough, though, they place 'Harvest' from *Blackwater Park* in-between 'Ending Credits' and 'Weakness'.) By and large, it's accurate to the studio versions, although there are some differences (such as more distinctive guitar parts on 'Windowpane' and a prolonged and more atmospheric jam during the middle of 'Closure'). Periodically, Wiberg's synths add extra nuances as well, which is why his presence during the angrier second set is greatly missed. Rather than play through all of *Deliverance*, too, they spice things up by devoting equal attention to it and *Blackwater Park*. Fan favourites like 'Master's Apprentices', 'The Leper Affinity', 'A Fair Judgement', 'Deliverance', and 'The Drapery Falls' are replicated wonderfully, with Åkerfeldt switching vocals styles flawlessly as the rest of the group nail every transition and timbre. Despite 'only [doing] two rehearsals and ... [being] pretty nervous' – as Méndez reminiscences in *Book of Opeth* – they put on one hell of a show.

In-between tracks, Åkerfeldt is charmingly tense yet confident as he introduces songs and/or adds typically humble and humorous banter (such as how he asks the audience to 'give us a big scream, will you?'). That earnestness, coupled with Joe Dyer's dynamic direction and the mood-shifting lighting scheme, makes it a thrilling watch from beginning to end. Likewise, the lengthy 'Making of *Deliverance* and *Damnation*' documentary is a delightfully low budget yet highly informative and filmic look into the creation of both records. A hodgepodge of studio footage and one-on-one interviews (with the whole quartet and Steven Wilson), it's a thorough and candid glimpse into the whole process that simultaneously humanises everyone and exposes how skilled and dedicated they are as artists. For all of those reasons – and more – *Lamentations* is indispensable.

Four years later (on 23 October 2007), *The Roundhouse Tapes* came out via Peaceville Records. The title is a nod to Iron Maiden's 1979 debut EP, *The Soundhouse Tapes*, and it marks both the final Opeth collection with Lindgren and the first with Axenrot. Upon release, Åkerfeldt proclaimed: 'The Roundhouse concert will always be a very memorable gig for us for many reasons, but most importantly, it caught the band at the peak of the *Ghost Reveries* tour'. Indeed, it does.

In contrast to *Lamentations*' relatively straightforward presentation, *The Roundhouse Tapes* is bookended with footage of fans waiting in line and/or being quizzed on the street; that technique helps contextualise how far the quintet has come by this point, as well as highlight the zany personalities of Opeth fans. Similarly, the direction is slightly more cinematic, with a wider array of camera angles, lighting, and effects (such as B&W and scratched film filters). There are more glimpses of the crowd, too, that reveal how consistently enthralled they are during the set, and Opeth display plenty of appealing imagery on a screen as well.

They acknowledge every album except for *Deliverance*, with the top picks being 'Ghost of Perdition', 'Windowpane', 'Face of Melinda', and 'When'. While the performances are top-notch, the sound quality can be a bit muddy at times; of course, that's a small complaint considering how well they pull off the newer material and give their oldest tracks more polish. Åkerfeldt seems more comical and self-assured when he talks, too. All in all, it's a great send-off for Lindgren (and initiation for Axenrot) whose DVD features—two artwork booklets, postcards, menu music written by Åkerfeldt and Wiberg, band interviews, fan interviews, soundcheck, and photo gallery—are fun, insightful, and communally enriching.

In Live Concert at the Royal Albert Hall – their first live commemoration with Åkesson – came about three years later, on 20 September 2010. Shot on 5 April of the same year, it was the standout part of their 'Evolution XX: An Opeth Anthology' tour. As mentioned previously, its cover – an homage to Deep Purple's *Concerto for Group and Orchestra* – was designed as a means for 'underlining the band's longstanding love for their prog-rock roots'. In the official press release, Åkerfeldt rejoices: 'It was a dream come true, and now afterwards, it still feels like a dream. We got it all on film, and this, our third live recording and DVD, might be my personal favourite ... Looking back at this night of celebration brings me fond memories of our 20th anniversary — this package is the delayed birthday present'. The vast amount of supplements that were available with the special editions (such as a two-disc DVD set; a set of four 180-gram LPs housed in two gatefold sleeves with exclusive artwork; an exclusive, numbered lithographs with artwork by Åkerfeldt and Travis Smith; a lengthy LP-sized booklet; and a triple-CD set) certainly testify to its importance.

Along the same lines, director Paul M. Green outdoes the previous two offerings with a far sleeker and more energising look. His camera never stops shifting from member to member, with a mixture of close-ups, wide angles, Dutch angles, and more acting as an active participant in the proceedings. Suitably, the larger stage allows them to double down on their theatrical and epic ambience via luxurious lighting, smoke machines, and projected videos and looped logos. Whereas *Lamentations* and *The Roundhouse Tapes* are terrific concert *movies*, this is an outstanding concert *film* (if that makes sense).

The first disc consists of a complete – and practically impeccable – playthrough of *Blackwater Park*, whereas the second presents a chronological trip through the rest of their discography (with one song per album being replicated). From *Orchid*'s 'Forest of October' and *My Arms, Your Hearse*'s 'April Ethereal', to *Ghost Reveries*' 'Harlequin Forest' and *Watershed*'s 'The Lotus Eater', they do a miraculous job revelling in their unrivalled career. That's particularly commendable because Åkesson had an issue with his pedals during that last song (as disclosed in *Book of Opeth*). He elaborates:

> We lost all sound for my guitar and the techs were trying everything to sort it out – we finally realised that the cameraman who was filming [Axenrot] had knocked the cables out of the amps. It was an extremely stressful situation, but Axe rode the high-hat the whole time and that kept the crowd going – so after a couple of minutes, when I was actually able to play my part, I could slide in easily and it worked out okay. It's typical that something like that happens when you're playing the Royal Albert Hall! Luckily, it all happened at the right time in the song when there was a natural space, and not mid-riff or some other place; that would have been much worse.

Predictably, the gargantuan audience claps and cheers during the start of every song, cementing how surreal and special it is to be able of such a once-in-a-lifetime night. While the group's instrumental attention to detail and accuracy isn't shocking, the relentless vigour of Åkerfeldt's growls is. After all, this is right before they formally abandoned that part of their sound with *Heritage* (and people began speculating that he couldn't do it anymore). While the quality of his death vocals has arguably diminished by now, his screams and howls are as robustly demonic as ever here.

The first disc is enhanced by a 40+ minute interview with Åkerfeldt in which he answers fan-submitted questions regarding Opeth's chemistry and history. Interestingly, his responses are intercut with concise clips of admirers talking about Opeth, the band hanging around the venue, and other pleasant inserts. Åkerfeldt is completely at ease and earnest, too, sitting in a red room and going into great detail about what fans want to know. Fortunately, the second disc is even better thanks to 'On Tour with Opeth', an equally extensive behind-the-scenes documentary that totally lives up to its name. It captures them lounging around on the bus, getting ready for shows, speaking about life on the road, meeting diehard followers, and much more. Paired with the rest of *In Live Concert at the Royal Albert Hall*, it's a lovely way to spend a relaxing evening.

Finally, there's *Garden of the Titans: Live at Red Rocks Amphitheater*, which took place in Morrison, Colorado on 11 May 2017 and was made available for purchase (by Nuclear Blast Entertainment/ Moderbolaget Records) on 2 November 2018. Curiously, they play only three tracks from *Sorceress* – 'Sorceress', 'The Wilde Flowers', and 'Era' – with the rest coming from earlier albums. Naturally, they perform each piece exceptionally well, with 'The

Devil's Orchard' and 'Cusp of Eternity' receiving deafening cheers (proving that *Heritage* and *Pale Communion* had become much more welcomed by the community over the past few years). Easily the best moment comes at the end, when Åkerfeldt's single purring guitar note instigates a rip-roaring rendition of 'Deliverance'.

The audio and video quality are great, too, with directors Ben and Julien Deka matching the professional and spirited style of *In Live Concert at the Royal Albert Hall*. Because the band is shrouded in darkness for most of their set – and aided by a lot of illuminated and projected theatrics – *Garden of the Titans* feels like the most legendary live release yet. At the same time, however, its lack of *any* bonus features or physical additions (there's just the two CDs and a choice of DVD or Blu-ray for the video version) makes it the least significant package of the four. Luckily, a few promotional trailers (or 'Episodes') were posted to YouTube before it came out, and they basically act like a mini documentary by exploring some backstage antics (with Devin Townsend) and preparation. 'Episode 4' is particularly enjoyable since it finds the troupe gallivanting at an amusement park, and it's a mystery as to why the series wasn't included on the home release.

To be fair, there were also two publication-exclusive live discs: 2011's *The Devil's Orchard* (*Live at Rock Hard Festival 2009*), which was a part of *Rock Hard* magazine #292, and 2017's *Live in Plovdiv* split EP with Enslaved, which was included with *PROG* #81. Together, they find the gang performing typically enthralling versions of classics such as 'The Devil's Orchard', 'Deliverance', 'Ghost of Perdition', 'The Leper Affinity', and 'The Grand Conjuration'. That said, they're not official Opeth releases – and they sound as good you'd expect – so they really only warrant a quick mention here.

Compilations and Extra Tracks

There have been several reissues and box sets over the years, such as 2006's *Collector's Edition Slipcase*, 2008's *The Candlelight Years*, 2009's *The Wooden Box*, 2014's Japan-only *The Collection*, and 2015's *Deliverance & Damnation Remixed*. However, none of them offer anything new or unique; rather, they merely compile previously released content, so there's no reason to discuss them here.

Therefore, the only thing left to look at is 'The Throat of Winter', a track they created for 2010's *God of War: Blood & Metal* EP that was used to promote the *God of War III* video game. Although the collection also houses entries from a half dozen other major acts – such as Dream Theater's 'Raw Dog', Trivium's 'Shattering the Skies Above', and Killswitch Engage's 'My Obsession' – 'The Throat of Winter' is perhaps the best of the bunch. At first, it's a frank acoustic folk rock tune with simple but intriguing guitar strums, backing effects, and cleanly sung melodies. The isolated mid-section arpeggios provide a sombre transition into the eerier second half; from there, trickier guitar work and percussion add tribal disorganisation that suits the chaos of the *God of War* series. It's palpably – and intentionally – disorganised, almost as if it's stitched together from a few leftover compositional fragments. Yet, it still packs Opeth's emblematic ability to make even the most feverish change-ups coherent. By no means a top-tier track, it deserves its place in the band's canon.

Bibliography

Åkerfeldt, Mikael. 'Chapter II.' *Opeth.com*,

Åkerfeldt, Mikael. 'Orchid Session Diary.' *Opeth.com*,

Åkerfeldt, Mikael. 'Chapter VIII.' *Opeth.com*,

Åkerfeldt, Mikael. 'Chapter X.' *Opeth.com*,

Åkerfeldt, Mikael. 'Deliverance – Diary.' *Opeth.com*,

Åkerfeldt, Mikael. 'MAYH Session Diary.' *Opeth.com*,

Åkerfeldt, Mikael. 'Morningrise Session Diary.' *Opeth*,

Åkerfeldt, Mikael. 'Watershed Diary.' *Opeth.com*,

Armin. 'Opeth – Mikael Åkerfeldt Writing New Material.' *Metal Storm*, 13 Aug. 2012. http://metalstorm.net/

Azevedo, Pedro. 'Opeth – My Arms, Your Hearse: Review.' *Chronicles of Chaos*, 7 Aug. 1998, http://www.chroniclesofchaos.com

Batmaz, Murat. 'Review: 'Opeth: Morningrise.'' *Sea of Tranquility*, 30 July 2005, https://www.seaoftranquility.org

Beecher, Russell, editor. *Book of Opeth*. ROCKET 88, 2020.

Blabbermouth. ' OPETH: 'Heritage' Album Details Revealed.' *blabbermouth.net*, 26 May 2011

Blabbermouth. ' OPETH's MIKAEL ÅKERFELDT On Next Album: It's Time To Go 'All In' With String Instrumentation.' *blabbermouth.net*, 4 Jan. 2014,

Blabbermouth. 'Guitarist Peter Lindgren Quits Opeth; Replacement Announced.' *blabbermouth.net*, 17 May 2007

Blabbermouth. 'Opeth Win Swedish Grammy!' *blabbermouth.net*, 19 Feb. 2003,

Blabbermouth. 'Opeth: 'the Roundhouse Tapes' Details Revealed.' *blabbermouth.net*, 20 Aug. 2007,

Blabbermouth. 'OPETH's 'Pale Communion' Pushed Back To August.' *blabbermouth.net*, 8 May 2014,

Bowar Heavy Metal Expert, Chad. 'Opeth Interview.' *About.com* , 6 Nov. 2015,

Davis, Dan. 'Ranked: Opeth's Discography From Best to Least Best.' *Metal Injection*, 21 Jan. 2015,

Dick, Chris. 'Opeth – 'Orchid.'' *Decibel Magazine*, 1 Feb. 2018,

Dick, Jonathan. 'Opeth Albums From Worst To Best.' *Stereogum*, 4 Oct. 2016,

Dolan, Jon, et al. '50 Greatest Prog Rock Albums of All Time.' *Rolling Stone*, Rolling Stone, 17 June 2015, https://www.rollingstone.com

Ewing, Jerry, and Hannah May Kilroy. 'The 100 Greatest Prog Albums of All Time: 100-81.' *PROG*, Louder, 6 Aug. 2014

Ewing, Jerry. 'Vote in Video of the Year Category.' *Prog*, Future Publishing Limited, 29 June 2017

Exposito, Suzy, et al. 'The 10 Best Metal Albums of 2019.' *Rolling Stone*, Rolling Stone, 11 Dec. 2019, https://www.rollingstone.com

FaceCulture. 'Opeth Interview – Mikael Åkerfeldt (Part 1).' *YouTube*, YouTube, 15 July 2011

Franklin, Dan. 'Dead Man Touring: Mikael Åkerfeldt Of Opeth Interviewed.' *The Quietus*, 21 Sept. 2016

Glass, Polly. 'Opeth Come Clean on What Sorceress Is Really About.' *Prog*, Louder, 27 Sept. 2016, https://www.loudersound.com/

Hartmann, Graham. 'Opeth Release Signature Beer XXV Anniversary Imperial Stout.' *Loudwire*, 7 Dec. 2015, https://loudwire.com/

Hatch, Sam 'Blammymatazz'. 'Mikael Åkerfeldt Interview – The House of Zazz.' *YouTube*, YouTube, 21 Sept. 2011,

Hill, John. 'Top 25 Progressive Metal Albums of All Time.' *Loudwire*, 28 June 2020, https://loudwire.com.

Howison, Kaydan. 'Opeth – In Cauda Venenum (Album Review).' *Wall Of Sound*, 26 Sept. 2019, https://wallofsoundau.com

katatonic_fear. 'Opeth Lyrics.' *Ultimate Metal – Heavy Metal Forum and Community*, 6 Dec. 2004, http://www.ultimatemetal.com

Kielty, Martin. 'Opeth Abandoned Tape for Pale Communion.' *Loudersound*, Louder, 28 Apr. 2014, https://www.loudersound.com

Lawson, Dom. 'How Opeth Conjured up Their Ghost Reveries.' *Metal Hammer*, Louder, 15 Sept. 2015, https://www.loudersound.com

Lawson, Dom. 'Opeth's Track by Track Guide to Sorceress.' *Metal Hammer*, Louder, 26 Aug. 2016, https://www.loudersound.com

Loudwire Staff. 'The 50 Best Metal Albums of 2019.' *Loudwire*, 3 Dec. 2019, https://loudwire.com

Loudwire Staff. 'Top 90 Hard Rock + Metal Albums of the '90s.' *Loudwire*, 14 Sept. 2020, https://loudwire.com

McCooe, Scott. 'Interview: Opeth.' *Metalupdate.com*,.

Mojjan. 'Interview with Peter Lindgren (English).' *Opeth FanClub Sweden*, 19 Oct. 2013, http://opethfanclub.se

Mudrian, Albert. 'Hear Exclusive New Opeth Song 'Cirkelns Riktning' Via Decibel Flexi Series.' *Decibel Magazine*, 2 Oct. 2019, https://www.decibelmagazine.com

Norton, Justin M. 'Q&A: Opeth on Pale Communion, Bad Taste, & Record Store Binges + Hear New Song 'Eternal Rains.'' *Stereogum*, 1 Aug. 2014, https://www.stereogum.com

Nuclear Blast America. ' IN CAUDA VENENUM.' *Nuclear Blast USA*, https://www.nuclearblast.com

Nuclear Blast Europe. 'OPETH – Initial Ideas and Diversity Behind 'Sorceress' (OFFICIAL INTERVIEW).' *YouTube*, YouTube, 6 Oct. 2016,

Odefjärd, Fredrik, director. *Opeth: Beyond Ghost Reveries*, 2006.

'Opeth – Prologue Lyrics.' *Metal Kingdom*, https://www.metalkingdom.net

Opeth Official. 'Opeth – about 'Hjärtat Vet Vad Handen Gör' / 'Heart in Hand' (Official Interview).' *YouTube*, YouTube, 18 July 2019,

'Opeth to Release 'In Live Concert at the Royal Albert Hall' DVD This September.' *Opeth.com*, 21 June 2010,

Palmerston, Sean. 'Opeth Blackwater Park.' *Exclaim!*, Exclaim! Media, 1 Feb. 2001, https://exclaim.ca

Pasbani, Robert. 'Opeth Interview 2014 – New Album, Satanism and What's

'Heavy." *Metal Injection*, 25 Mar. 2014, https://metalinjection.net

Pasbani, Robert. 'Opeth Pale Communion Album Art Revealed!' *Metal Injection*, 27 May 2014, https://metalinjection.net

The Pit. 'Opeth – New Album Pale Communion (Interview Part 1).' *YouTube*, YouTube, 31 July 2014,

Porter, Christopher. 'Progressing Past the Metalocalypse: Opeth.' *The Washington Post*, WP Company, 4 Mar. 2019, https://www.washingtonpost.com

Prog Sphere. 'Opeth Albums Ranked from Less Great to Great [REVISITED].' *Prog Sphere*, 15 Dec. 2017, https://www.prog-sphere.com

Reapxes. 'Hidden Lyrics in The Funeral Portrait.' *Reddit*, 28 Apr. 2019, https://www.reddit.com.

Rees, Jen, et al. 'Interview with Fredrick from Opeth about Pale Communion and Their Upcoming Australia Tour.Jen Rees, Jordan Sibberas and Kit Lindsey.' *Music Injection*, 12 Apr. 2015, https://musicinjection.com.au

Roadrunner Records. 'Opeth Part Ways with Keyboardist per Wiberg.' *RoadrunnerRecords.com*, 7 Apr. 2011.

Rose, Jonathon. 'EVERY OPETH ALBUM, RANKED FROM BEST TO WORST.' *Metal Wani*, 27 Aug. 2016, https://metalwani.com

Rosenthal, Jon. 'Godhead's Lament: 20 Years of Opeth's 'Still Life,' an Interview with Mikael Åkerfeldt.' *Invisible Oranges – The Metal Blog*, 18 Oct. 2019, https://www.invisibleoranges.com

Savić, Niko. 'Opeth: An Interview with Mikael Åkerfeldt.' *Prog Sphere*, 17 Oct. 2016, http://www.prog-sphere.com

Savić, Niko. 'OPETH's New Album Could Be Called 'Nux Vomica." *Prog Sphere*, 3 Aug. 2014, https://www.prog-sphere.com

Scarlett, Elizabeth, et al. 'Metal Hammer Critics' Top 50 Albums of 2008.' *Metal Hammer*, Louder, http://www.metalhammer.co.uk

Schafer, Joseph. ' Interview: Mikael Åkerfeldt (Opeth).' *Invisible Oranges* , 22 July 2014, https://www.invisibleoranges.com

Jordan Blum's ultimate Opeth Playlist

This is easily the most difficult playlist I've had to compile for one of my books, as Opeth truly have classic tracks strewn throughout their whole catalogue. What's more, several albums deserve to be represented in their entirety. Alas, that's really not possible, so the following list is my best attempt to highlight the greatest Opeth songs within the widest breadth of their career. As with my album rankings below, you'll notice that I mostly favour the band's output from the 2000s; still, there are a few undeniable gems from the 1990s and 2010s as well, and I'd love to compare my playlist with yours!

1. 'Ghost of Perdition'
2. 'Deliverance'
3. 'Eternal Rains Will Come'
4. 'The Moor'
5. 'Still Day Beneath the Sun'
6. 'A Fair Judgement'
7. 'Patterns in the Ivy II'
8. 'Windowpane'
9. 'Master's Apprentices'
10. 'The Drapery Falls'
11. 'To Bid You Farewell'
12. 'When'
13. 'Face of Melinda'
14. 'Moon Above, Sun Below'
15. 'To Rid the Disease'
16. 'Hours of Wealth'
17. 'Faith in Others'
18. 'Will O the Wisp'
19. 'The Devil's Orchard'
20. 'Dignity'

Opeth albums ranked from best to worst

My album ranking will probably be more controversial than my playlist.
Granted, Opeth's middle period – which is widely considered to be their peak
– is completely represented in the top half. Plus, if you've made it this far,
you already know how much I adore *Pale Communion*; think *Heritage* and
Sorceress could've been better; and view the group's first two LPs as important
stepping stones more than as excellent collections. Undoubtedly, fans who
prefer Opeth's black metal side, as well as those who prefer Opeth's post-
growling phase, will see things differently. By all means, let me know where
you'd place the records on your list.

1. Ghost Reveries
2. Pale Communion
3. Still Life
4. Blackwater Park
5. Damnation
6. Deliverance
7. Watershed
8. In Cauda Venenum
9. Sorceress
10. My Arms, Your Hearse
11. Heritage
12. Morningrise
13. Orchid

On Track series

Tori Amos – Lisa Torem 978-1-78952-142-9
Asia – Peter Braidis 978-1-78952-099-6
Barclay James Harvest – Keith and Monica Domone 978-1-78952-067-5
The Beatles – Andrew Wild 978-1-78952-009-5
The Beatles Solo 1969-1980 – Andrew Wild 978-1-78952-030-9
Blue Oyster Cult – Jacob Holm-Lupo 978-1-78952-007-1
Marc Bolan and T.Rex – Peter Gallagher 978-1-78952-124-5
Kate Bush – Bill Thomas 978-1-78952-097-2
Camel – Hamish Kuzminski 978-1-78952-040-8
Caravan – Andy Boot 978-1-78952-127-6
Cardiacs – Eric Benac 978-1-78952-131-3
Eric Clapton Solo – Andrew Wild 978-1-78952-141-2
The Clash – Nick Assirati 978-1-78952-077-4
Crosby, Stills and Nash – Andrew Wild 978-1-78952-039-2
The Damned – Morgan Brown 978-1-78952-136-8
Deep Purple and Rainbow 1968-79 – Steve Pilkington 978-1-78952-002-6
Dire Straits – Andrew Wild 978-1-78952-044-6
The Doors – Tony Thompson 978-1-78952-137-5
Dream Theater – Jordan Blum 978-1-78952-050-7
Elvis Costello and The Attractions – Georg Purvis 978-1-78952-129-0
Emerson Lake and Palmer – Mike Goode 978-1-78952-000-2
Fairport Convention – Kevan Furbank 978-1-78952-051-4
Peter Gabriel – Graeme Scarfe 978-1-78952-138-2
Genesis – Stuart MacFarlane 978-1-78952-005-7
Gentle Giant – Gary Steel 978-1-78952-058-3
Gong – Kevan Furbank 978-1-78952-082-8
Hawkwind – Duncan Harris 978-1-78952-052-1
Roy Harper – Opher Goodwin 978-1-78952-130-6
Iron Maiden – Steve Pilkington 978-1-78952-061-3
Jefferson Airplane – Richard Butterworth 978-1-78952-143-6
Jethro Tull – Jordan Blum 978-1-78952-016-3
Elton John in the 1970s – Peter Kearns 978-1-78952-034-7
The Incredible String Band – Tim Moon 978-1-78952-107-8
Iron Maiden – Steve Pilkington 978-1-78952-061-3
Judas Priest – John Tucker 978-1-78952-018-7
Kansas – Kevin Cummings 978-1-78952-057-6
Led Zeppelin – Steve Pilkington 978-1-78952-151-1
Level 42 – Matt Philips 978-1-78952-102-3
Aimee Mann – Jez Rowden 978-1-78952-036-1
Joni Mitchell – Peter Kearns 978-1-78952-081-1
The Moody Blues – Geoffrey Feakes 978-1-78952-042-2
Mike Oldfield – Ryan Yard 978-1-78952-060-6
Tom Petty – Richard James 978-1-78952-128-3
Porcupine Tree – Nick Holmes 978-1-78952-144-3
Queen – Andrew Wild 978-1-78952-003-3
Radiohead – William Allen 978-1-78952-149-8
Renaissance – David Detmer 978-1-78952-062-0
The Rolling Stones 1963-80 – Steve Pilkington 978-1-78952-017-0

The Smiths and Morrissey – Tommy Gunnarsson 978-1-78952-140-5
Steely Dan – Jez Rowden 978-1-78952-043-9
Steve Hackett – Geoffrey Feakes 978-1-78952-098-9
Thin Lizzy – Graeme Stroud 978-1-78952-064-4
Toto – Jacob Holm-Lupo 978-1-78952-019-4
U2 – Eoghan Lyng 978-1-78952-078-1
UFO – Richard James 978-1-78952-073-6
The Who – Geoffrey Feakes 978-1-78952-076-7
Roy Wood and the Move – James R Turner 978-1-78952-008-8
Van Der Graaf Generator – Dan Coffey 978-1-78952-031-6
Yes – Stephen Lambe 978-1-78952-001-9
Frank Zappa 1966 to 1979 – Eric Benac 978-1-78952-033-0
10CC – Peter Kearns 978-1-78952-054-5

Decades Series

The Bee Gees in the 1960s – Andrew Mon Hughes et al 978-1-78952-148-1
Alice Cooper in the 1970s – Chris Sutton 978-1-78952-104-7
Curved Air in the 1970s – Laura Shenton 978-1-78952-069-9
Fleetwood Mac in the 1970s – Andrew Wild 978-1-78952-105-4
Focus in the 1970s – Stephen Lambe 978-1-78952-079-8
Genesis in the 1970s – Bill Thomas 978178952-146-7
Marillion in the 1980s – Nathaniel Webb 978-1-78952-065-1
Pink Floyd In The 1970s – Georg Purvis 978-1-78952-072-9
The Sweet in the 1970s – Darren Johnson 978-1-78952-139-9
Uriah Heep in the 1970s – Steve Pilkington 978-1-78952-103-0
Yes in the 1980s – Stephen Lambe with David Watkinson 978-1-78952-125-2

On Screen series

Carry On… – Stephen Lambe 978-1-78952-004-0
David Cronenberg – Patrick Chapman 978-1-78952-071-2
Doctor Who: The David Tennant Years – Jamie Hailstone 978-1-78952-066-8
Monty Python – Steve Pilkington 978-1-78952-047-7
Seinfeld Seasons 1 to 5 – Stephen Lambe 978-1-78952-012-5
James Bond – Andrew Wild 978-1-78952-010-1

Other Books

Babysitting A Band On The Rocks – G.D. Praetorius 978-1-78952-106-1
Derek Taylor: For Your Radioactive Children – Andrew Darlington 978-1-78952-038-5
Iggy and The Stooges On Stage 1967-1974 – Per Nilsen 978-1-78952-101-6
Jon Anderson and the Warriors – the road to Yes – David Watkinson 978-1-78952-059-0
Nu Metal: A Definitive Guide – Matt Karpe 978-1-78952-063-7
Tommy Bolin: In and Out of Deep Purple – Laura Shenton 978-1-78952-070-5
Maximum Darkness – Deke Leonard 978-1-78952-048-4
Maybe I Should've Stayed In Bed – Deke Leonard 978-1-78952-053-8
Psychedelic Rock in 1967 – Kevan Furbank 978-1-78952-155-9
The Twang Dynasty – Deke Leonard 978-1-78952-049-1

and many more to come!

Would you like to write for Sonicbond Publishing?

We are mainly a music publisher, but we also occasionally publish in other genres including film and television. At Sonicbond Publishing we are always on the look-out for authors, particularly for our two main series, On Track and Decades.

Mixing fact with in depth analysis, the On Track series examines the entire recorded work of a particular musical artist or group. All genres are considered from easy listening and jazz to 60s soul to 90s pop, via rock and metal.

The Decades series singles out a particular decade in an artist or group's history and focuses on that decade in more detail than may be allowed in the On Track series.

While professional writing experience would, of course, be an advantage, the most important qualification is to have real enthusiasm and knowledge of your subject. First-time authors are welcomed, but the ability to write well in English is essential.

Sonicbond Publishing has distribution throughout Europe and North America, and all our books are also published in E-book form. Authors will be paid a royalty based on sales of their book. Further details about our books are available from www.sonicbondpublishing.com. To contact us, complete the contact form there or email info@sonicbondpublishing.co.uk